# COVENTRY IN 50 BUILDINGS



DAVID MCGRORY

AMBERLEY

*To my late friend Raymond Holl, Coventrian, twice master of Coventry Freeman's Guild, Master of the London Freemen, holder of the Medal of the British Empire.*

First published 2017

Amberley Publishing, The Hill, Stroud
Gloucestershire GL5 4EP

www.amberley-books.com



British Library Cataloguing in Publication Data.
A catalogue record for this book is available from the British Library.

ISBN 978 1 4456 6578 8 (print)
ISBN 978 1 4456 6579 5 (ebook)

Origination by Amberley Publishing.
Printed in Great Britain.

Appointed GPSR EU Representative: Easy Access System Europe Oü, 16879218
Address: Mustamäe tee 50, 10621, Tallinn, Estonia
Contact Details: gpsr.requests@easproject.com, +358 40 500 3575

# Contents

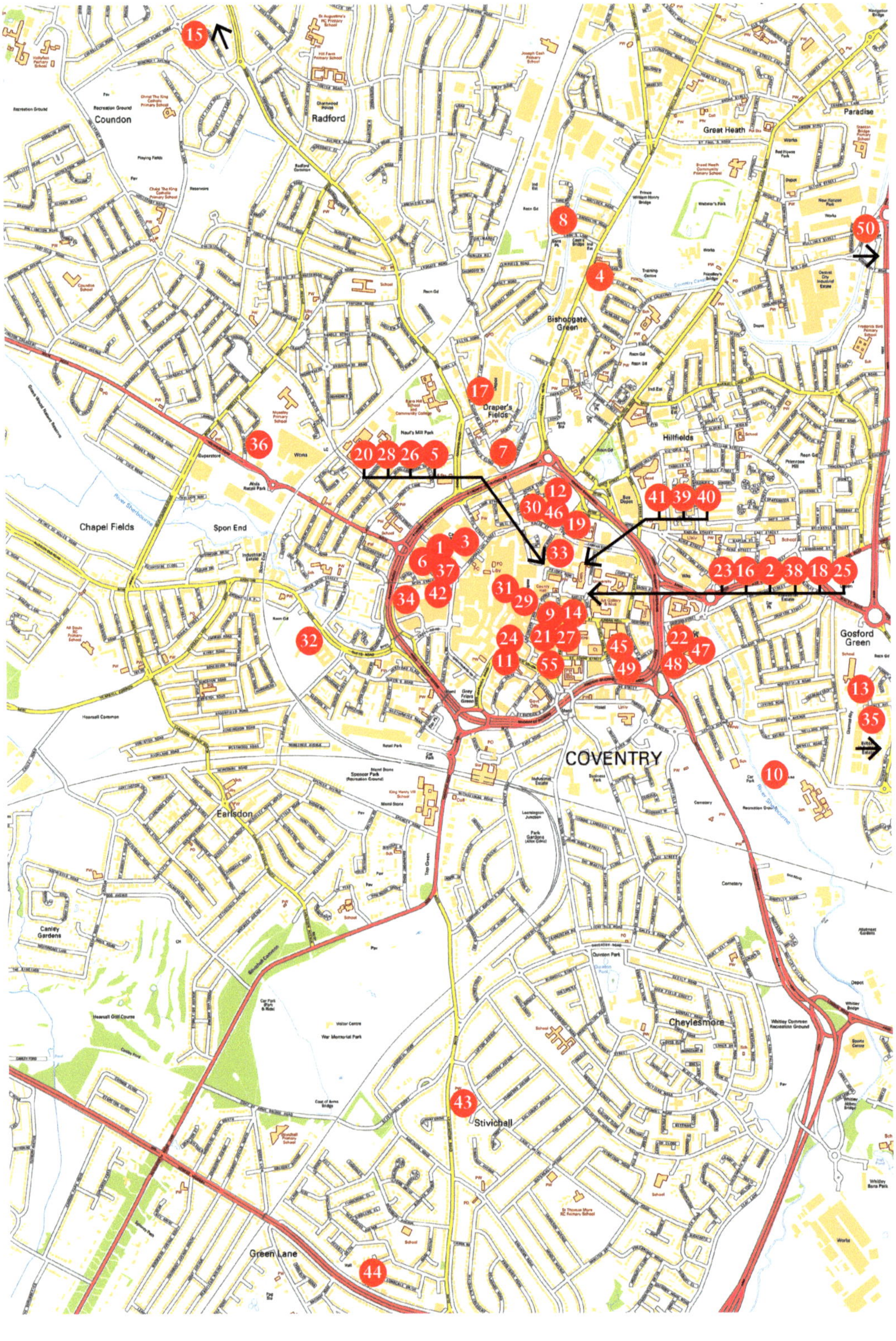
Coundon
Radford
Great Heath
Paradise
Bishopgate Green
Draper's Fields
Hillfields
Chapel Fields
Spon End
Gosford Green
COVENTRY
Earlsdon
Canley Gardens
Cheylesmore
Stivichall
Green Lane

# Key

1. Bablake School
2. No. 22 Bayley Lane
3. Belgrade Theatre
4. Bird Grove
5. Blue Coat School
6. Bonds Hospital
7. Canal Warehouses
8. Cash's Model Factory
9. Castle Grounds, No. 7 Little Park Street
10. Charterhouse Priory of St Anne
11. Cheylesmore Manor Gatehouse
12. Cook Street Gate
13. Coombe Abbey
14. Council House
15. Coundon Hall
16. County Hall
17. Daimler Buildings
18. Drapers Hall
19. Fire Station
20. Flying Standard
21. Fords Hospital
22. Frederick Lancaster Library
23. Golden Cross
24. Greyfriars
25. Herbert Art Gallery & Museum
26. Holy Trinity
27. Kirby House
28. Lych Gate Cottages
29. National Westminster Bank
30. Old Grammar School
31. Precinct
32. Premier Inn
33. Ribbon Factory
34. Rotherham House Spon Street
35. St Bartholomew Binley
36. St Catherine's Well
37. St John the Baptist
38. St Mary's Guildhall
39. St Michael (New)
40. St Michael & All Saints
41. St Michael's House, No. 11 Priory Row
42. Spon Street
43. Stivichall Church
44. Stivichall Grange
45. Stone House
46. Swanswell Gate
47. University Science Block
48. Whitefriars
49. Whitefriar's Gate
50. Wyken Church

# Introduction

Coventry's buildings have gone through some very tough times: bombing and development. The bombs took out significant sections of the city, mainly the area that now contains the first pedestrian shopping precinct in Europe. These raids destroyed buildings from the fourteenth to twentieth century. Most pre-war guides show that few of the city's most significant buildings were lost. Apart from them Coventry once had hundreds of timbered buildings, all significant in their own right. As few bothered about these ancient domestic dwellings, in 1914 the Coventry City Guild was set up to protect them, its role continued today by the Coventry Society.

In 1925 it was reported that the secretary of the Society for the Protection of Ancient Buildings had visited Coventry regarding the preservation of its ancient buildings, especially regarding planned street schemes. The Corporation were asked if they would appoint a special committee, 'to watch and report on matters affecting the beauty of the city, especially with regard to its ancient buildings.' The Corporation did not think this was 'desirable'.

Apart from bombs, most destruction lies with individuals, developers and the Corporation/council. In 1929 demolition took place on a huge scale for Corporation Street. Destruction continued in 1936 when Coventry's favourite ancient street, Butcher Row, and its picturesque side streets were flattened to make way for Trinity Street. Around 300–400 timbered buildings were destroyed to give easier access for the motor vehicle.

After this, small acts of restoration took place. The fifteenth-century Palace Yard, in danger of demolition and turned down by the council, was saved and restored by a group of local citizens. Two beautiful Elizabethan buildings were restored in the High Street only to be bombed in 1940, along with Palace Yard. Leading up to the war, schemes for road widening had already begun in Smithford Street, Cross Cheaping and High Street. In 1936 the city set up its own architect department, led by twenty-six-year-old Donald Gibson. Gibson put forward radical plans for rebuilding the city centre, including the demolition of a large number of historic buildings.

The bombing meant the plans were fulfilled sooner, starting with Broadgate then the Precinct. In 1946 there were 350 identifiable pre-seventeenth-century buildings in the city. Twenty years later only thirty-four remained. There were more; they survived, hidden. Some can be seen in Gosford Street, restored recently as part of the excellent Fargo development, and the excellent Weavers House in Spon End. Other timbered buildings still lie hidden in the Burges. In the 1960s the council restored Cheylesmore Manor Gatehouse and Whitefriars. The best example of council restoration was Spon Street. Recently, however, the addition of modern higher buildings, fast-food restaurants, tarmac and street parking has damaged the original vision.

One thing that can be said of Gibson and Arthur Ling's precinct is that it was actual planning. It was all part of a concept; Ling changed it by adding height with blocks of flats. Basically, however, it did have shape and form, it followed a pattern and still stands the test of time. Most development now in the centre is about squeezing boxes into holes. More and more student accommodation is being built in the city centre with apparently no thought. A multistorey car park is planned next to Ford's Hospital because student towers are built on busy car parks. St John's Church, Bond's Hospital and Bablake have been dwarfed by a student block that blocks out the sky. A new student block in Hales Street completely destroys the perspective so carefully thought out originally for Trinity Street, boxing in the planned opening up of the River Sherbourne. Students definitely add something to the city, but those who design and site their accommodation do not. One tends to think it would have worked better if a student village had been created in the Friar Gate area. Then the centre could have been developed in a thoughtful manner for the people and the students.

Many still see Coventry as all concrete held together by an ugly ring road and if you travel the ring road you can understand why. However, scattered within the wall of glass and concrete are many fine buildings and a fine city, despite its ongoing mistreatment. Coventry brings in £449 million a year from its growing tourism; tourists love Coventry – they mainly come to see our old buildings, not our tower blocks!

If you can't find your favourite building here, it is because Coventry has many more significant and interesting buildings than there is space for.

The flow of Trinity Street gets blocked and Millennium Place cramped by this student development.

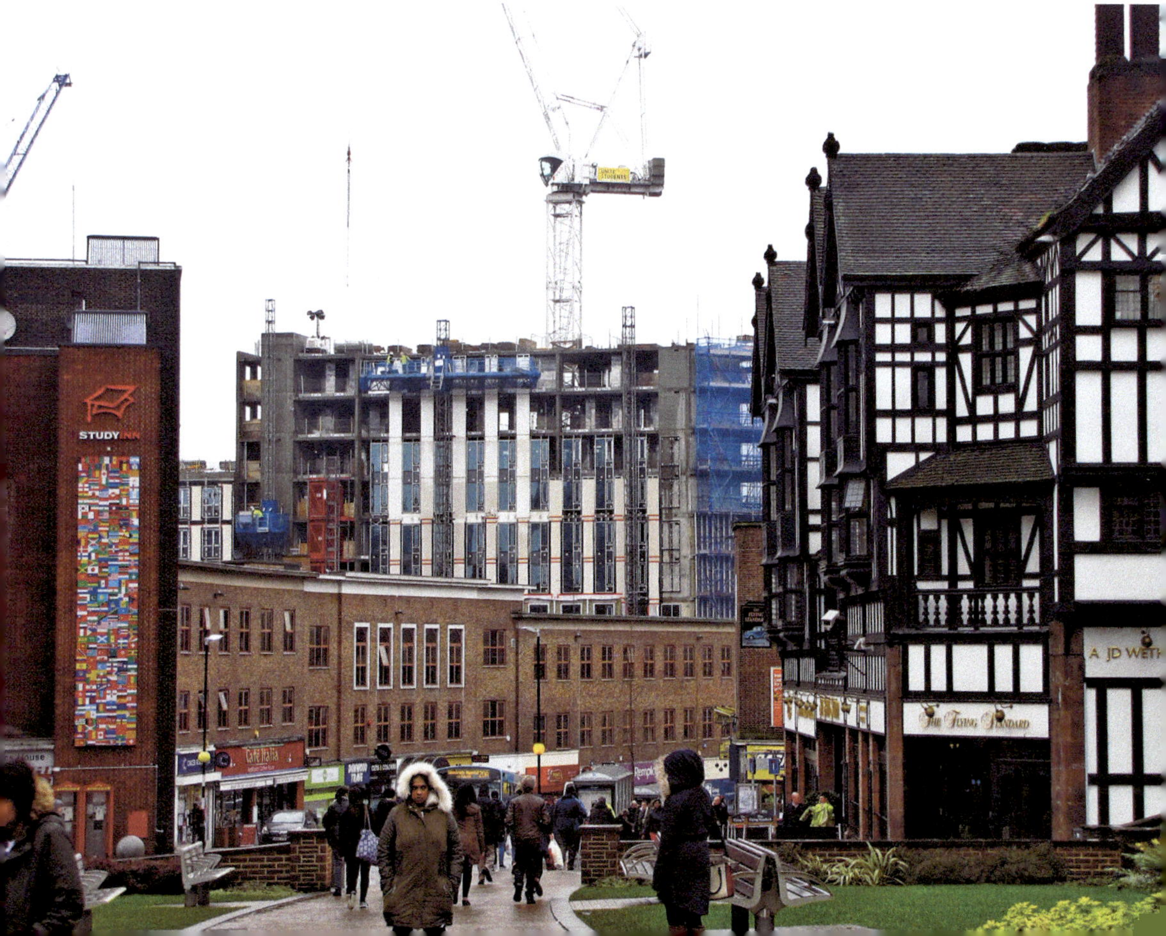

# The Fifty Buildings

## 1. Bablake School

The register of old Bablake School stated, 'In the year of Our Lord God, 1560, then being Mayor of the City of Coventry, Mr Richard Smith, the hospital of Bablake was erected.'

On 7 April 1563 an indenture was made to the foundation by Thomas Wheatley, ex-mayor, ironmonger and card maker of Coventry. It was said he sent a servant to Spain to purchase some steel gads and on arrival the barrels contained silver ingots. The servant didn't know who he had purchased them off so Wheatley kept them in case of enquiry – none came. He gave the profit of the ingots and much of his fortune to charitable purposes, including this school. This was often accepted as the source of the original foundation and the school has used Wheatley's arms, so it was believed he actually founded it, which is incorrect.

Bablake School as seen from Hill Street.

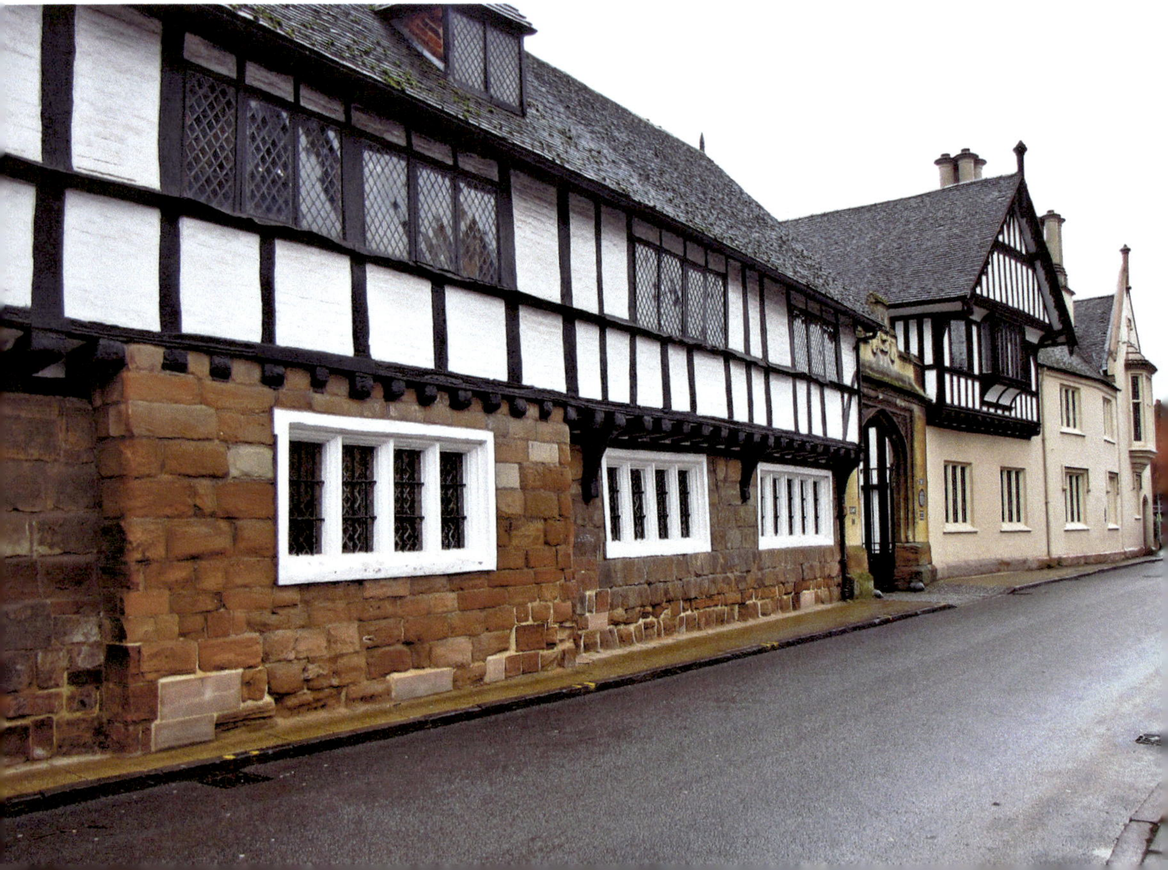

Bablake School or more rightly Bablake Hospital or Blue Coat Boys Hospital was established in 1560 as a Blue Coat School by the mayor and council using charitable contributions. Blue Coat schools were started in the sixteenth century as charitable schools for poor or foundling children – blue for charity and because they wore blue frock coats. It was to this institution that Wheatley gave his gift. Later the council who administered it gave a yearly grant of £40.

Some now claim it dates from the fourteenth century. The previous school in the quadrangle was attached to the College of St John and was set up and funded by the Trinity Guild for guildsmen's children and was run by the priests of St John's. This school was dissolved by the Chantries Act of December 1547. The later school, as recorded on the register, is a 'hospital', a school for children of the needy! Whether one can claim this is a continuous institution is debateable.

In 1890 the school moved to Coundon Road and the boy's old uniform, the blue coat, yellow petticoat, stockings and round black tasselled cap were changed for a blue Eaton-style vest, trousers, yellow stockings and straw hat. It was turned into a museum in the late 1930s. Today it is school offices.

The present building is part of the east range of the Bablake quadrangle and dates from the fifteenth and early sixteenth centuries. In 1581 it was described as having a hall, kitchen, three offices below and chambers and lodgings above.

Looking across Bablake quadrangle at Bablake School.

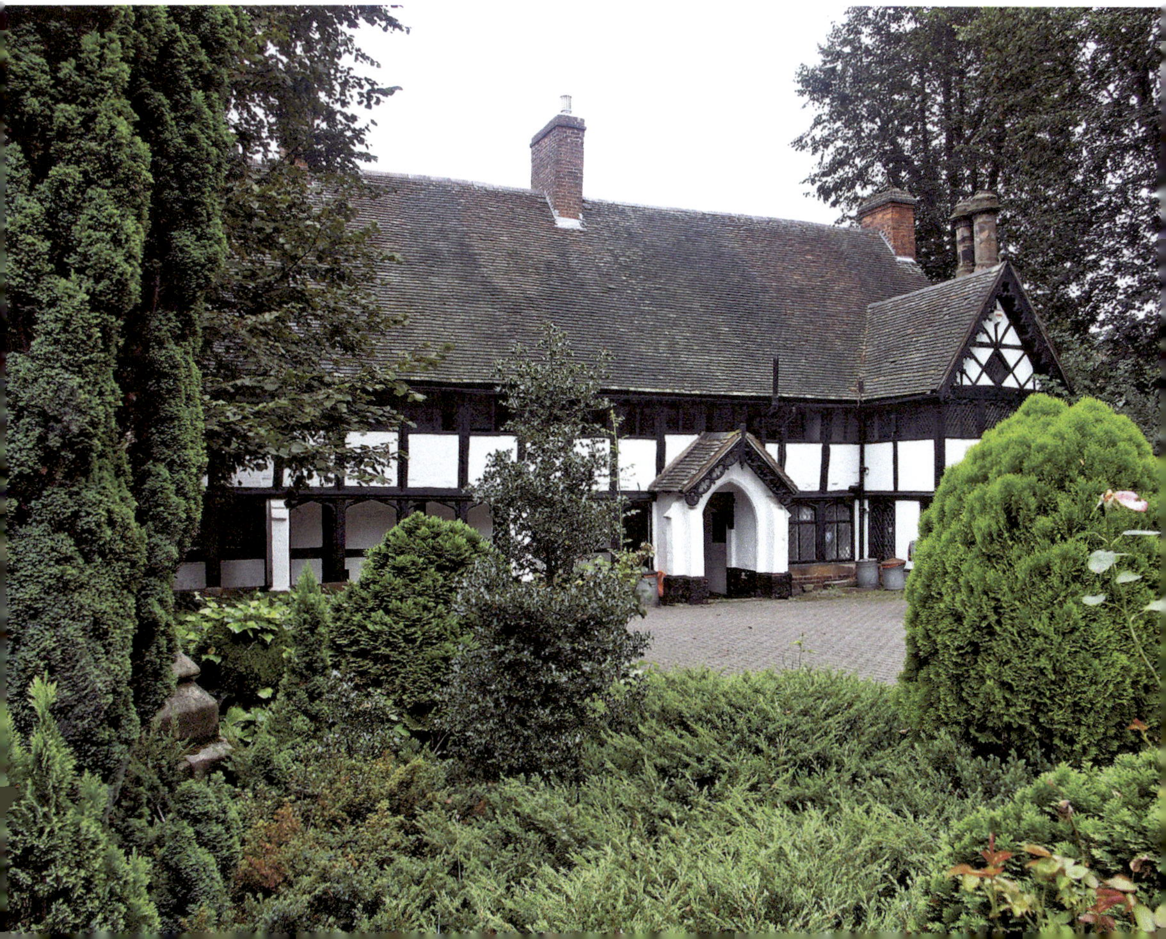

## 2. No. 22 Bayley Lane

Number 22 is the only remaining timbered house in Bayley Lane. Dating from the close of the fifteenth to the seventeenth century, the building has a fine carved corner post and a jettied upper storey, first-floor buttress shafts, carved tracery and a dragon beam inside. It has seventeenth-century chimney stacks and Victorian lower windows. The decorative bargeboards on the gable end placed there in 1822 originated on the buttery (building for wine butts, etc.), which straddled No. 22 and the guildhall. They were drawn by the great Victorian architect Pugin, along with the corner post.

Up until 1862 it was the shop of John Gibson, baker; when he died his wife Mary continued the business. From 1913 John Owen lived here, he was verger of St Michael for thirty-seven years and gave out the church's annual bread dole. He was followed by William Bourne, a baker and known as the oldest Freeman in Coventry; he died in 1917 and afterwards it became a curio shop. In 1939 the Corporation planned to demolish it with the buildings above and build upon Castle Yard and Hay Lane. It was for many years occupied by Browett solicitors and recently a plan to turn it into student flats was blocked. Since then the building has been left to deteriorate.

No. 22 from Bayley Lane, a fine building in need of restoration and a proper use.

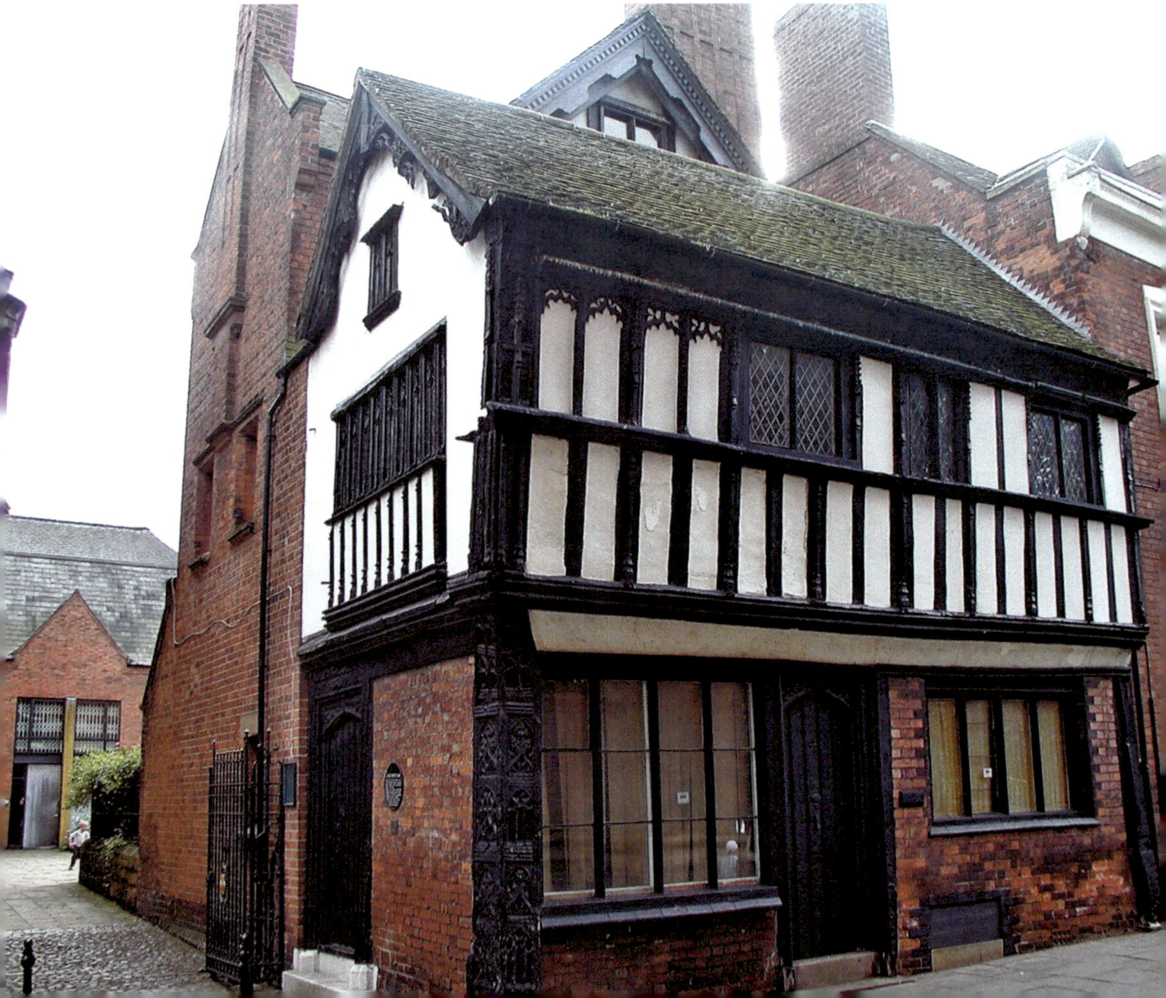

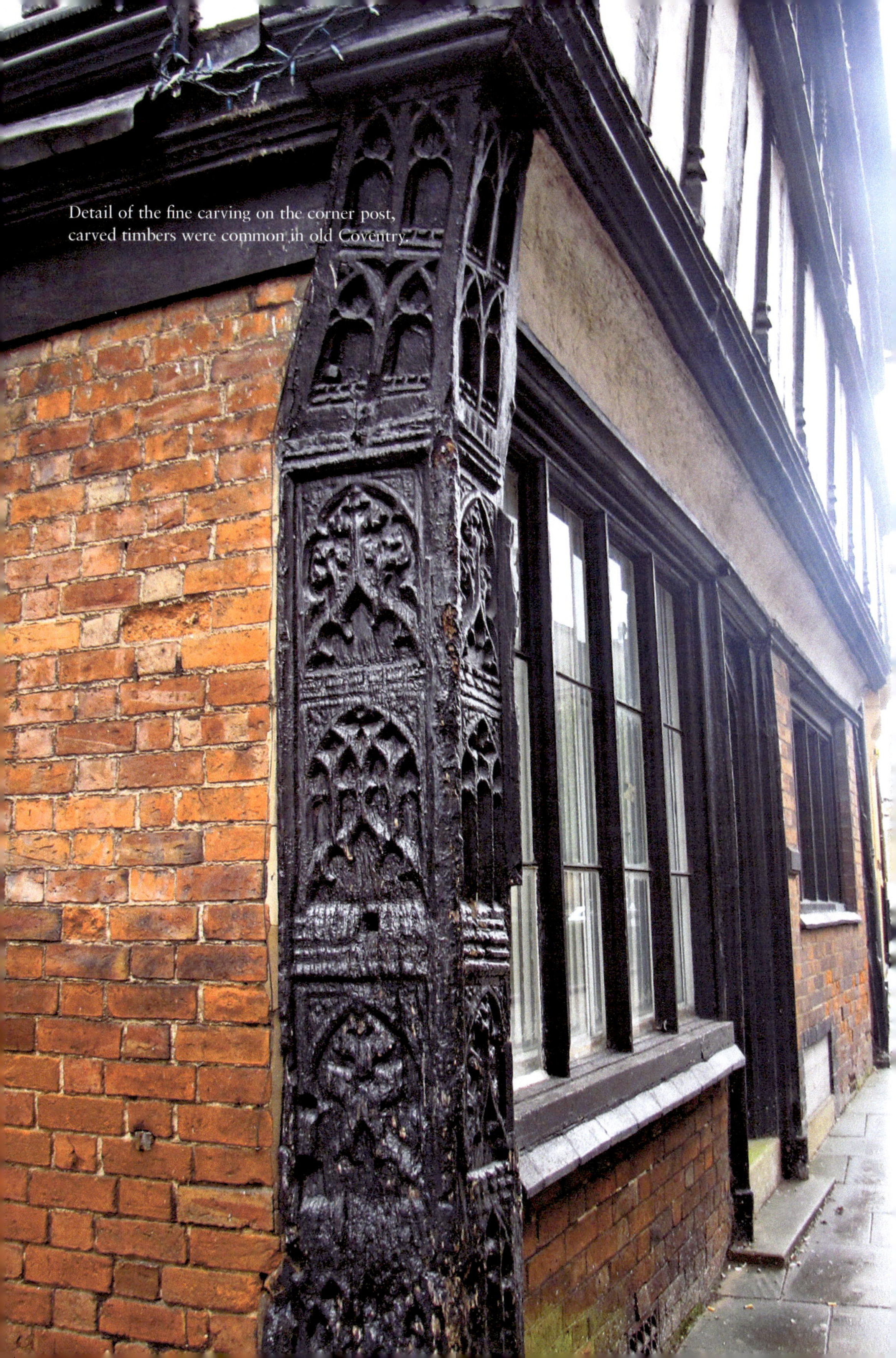

Detail of the fine carving on the corner post, carved timbers were common in old Coventry.

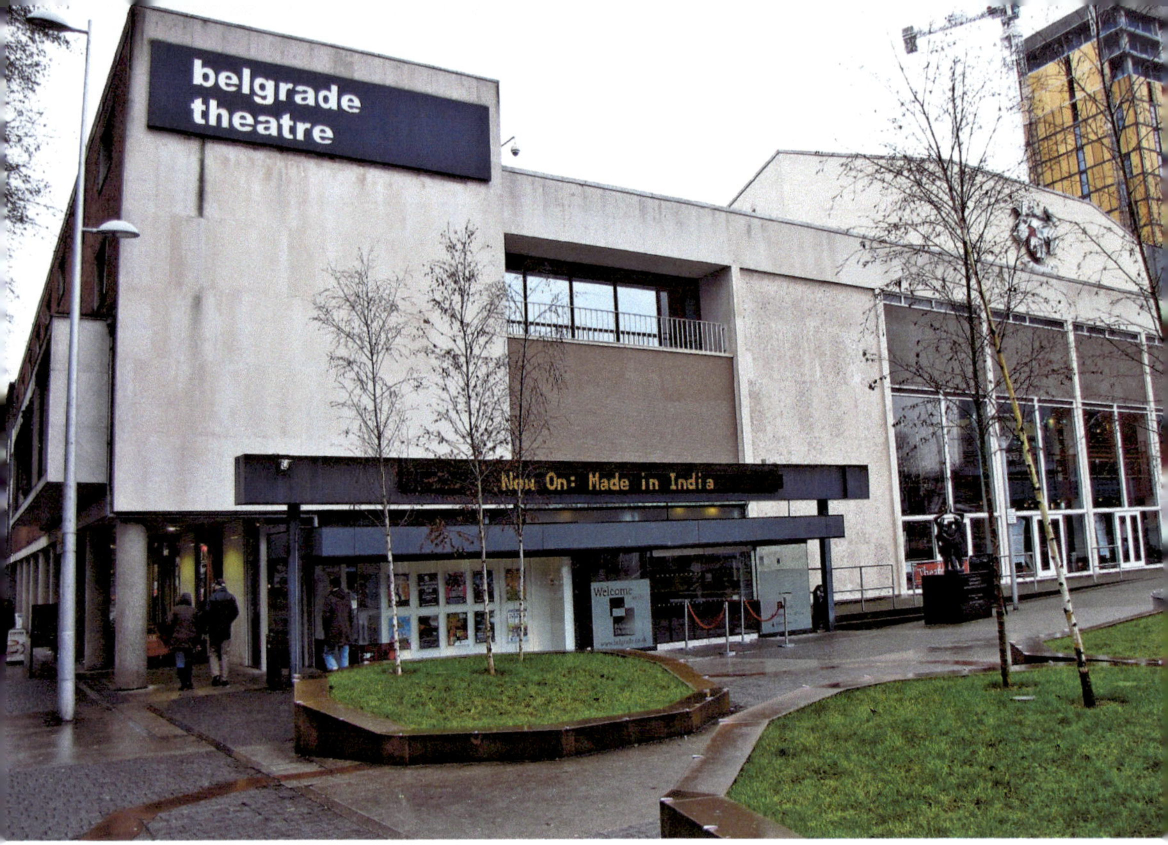


The Belgrade Theatre, from Upper Well Street.

## 3. Belgrade Theatre

The Belgrade was the first post-war professional theatre built in Britain. Opened in March 1958, it takes its name from Coventry's twin city Belgrade, then in Yugoslavia. Yugoslavia presented £6,000 worth of beech wood to Coventry for rebuilding; much was used for the new roof in the guildhall and the rest in the Belgrade. The theatre was designed by Arthur Ling, the city architect, and cost £203,000.

It originally had its own company of actors and became renowned under its first director, Brian Bailey; early company members included Sir Trevor Nunn, Sir Ian McKellen, Dame Joan Plowright, Michael Crawford, Frank Finlay and Leonard Rossiter. The theatre reopened in September 2007 after undergoing a £12-million refurb with a seven-storey extension providing a second auditorium. Importantly, although not taking place here, the Belgrade has kept Coventry's mystery play tradition alive and it was also a pioneer of youth theatre.

## 4. Bird Grove, No. 28 George Eliot Road

Bird Grove was a semi-detached Georgian house in Foleshill – only half of it remains. It was the residence of Mary Ann Evans, better known as the novelist George Eliot, who lived here for eight years from March 1841 with her father Robert Evans. Mary Ann started her literary career at Bird Grove. The alcove where she sat writing still exists with its small window that once overlooked Coventry's spires. Here she sat by a figure of Christ for two years translating Strauss's *Life of Jesus*. Her neighbours, Abijah and Elizabeth Pears, introduced her to Elizabeth's brother, Charles Bray, and his wife Caroline at Rosehill on Radford Road. It was this meeting with the Brays and their circle of intellectual friends that led to the life-changing creation of 'George Eliot' as we know her today.

Bray, a social reformer, bought the *Coventry Herald* as his political mouthpiece and while at Bird Grove Mary Ann wrote her first original works for it. One written in 1847 called *Vice and Sausages* was a satire on John Vice (Coventry's chief constable) and a scandal involving Coventry butchers. Robert Evans died here in 1849; Mary Ann went to the Continent with the Brays and afterwards moved to London.

In December 1860, the house was described as comprising of a

> Drawing Room, 30 ft. by 20 ft. with Bay Windows; a Dining Room 34ft by 16 ft.; Best and Servants Kitchen, Butler's Pantry, with excellent Cellarage, Five Bed Chambers, with Bath Room, Water Closet, and Servant's Chamber. The Outbuildings comprise a Carriage House, Harness Room, Stable, Shed, and Pig Sty's, and adjoining the House are a Conservatory and Vinery.

Joseph Cash Jr then lived here until his death in 1880. He was the nephew of John Cash, one of the founders of J & J Cash, the famous silk weavers. Joseph's son Joseph (another Jr)

Bird Grove as it was in Mary Ann's time. Its name comes from the many birds that lived here.

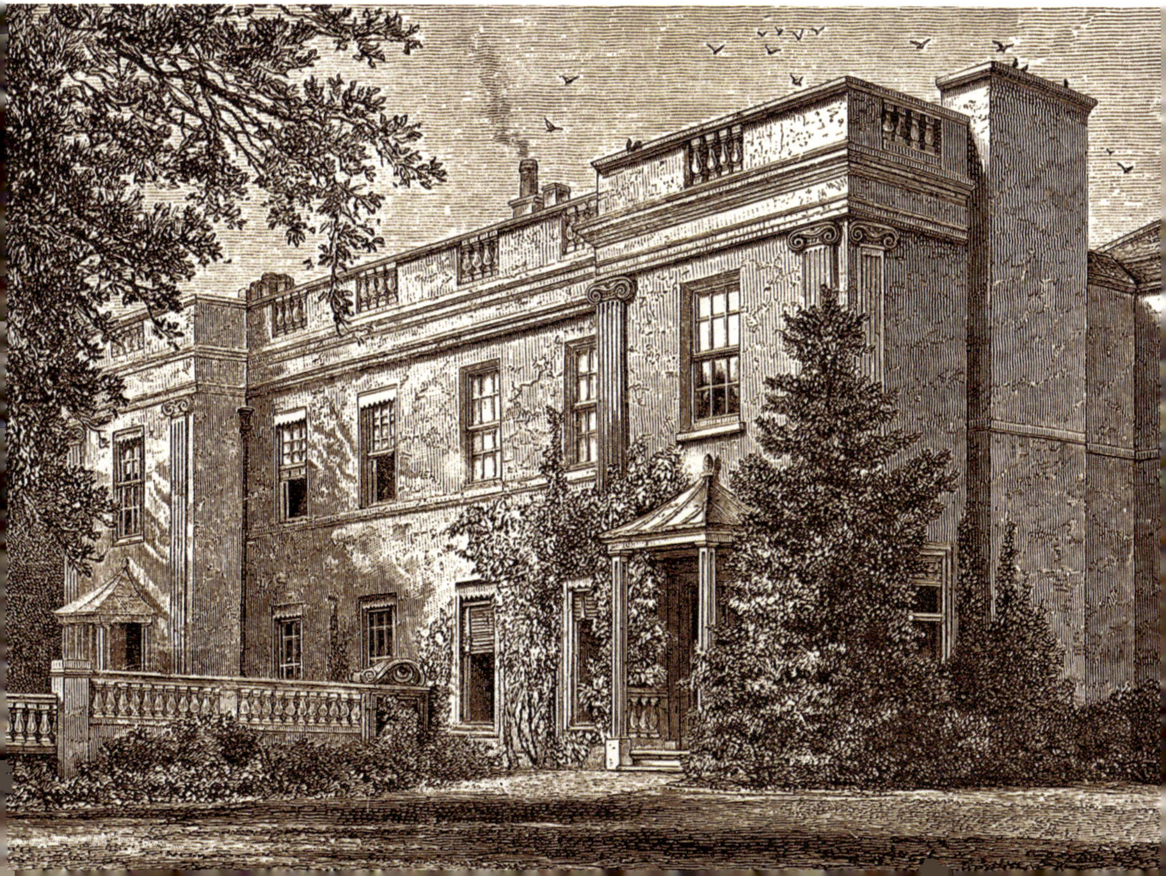

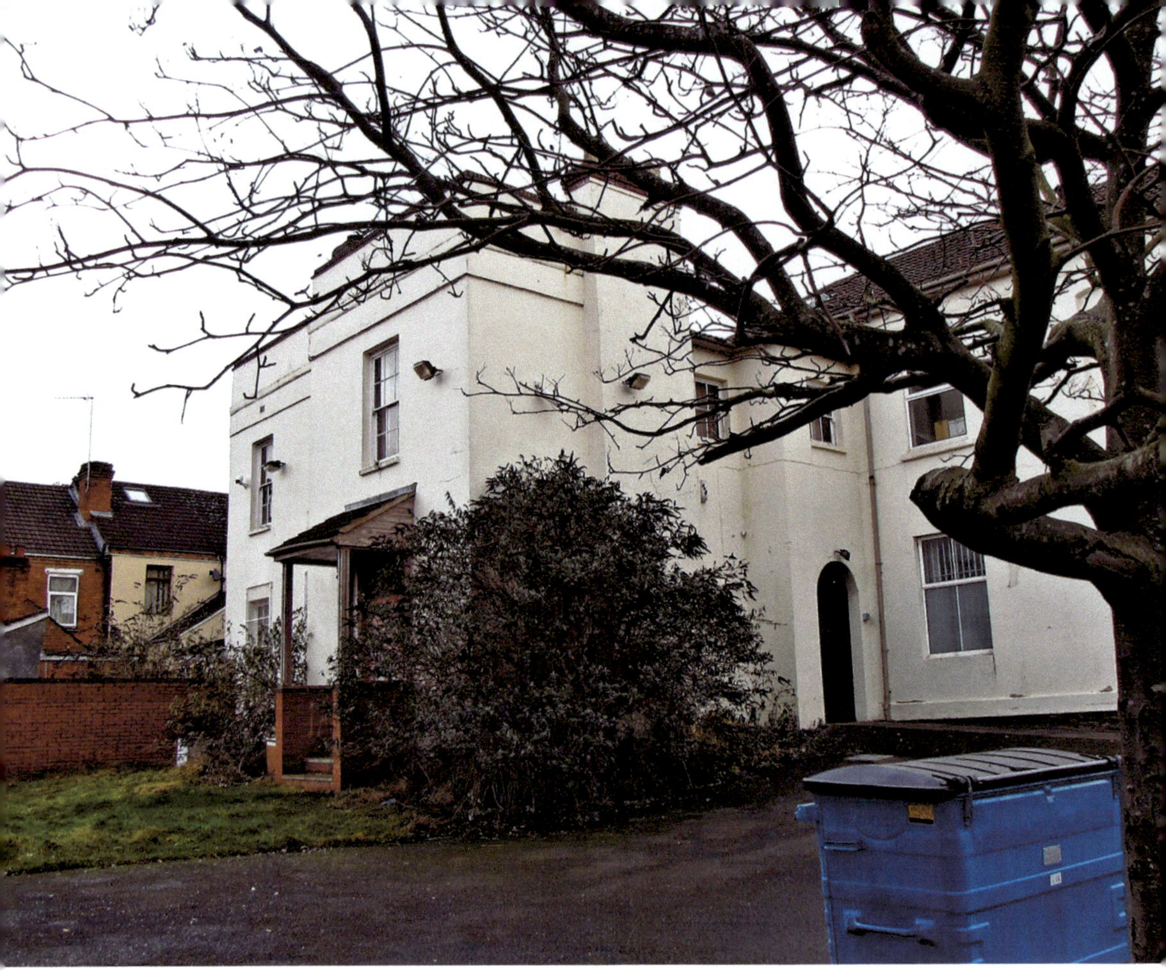

Bird Grove today swamped by housing, and minus half the original building. Mary Ann sat by the window over the curved door.

took over the building after his death. Although set in extensive grounds, over time the Cash's purchased land to protect their view as the city encroached.

This Joseph Cash, silk manufacturer, JP and formerly of J & J Cash Ltd went bankrupt in 1900 after investing in numerous unprofitable ventures. In 1942 the building was acquired by the council and the following year turned into a boys' hostel. It has since been many things, including an evangelical school. It now stands empty.

## 5. Blue Coat School

Blue Coat Charity School was founded in around 1714 as an industrial school to educate poor girls, mainly orphans, and place them in service. The school was closely linked to Holy Trinity and sermons here and St Michael's raised funds for its running.

In 1855 the original school room was unstable due to being built on the priory ruins. The Blue Coat School Charity bought two unoccupied houses and the original brick school at the end of Priory Row, then hired local architect James Murray to design a new school in the fashionable Gothic style. It was said at the time that it was intended to be one of the most beautiful buildings

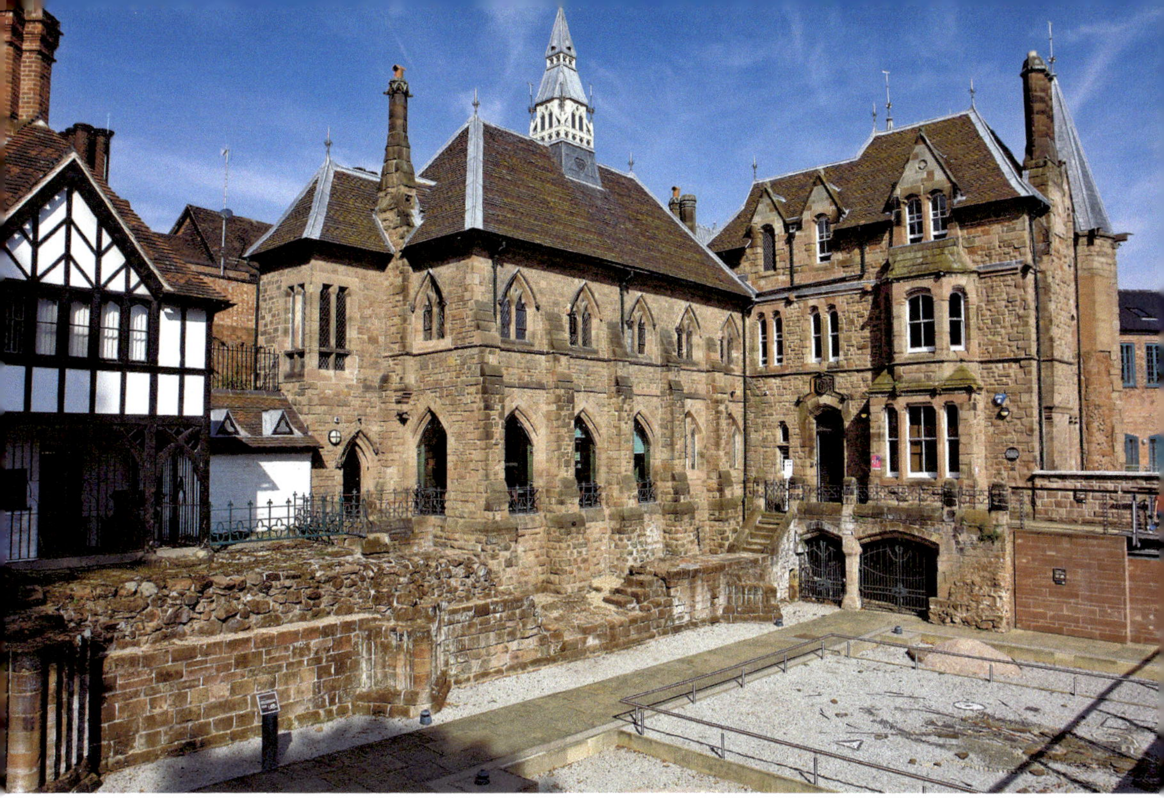

*Above*: Blue Coat School across Priory Gardens, the ruins of the priory can be seen below it. It also includes a section of the west tower of the priory.

*Below*: Blue Coat's attractive schoolroom with its beautiful roof.

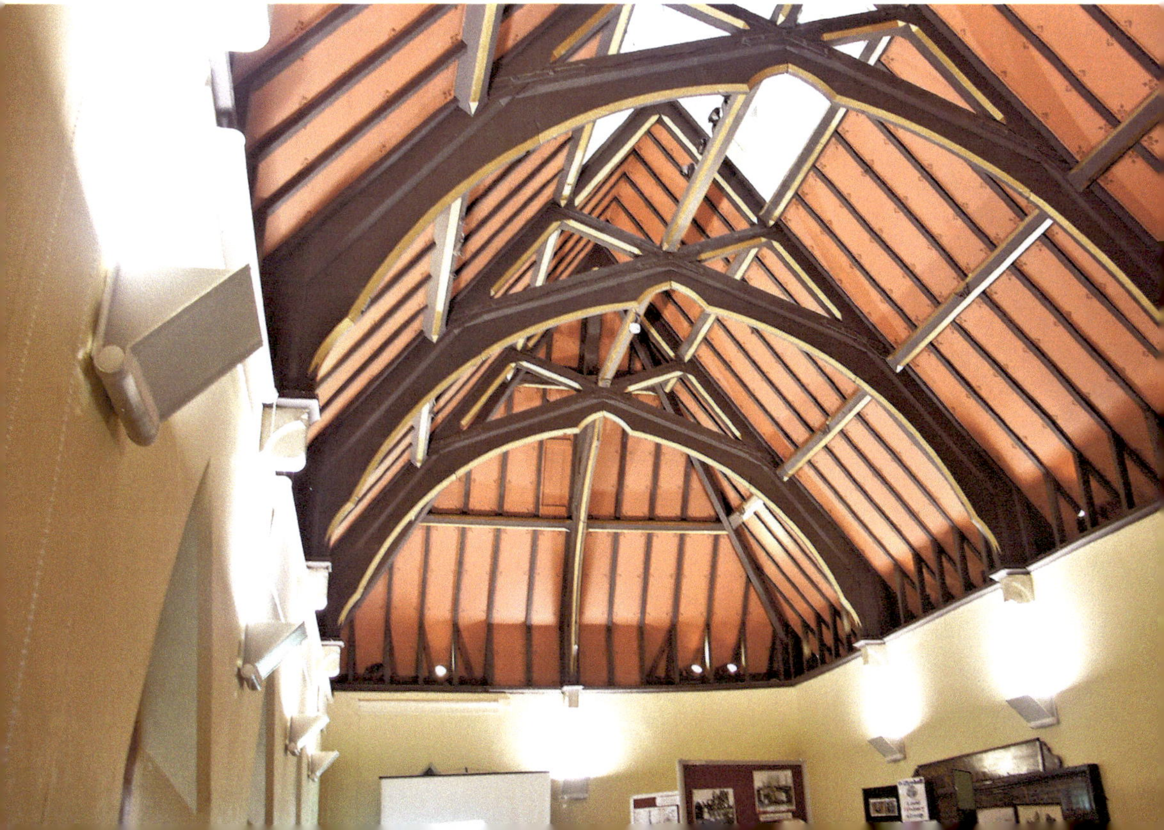

in the city. When clearing the site, the entrance of the Priory Cathedral of St Mary was discovered. Work began in 1856 and was completed the following year by public subscription.

In 1859 it held fifty girls who were taught the Bible and the three Rs. Six senior girls boarded for a year under the matron, who taught them domestic duties. By the turn of the twentieth century it was a girls' orphanage, until they were evacuated in 1940, never to return. In March 1940 it was given by the trustees to the council, who rented it out as a canteen and lost property department for public transport workers. This continued until the early 1970s. It stood empty from 1990 until restored under the council's Phoenix Initiative and became the Holy Trinity Church Centre, re-establishing its old link between the school and the church.

## 6. Bonds Hospital

During his mayoralty in 1497, Thomas Bond (a draper) gave the Corporation landed property to the value of £49 11*s* 7*d* per year to found a Bede house at Bablake for ten poor men and one poor woman to attend them. An archive manuscript gives 1497 as the actual date of foundation but another foundation date given is 1506. This is probably the date

Bond's Hospital with its attractive close studded timberwork.

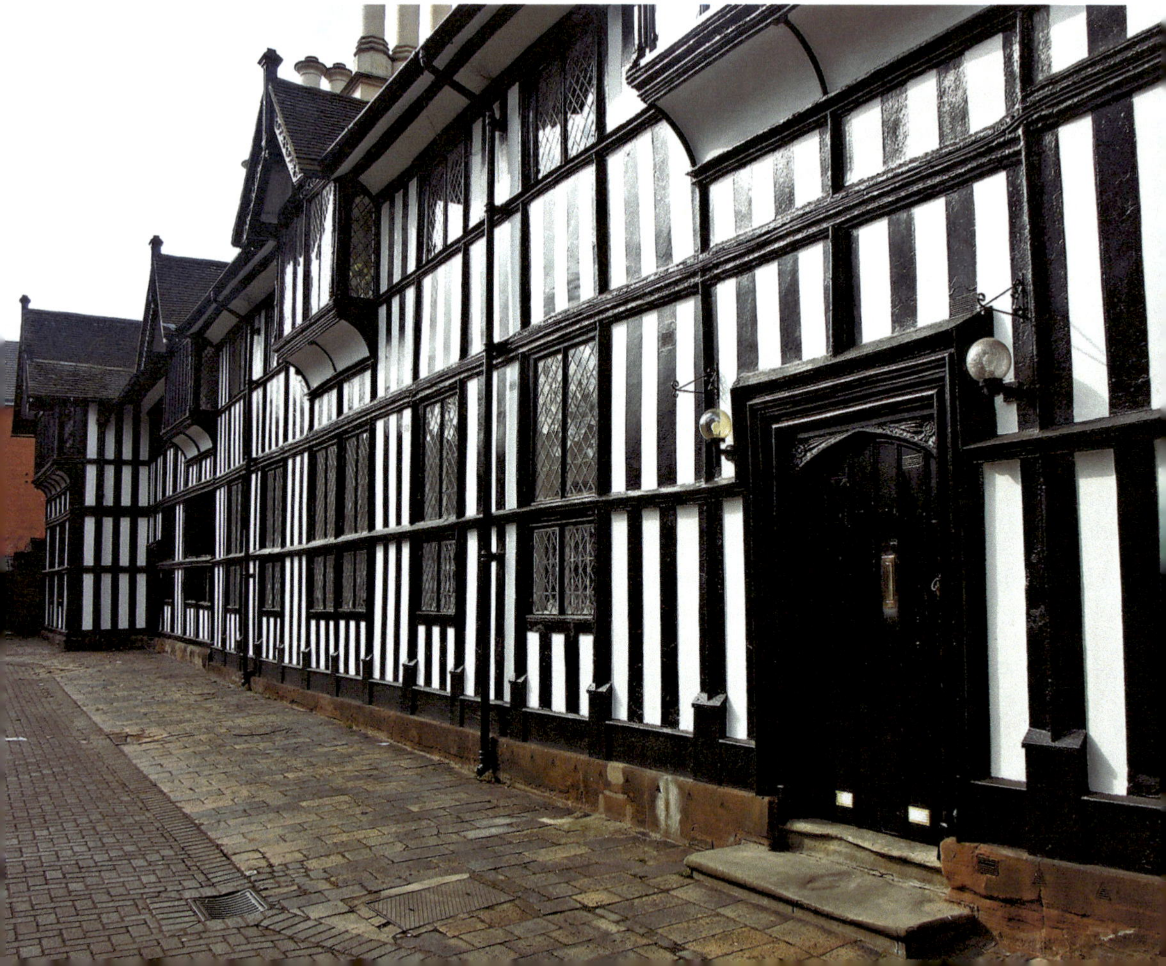

of the actual erection of the building and its first admissions, as it would have taken a few years for rent to accumulate to build it. Each man was to receive, 'every year a gown of black, with a hood,' and a small sum of money weekly.

The first inmates were required to attend daily matins, mass and evensong and a chaplain was employed to look after their spiritual needs, and to pray for the souls of the founder, his father, grandfather, and all Christians. An order for the suppression of all such houses was made in 1547. Both Bond's and Ford's were included in the closures. But, on the city claiming suffering would ensue, the order was withdrawn and both institutions were granted to the mayor, bailiffs, and commonalty at a rent of 1*d* a year. In 1609 the buildings and land that maintained the house were said to have been concealed from the Crown and restitution or purchase was demanded. The council chose the latter.

In 1894 there were sixty almsmen receiving 6*s* weekly – eighteen were residents. They had two nurses, a common kitchen, and a common sitting room. The property and charity were administered by trustees and two councillors attended each Sunday, when the roll was called and the almsmen paraded in their black hooded gowns to St John's. The hospital was enlarged in 1816, but by 1830 large parts were dilapidated. In 1832–34 the building was extensively restored by Rickman and Hutchinson. Much of the old timber was reused

Looking across Bablake quadrangle. Bond's is left. Note the student block encroaching.

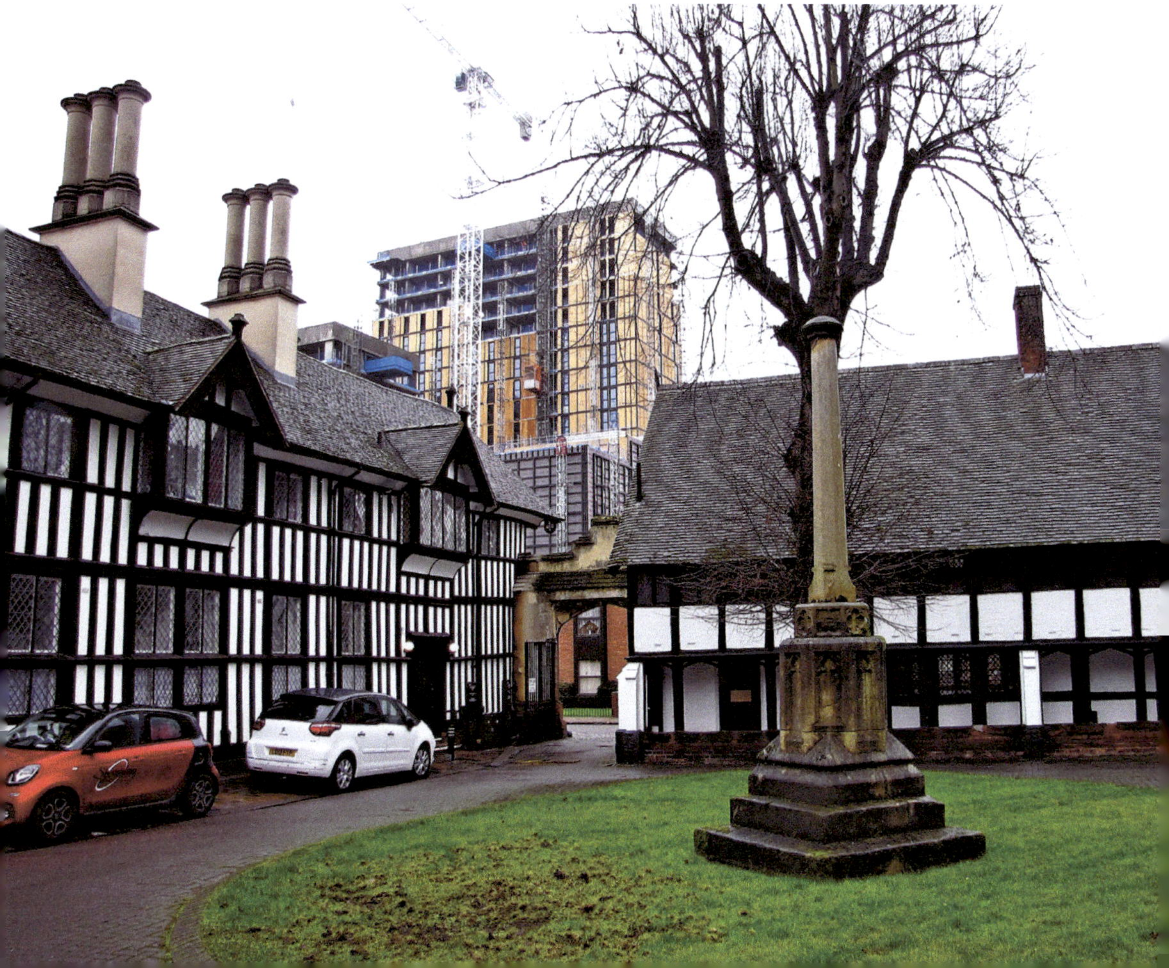

in its construction – the carved window lintels are original but the barge-boards are copies. The lower windows are not in their original position and chimneys were added. In 1846–47 Rickman and Hutchinson added the Tudor-style Hill Street frontage built over the city wall – a fragment can be seen in the side of the building. The building today still fulfils its original purpose.

## 7. Canal Warehouses

In 1768 a contract was drawn up by Coventry Canal Co. to dig a canal between Coventry and Fradley; James Brindley was appointed its engineer. On 10 August 1769 the first boatloads of coal came into Coventry from the Bedworth coal fields, cheered into the basin by thousands. The buildings around the basin in Bishop Street were constructed in 1788 by Coventry Canal Co. These consisted of coal bunkers, warehouses, a weighbridge and Canal House, the centre of administration – now demolished. The large warehouse on the city centre side was rebuilt in 1914 and bore the words 'GRAND UNION WAREHOUSE'. This title dated from 1930 when the Grand Union Canal Carrying Co. acquired the buildings. It was restored in 1995 by Coventry City Council, who developed artist studios, offices and craft shops here. The initial ambitions to hold regular events weren't maintained and despite its attractiveness it now has few businesses – the largest is the *Coventry Telegraph* offices by the warehouse and a popular bar and music venue in the coal bunkers called The Tin.

This white housing tower adds interest as it reflects in the water, some days, however, it just looks wrong! Artist studios are mainly in the warehouse on the right.

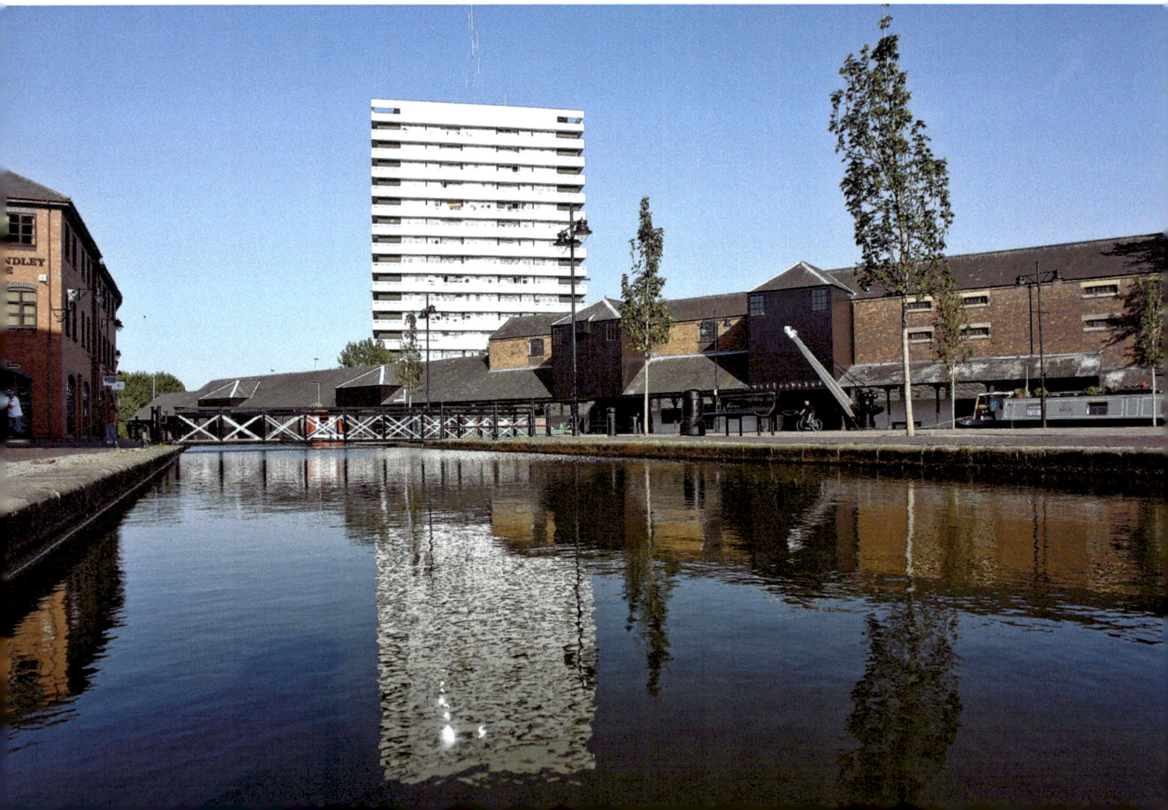

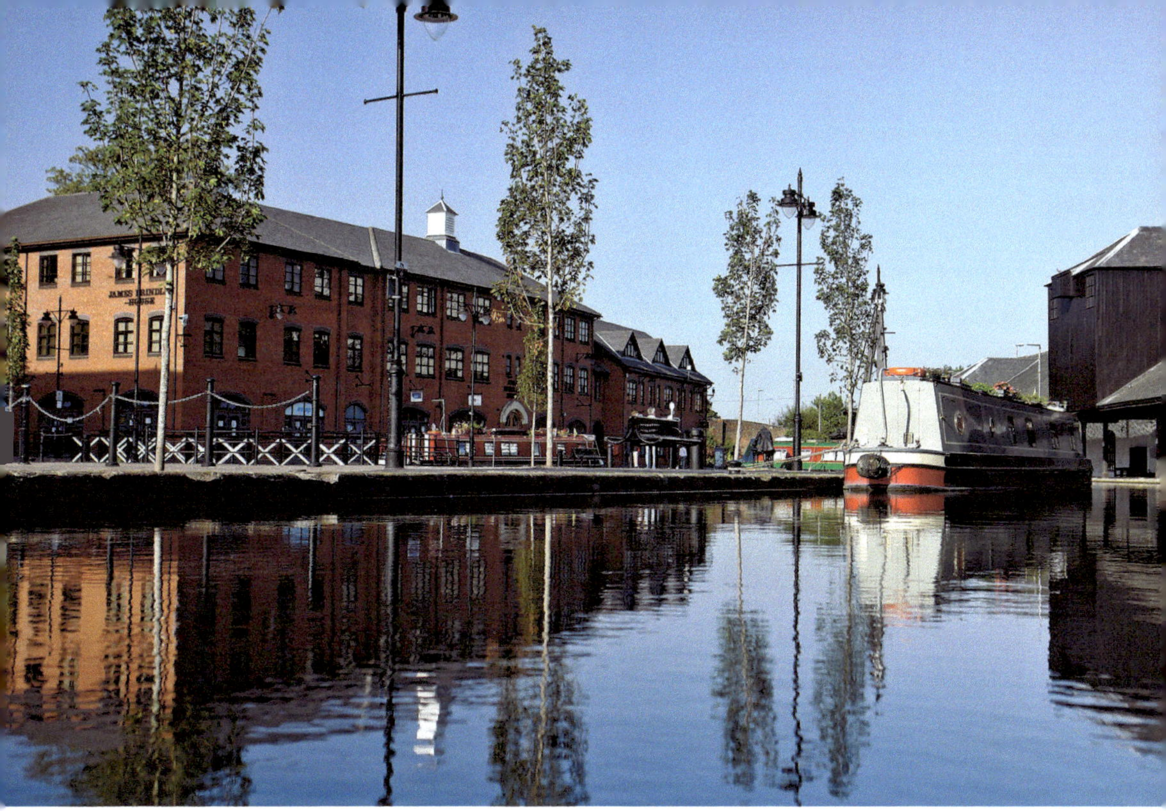

The shop units are on the left; this is a forgotten attractive place.

## 8. Cash's Model Factory, Cash's Lane

Built at Kingfield by the canal in 1857 by Quakers John and Joseph Cash, it was designed by James Murray of Priory Row in the Jacobean style. This early cottage factory for Cambric Frilling (later silk) weavers was an L-shaped terrace of two-storey homes with third-storey windowed 'top shops'. They were created to maintain the workers' independence within the factory system. Each house/shop was rented out and had small individual gardens. The terrace originally had forty-six units with a gable at either end and two gables in centre. The loom rooms in the upper terrace, entered by a ladder, held a Jacquard loom powered by a rotating shaft that ran through the building.

It appears that the original concept of the weaver having his own individual workshop never worked out, for in 1862 an employee named William Andrews wrote:

> Their cottage factory system for which they built the house at Kingfield's has been a complete failure. They could obtain no rent from the tenants unless they found work for them – now at great cost they have knocked out the partition walls of the shops and converted the top of the buildings into one large factory … the houses underneath now form merely cottages for the weavers…

The canal-facing section received the most alteration, whereas the Cash's Lane side, because of its internal design, was more difficult to alter. Its failure was down to bad timing, being completed by 1860 when a tariff on foreign imports was dropped, crippling the trade. If it

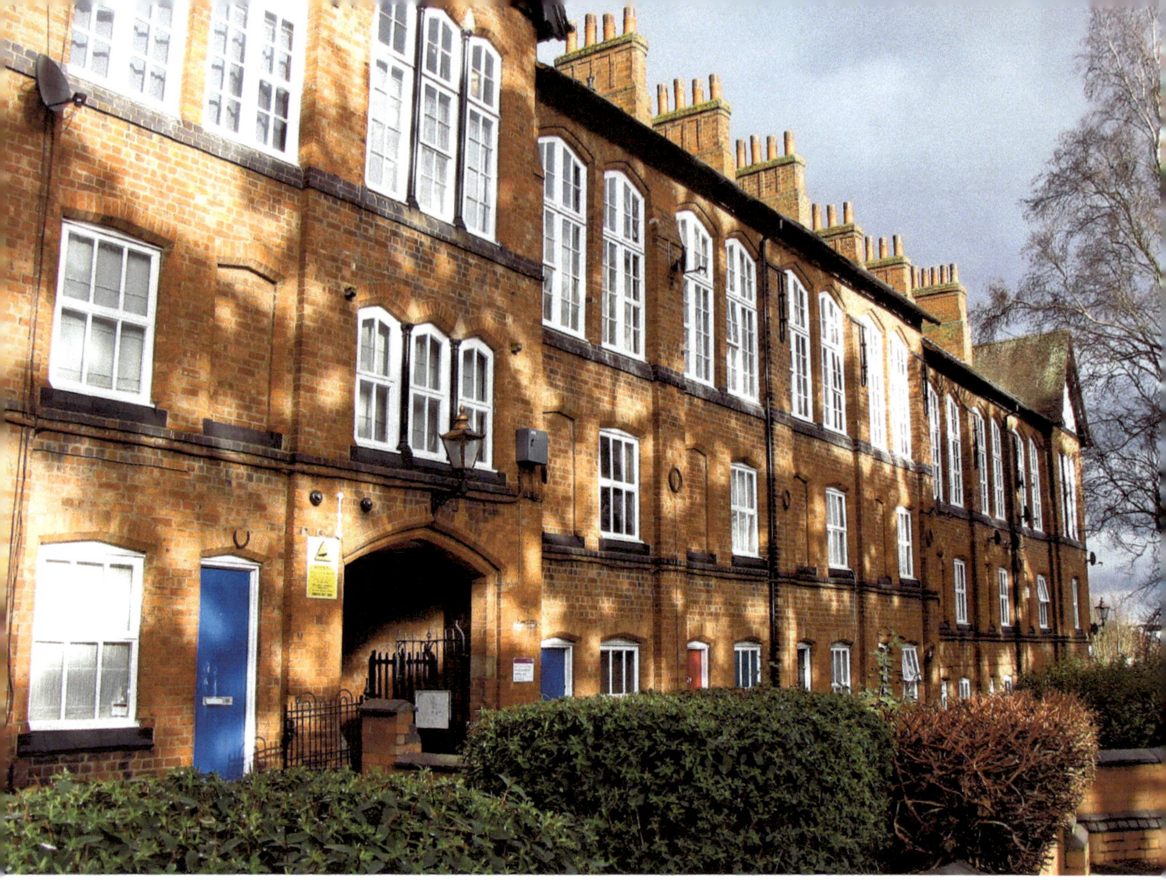

*Above*: Taken from Cash's Lane, this is a rare thing, an attractive factory.

*Below*: Cash's factory taken around 1900. Cows were usually seen in the field opposite, a truly rural industrial scene.

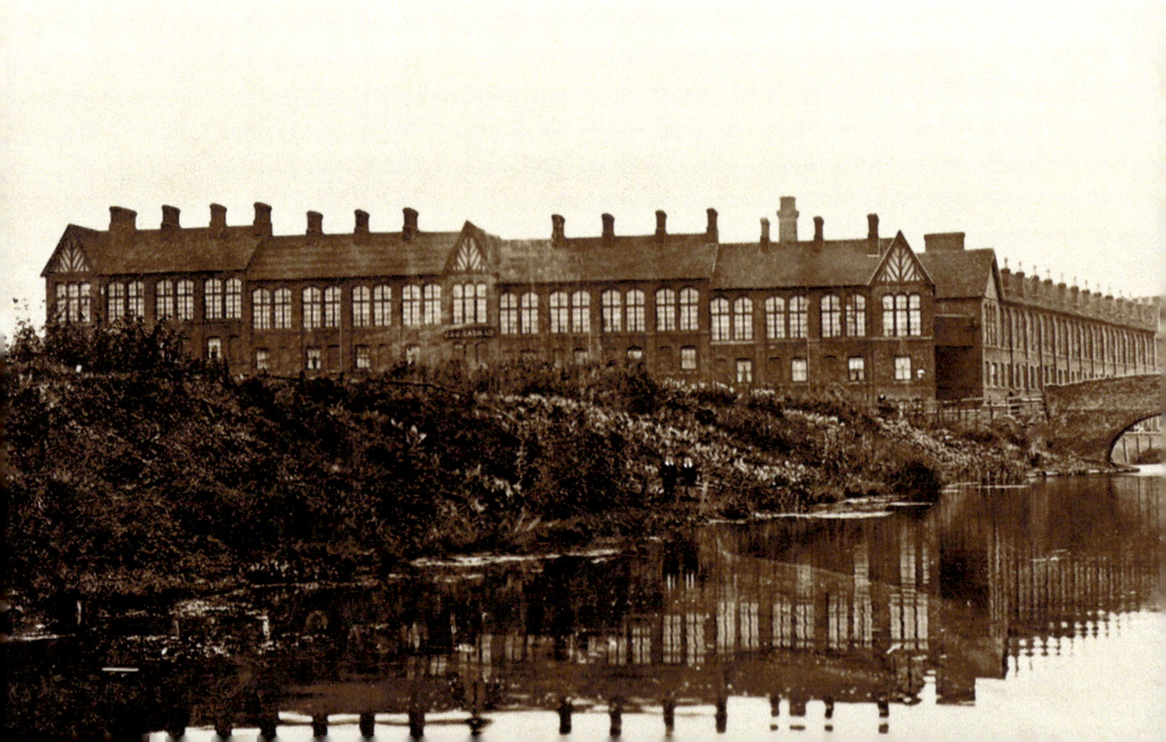

wasn't for this, Cash's intended to extend their factory to 300 units. Cash's continued on this site up until two years ago and now the Chinese-owned company creates its beautiful silks and tags in Tile Hill. Their unique cottage factory has now been turned into housing.

## 9. Castle Grounds

Number 7 Little Park Street, now 'the Castle Grounds', was built for Thomas Bird, a silk ribbon manufacturer, between 1720 and 1746. Bird's family brought silk weaving into the city at the end of the seventeenth century with the assistance of Huguenots and established the first works in 1703. Before he died in 1746 he employed over 2,000 people. His son Alderman John Bird continued in the house and trade. John's wife Judith was the aunt of William Wilberforce, famed for his stance against slavery. The couple's son William Wilberforce Bird lived here and served the city as an MP from 1796 to 1802. He was a champion of the Coventry Blues, the Whigs. He went bankrupt in 1804 and in 1810 held a government post in Africa. From 1881 until 1978 the building was the home of the Manchester Unity Club, order of Oddfellows and around 1981 was sold to the Coventry Building Society. The building deteriorated over the '80s, and in 1997 was converted into a pub by Wolverhampton and Dudley Breweries. This building was originally called the Varsity and has recently been renamed the Castle Grounds.

The Bird residence, now a favourite student watering hole.

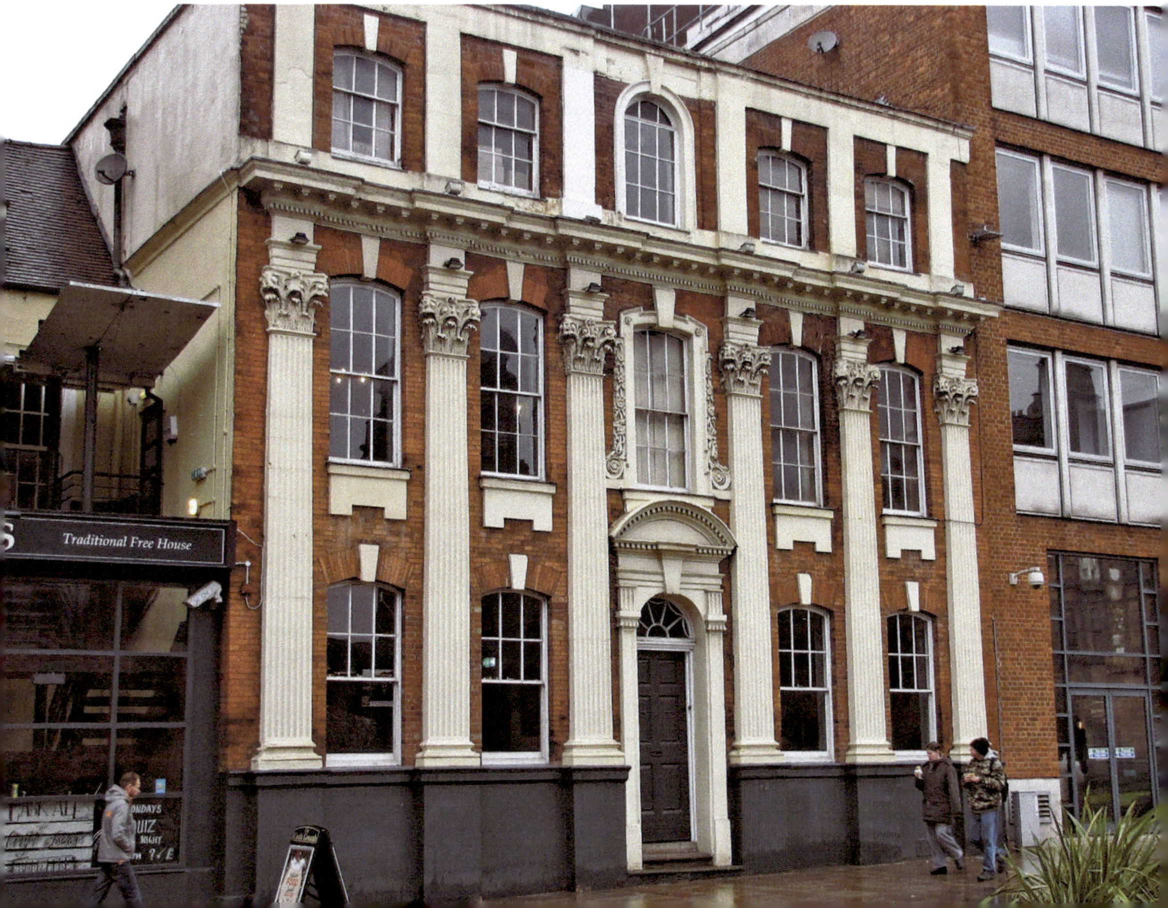

## 1c. Charterhouse Priory of Saint Anne, London Road

Charterhouse was named after the main Chartreuse in France. It was founded in 1381 by William Lord Zouch of Harringworth, who obtained from Sir Baldwin Freville 14 acres of land within the manor of Shortley. Zouch secured the co-operation of Richard II and nominated him as principal founder of the house. He then procured John Luscote, prior, Palmer, the procurator, John Netherby, vicar of the house, and Edmund Balling from the Charterhouse in London. They came to Coventry and established themselves at the hermitage of St Ann, which already existed somewhere on the site. They were then joined by three more monks from the Carthusians at Beauvale, and four who had recently joined the order. This small group established the order in Coventry.

Lord Zouch died leaving an endowment of £60 a year. His role was taken over by Richard Luffe, mayor of Coventry, John Botoner, John Bockingham, Bishop of Lincoln and Adam Botoner (mayor in 1377 and 1385), and others. Richard Luffe and John Botoner gave 400 marks towards building the church, cloisters and cells for the monks. The monks lived in their individual cells and only met at appointed times. King Richard, as the proclaimed founder, came to the city in 1385 with Queen Anne to lay the foundation stone, also bestowed upon it gifts of land and properties. The discipline in these houses was very severe: from cell to church and back again, with study and manual labour, and conversation was limited to 'talking days'. Despite this the Carthusians spared no expense on the decoration of their monasteries, and there were some very artistic and learned men among them. One such was Nicholas of Hereford, a close companion of reformer John Wycliffe who helped him translate the Bible into English. He retired to the Charterhouse in 1417 and died here in 1420. One noted visitor was Thomas Mowbray, Duke of Hereford, who attended its church for three masses before his expected combat on Gosford Green in 1398.

The monastery continued to grow in importance until its suppression in 1539, and in 1542 the last prior, John Bochard, passed the monastery, church and buildings to Richard Andrews, gent, and Leonard Chamberleyn. The church was demolished and sold on and the prior's hall and refectory were converted into a residence. In 1567 Henry Waver, a mercer, died in occupation, leaving it to his son Richard, who sold it in 1569 to Robert Dudley, Earl of Leicester. Leicester sold it to Thomas Riley, who sold it on to Sampson Baker who occupied the house. It then passed to Edward Holt of Dudston, whose son Sir Thomas Holt of Aston sold it to Richard Butler of Coventry. Butler sold it to a Londoner named Lodge. It was purchased from him by Edward Hill, whose son Edward left it to his nephew, also called Edward Hill. This Edward Hill left three daughters; one, named Ann, married Henry Inge, who became owner in 1733. From him it passed to Edward Inge, Coventry town clerk, then to his brother John. During John's ownership two vicars of St Michael's occupied it. Later in 1838 the estates of Edward Inge were sold under decree of the Court of Chancery to William Grant, silk dyer of Coventry, for £4,536.

On Grant's death it was sold in 1848 to John and Francis Wyley, wholesale chemists of the city. The property was in a dilapidated condition and substantial repairs were made, and it was converted into a double residence. The northern section in 1880 was tenanted by Mrs Laxon, and the southern half by Francis Wyley, councillor, alderman and mayor.

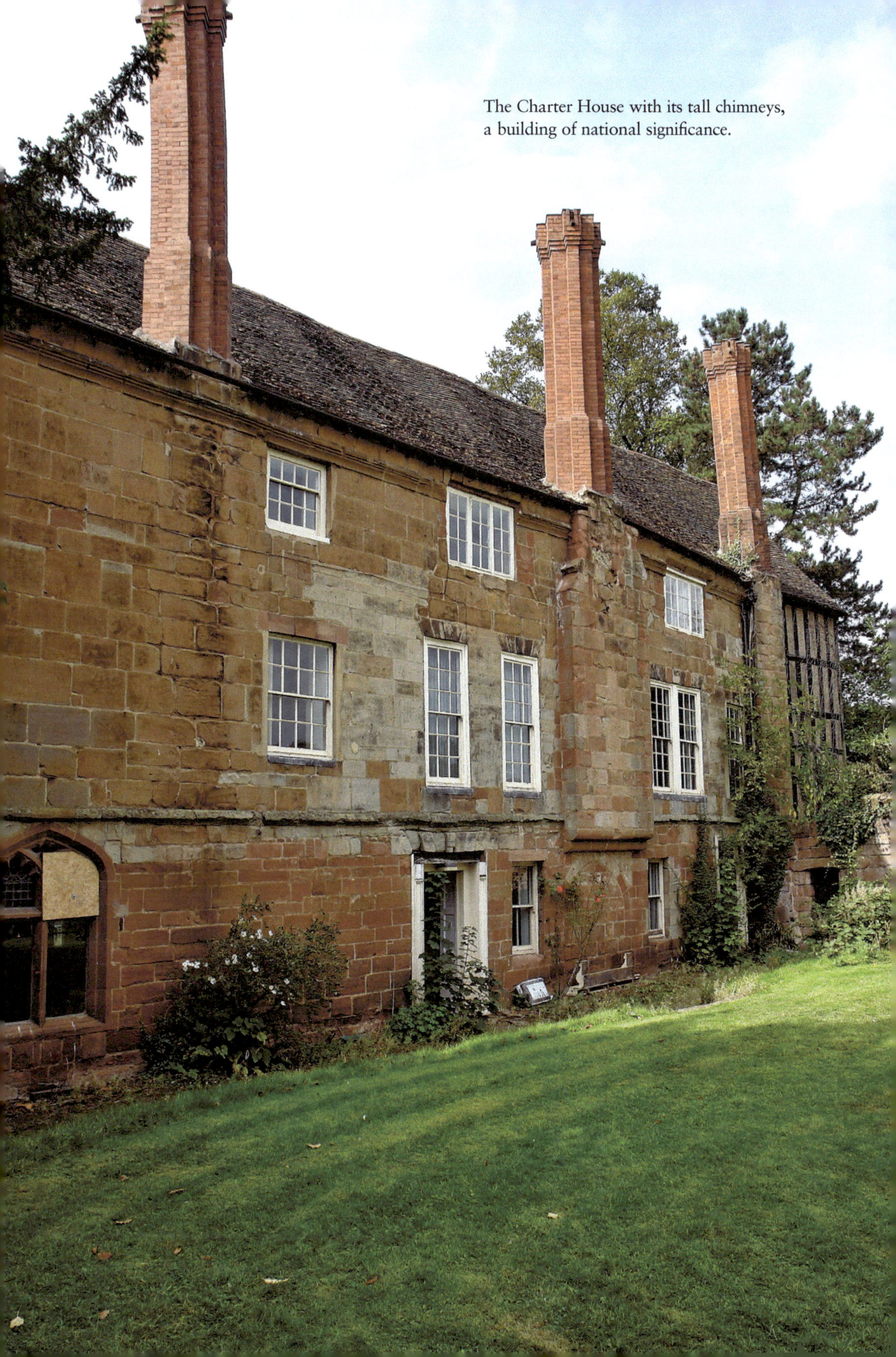

The Charter House with its tall chimneys, a building of national significance.

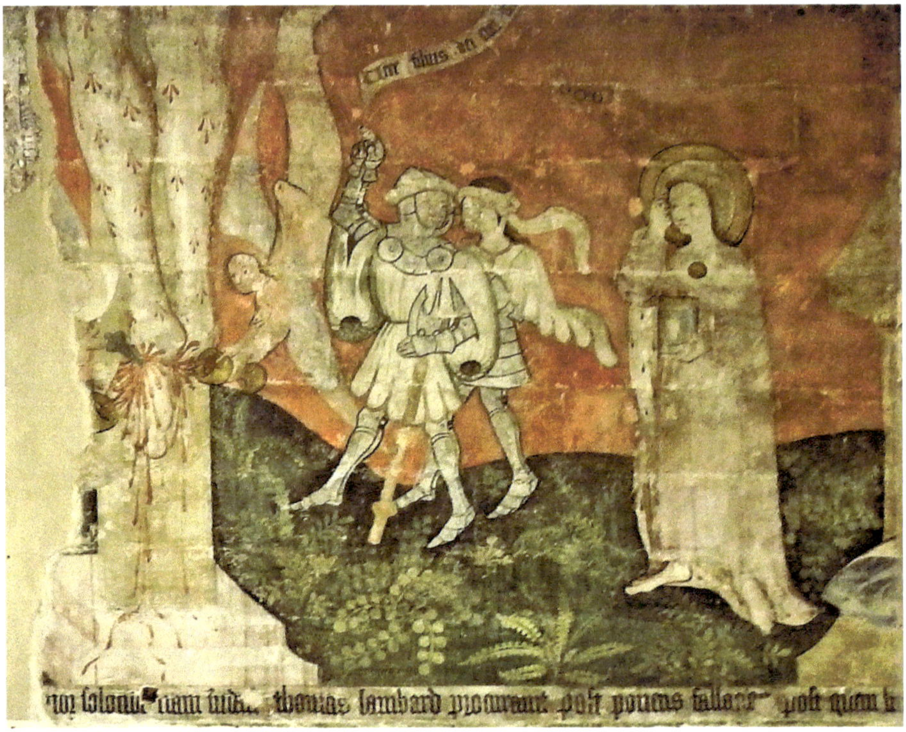

*Above*: A section of the medieval crucifixion scene showing an angel collecting Christ's blood and a noble in armour taking the place of Longinus. This painting covered the entire wall off the open hall, until it was cut off when the upper floor was added in the sixteenth century.

*Below*: Beautiful sixteenth-century wall paintings also survive in the Charterhouse.

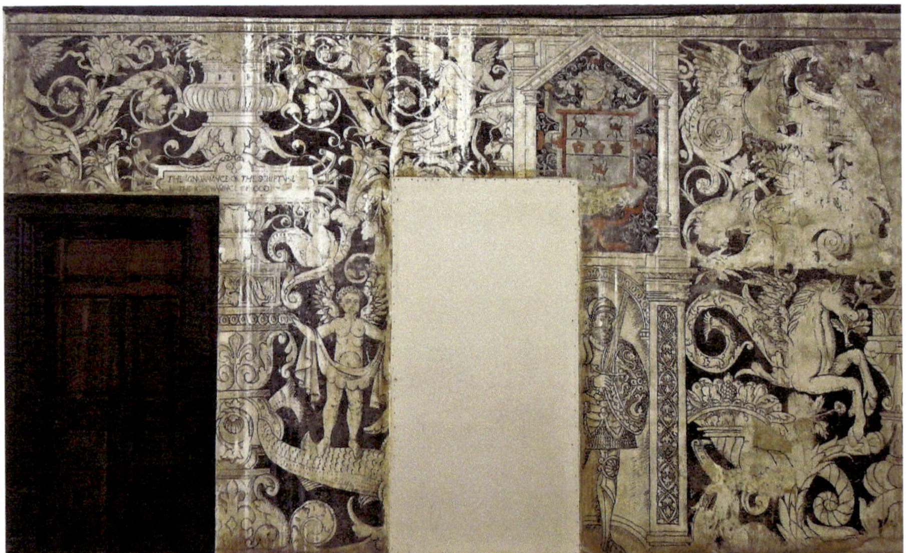

Sir William Wyley took over the building in 1889 and left it as we know it today, a medieval and Tudor house. Wyley uncovered the remarkable wall paintings, including the huge lower section of Christ crucified on the south wall, dating to around 1417. He was a council member from 1876 to 1888 and unusually, while not a councillor, he was elected mayor twice. He was one of Coventry's most prominent citizens.

In his will, from 1940, Wyley gave the Charterhouse and its grounds to the city with a wish that it was made into a museum and park for the people. The council didn't follow Wyley's wishes but gave his home over to various tenants, ending with Coventry City College. When the college left in 2009, the building was left empty, and in 2011 offered for sale. This was met with opposition. It was hoped the council would step in; nothing was forthcoming, its future looked uncertain. In 2011 a group formed to save it, the Charterhouse Preservation Society, who were passed possession in 2012. It is now part of the Historic Coventry Trust and has gained funding from the National Heritage Fund. Future plans include a museum, education centre and Heritage Park. Ian Lush, the chief executive of the Architectural Heritage Fund, said of it, 'This is a building of International significance.' Thankfully Sir William Wyley's vision for his beloved home is after seventy-six years is finally coming true.

## 11. Cheylesmore Gatehouse

Cheylesmore Gatehouse could have been so much more, for until the 1950s part of its original main hall still stood. What we see today, the gateway, is all that remains of a moated royal residence built of stone and timber. Due to war demands in 1942 a nearby engineering firm decided to knock down the old building adjoining the gatehouse. Tiles were pulled off and the ceiling ripped down revealing an ancient timbered roof. Local historian J. B. Shelton brought in experts and work was halted.

The Ministry of Ancient Monuments recommended the building be listed as an Ancient Monument in 1943. In 1944 historian Phillip Chatwin wrote,

> The old half-timber building spanning the roadway has been always known as 'The Manor House'. No one seems to have realised that a row of cottages within ... crowned by ribbon weaving rooms, was actually the Hall of the Manor House ... Admittedly there was the medieval chimney at the far end, but directly the plaster ceilings were removed the wonderful 14th century roof became apparent ... The roof is undoubtedly a 'gem' and we look forward to the time when some of the old glory of the hall can be recovered. The roof is remarkable in two ways for not only is the timberwork a grand piece of medieval construction, but the tiles which covered it with its ridge complete are medieval too. Such a condition of things is unique in the Midlands and a very great rarity in the country as a whole.

The most remarkable thing about this hall, which belonged to Queen Isabella and the Black Prince, is it didn't survive – it was demolished in 1956. Why? It was said for 'necessary development' – the site lay untouched for over forty years.

Fortunately the gatehouse survived, possibly because it had been subdivided into two cottages and was still occupied, having been relet in 1939. The gatehouse was dismantled and carefully restored by the council in 1965 and was found to stand on an earlier fourteenth-century building

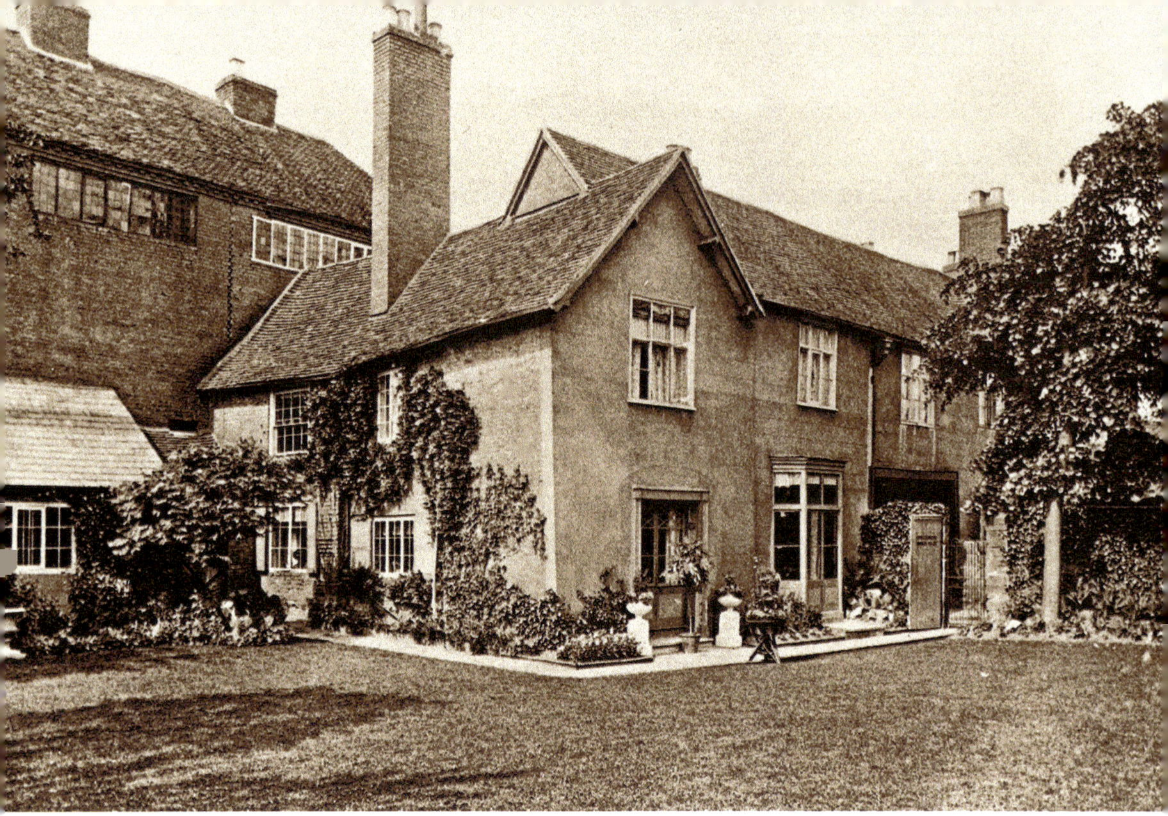

*Above*: Taken around 1890, this photograph shows the gatehouse when it still formed two cottages and to the left the main hall can be seen still standing.

*Below*: A rear view of the gatehouse a seen today.

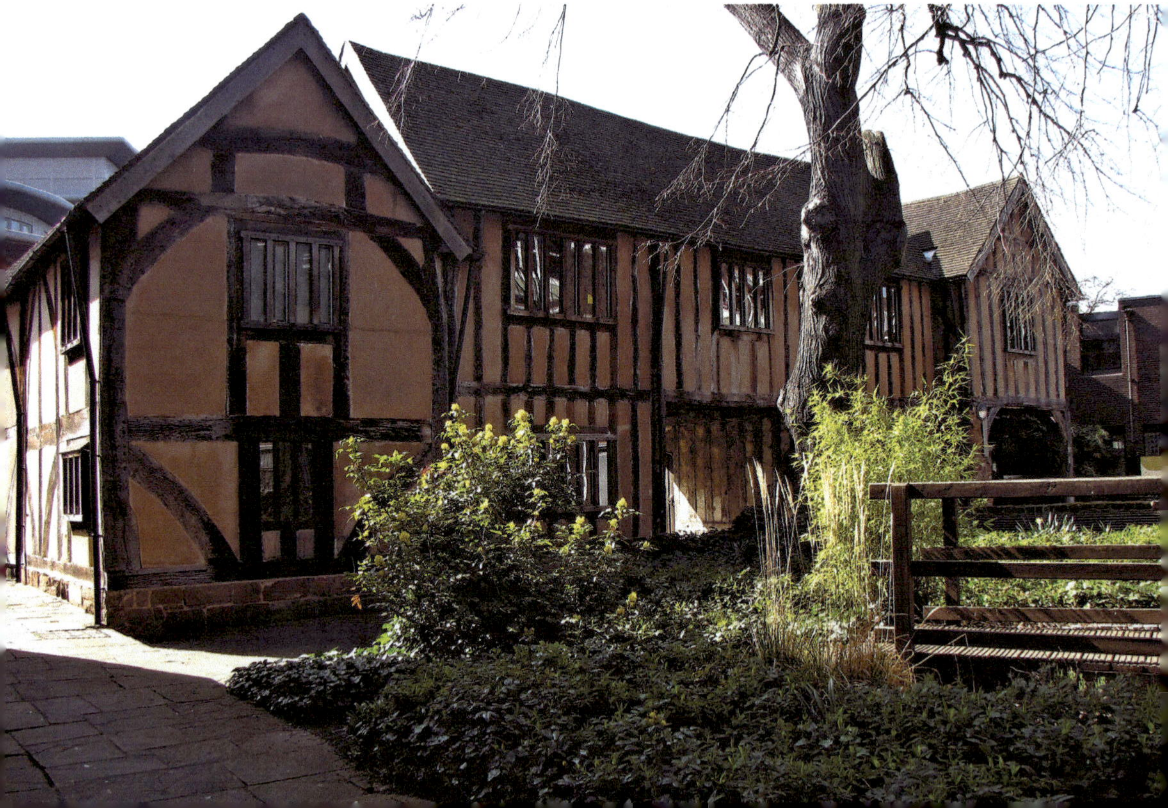

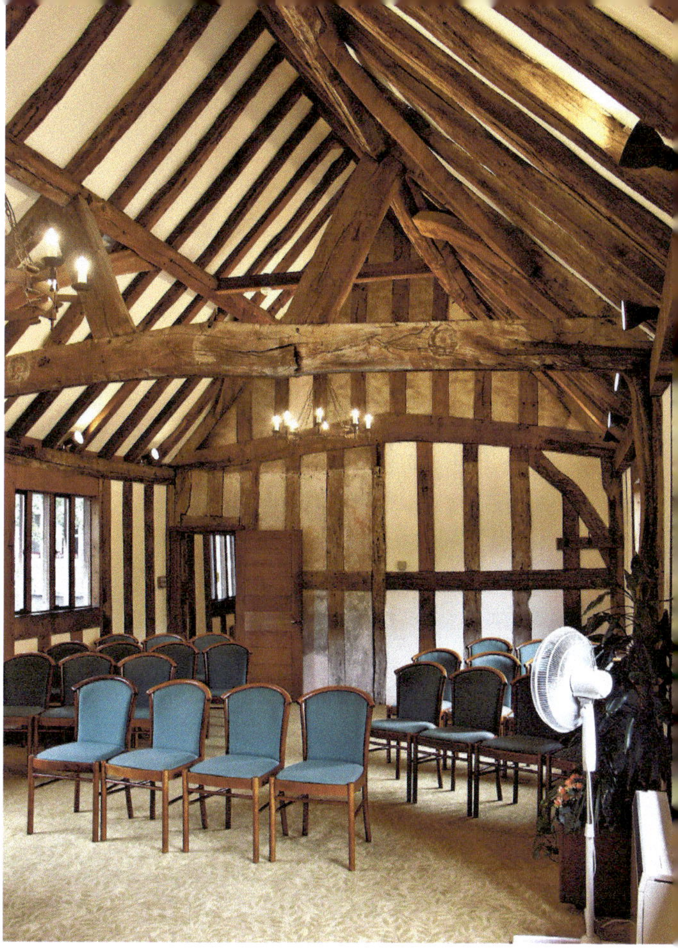

A fine timbered room inside.

and below that a twelfth-century agricultural building. It is generally described as a sixteenth-century manor gatehouse with two attached fourteenth-century wings – the north wing having a fifteenth-century floor. It is now the oldest register office in the country.

## 12. Cook Street Gate

Coventry's city wall was 'slighted' in 1662 by order of Charles II because it had withheld his father. The city gates lasted longer, until in 1762 when an Act of Parliament was passed for widening the streets. Writing in the nineteenth century, William Reader the Coventry antiquarian stated,

> Five of the principal gates which the Earl of Northampton had left out to the city were now to experience the ruthless violence of a careless Corporation. Instead of permitting these ancient and noble ornaments of the city to remain, and making roads to pass by the sides (as was the case at Warwick), they, under the pretence that loaded waggons could not pass through the arches, levelled these beautiful monuments of antiquity to the ground.

The last major gate demolished was Mill Lane Gate in 1849, which left just Swanswell and Cook Street Gate. Cook Street Gate is believed to have been built in the first quarter of the

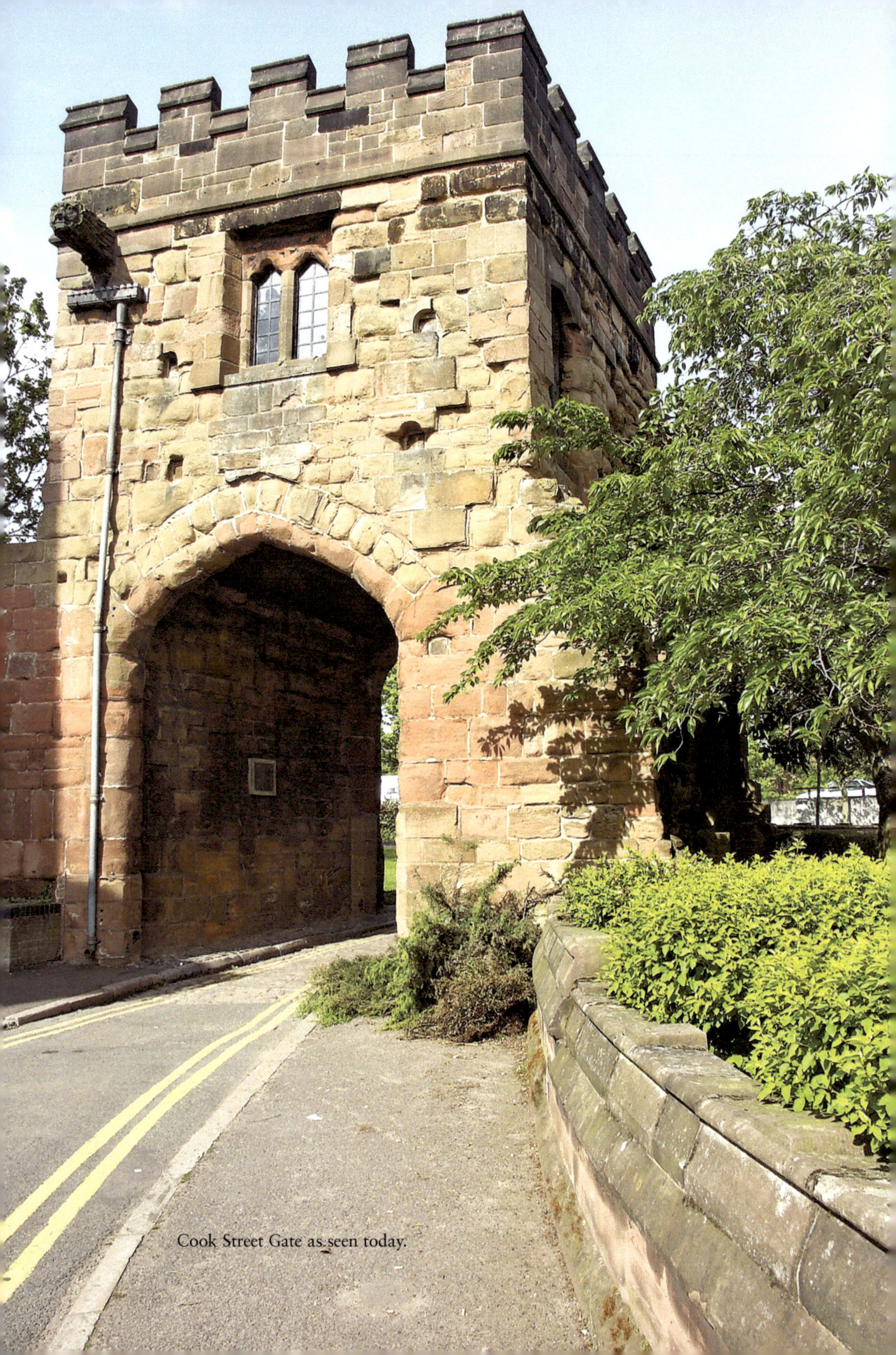

Cook Street Gate as seen today.

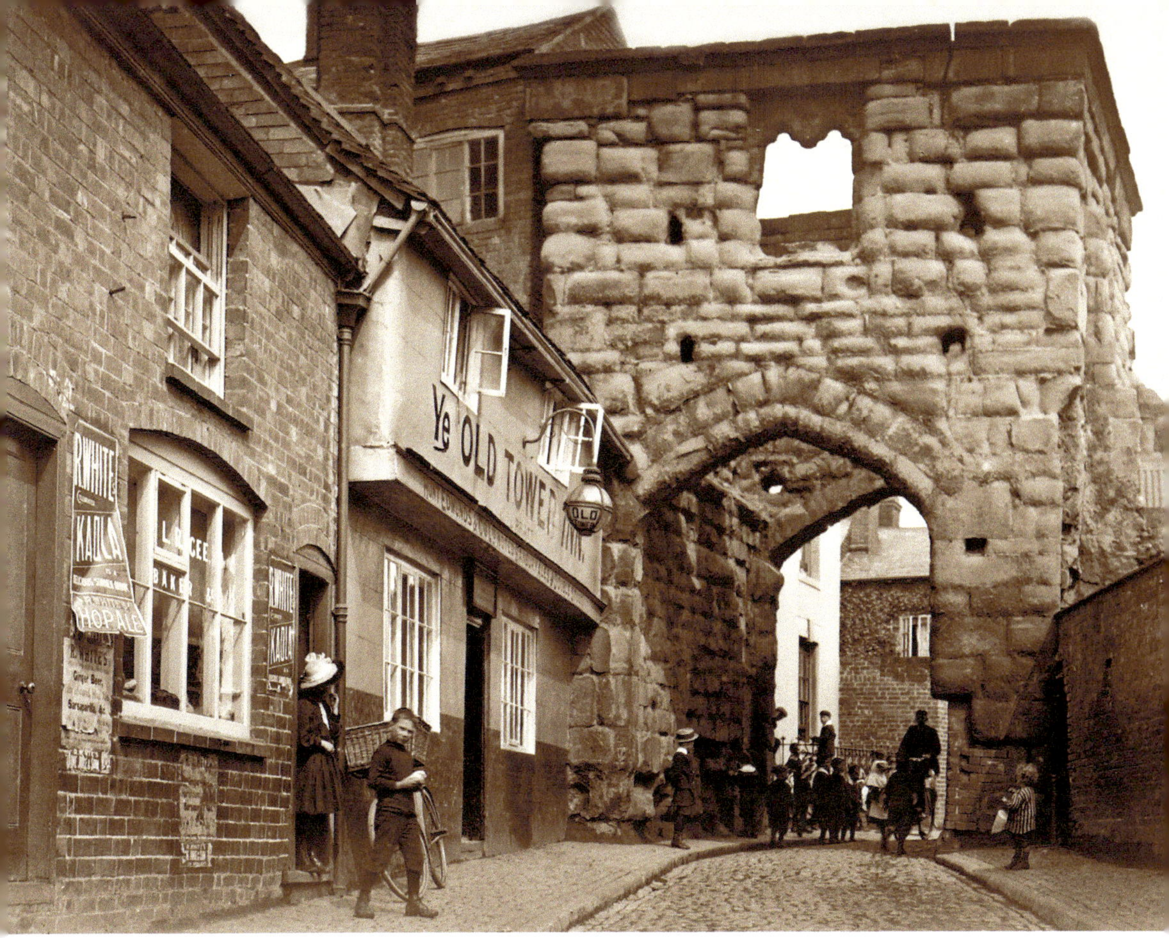


Cook Street Gate as it was. The medieval Tower Inn on its left was given by the brewery to the safe keeping of the city. It was demolished in 1963.

fourteenth century and possibly changed later that century. Work on the adjacent city walls began around 1352 and a licence to add battlements was granted in 1363. Built of local sandstone, it has a four-centred arch, side buttresses and twentieth-century battlements. There is a copy of a gargoyle on the tower and an elephant and castle carved inside. Grooves suggest it had a portcullis. It is the oldest functioning gate in the city, in that it still straddles a road.

In 1833 the Corporation rented it to a Miss Bibbins. At the beginning of the twentieth century it was purchased by Colonel William Wyley who, in 1913, presented it to the city. By 1916 it was in a 'dangerous' condition. A public appeal was made and in 1918, it was restored. The gate has recently been given over to the Historic Coventry Trust as it is seen as no longer of any 'strategic value'.

## 13. Coombe Abbey

The Cistercian abbey of Coombe was founded in 1150 by Richard de Camvill. In 1290 land was given in Harbury, Binley, and Hopsford and in that same year Edward I granted the abbot free warren over his manors of Combe, Binley, Copston, Ernsford, Radbourn, Withybrook, and Wolvey. By 1291 Coombe was the wealthiest house in Warwickshire.

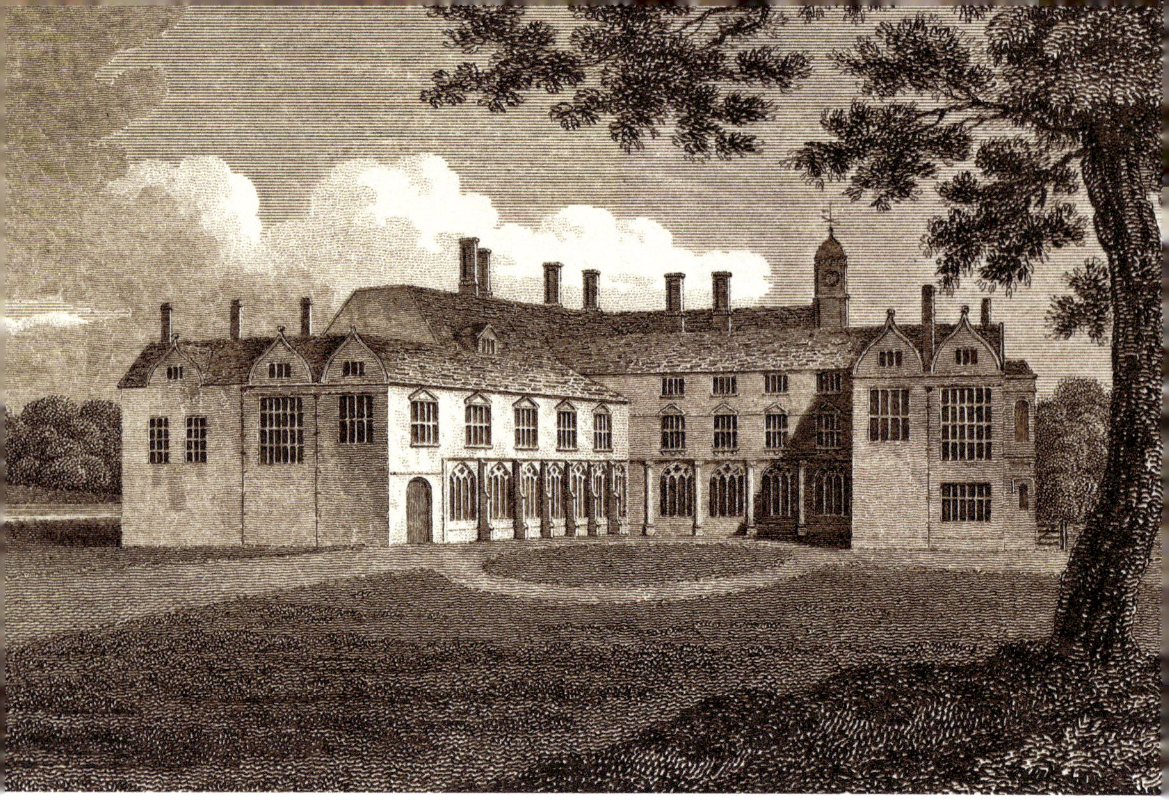

*Above*: This engraving from 1810 shows how the building hadn't changed since the sixteenth century.

*Below*: Coombe from the lakeside as it appears today, unchanged since the Craven days.

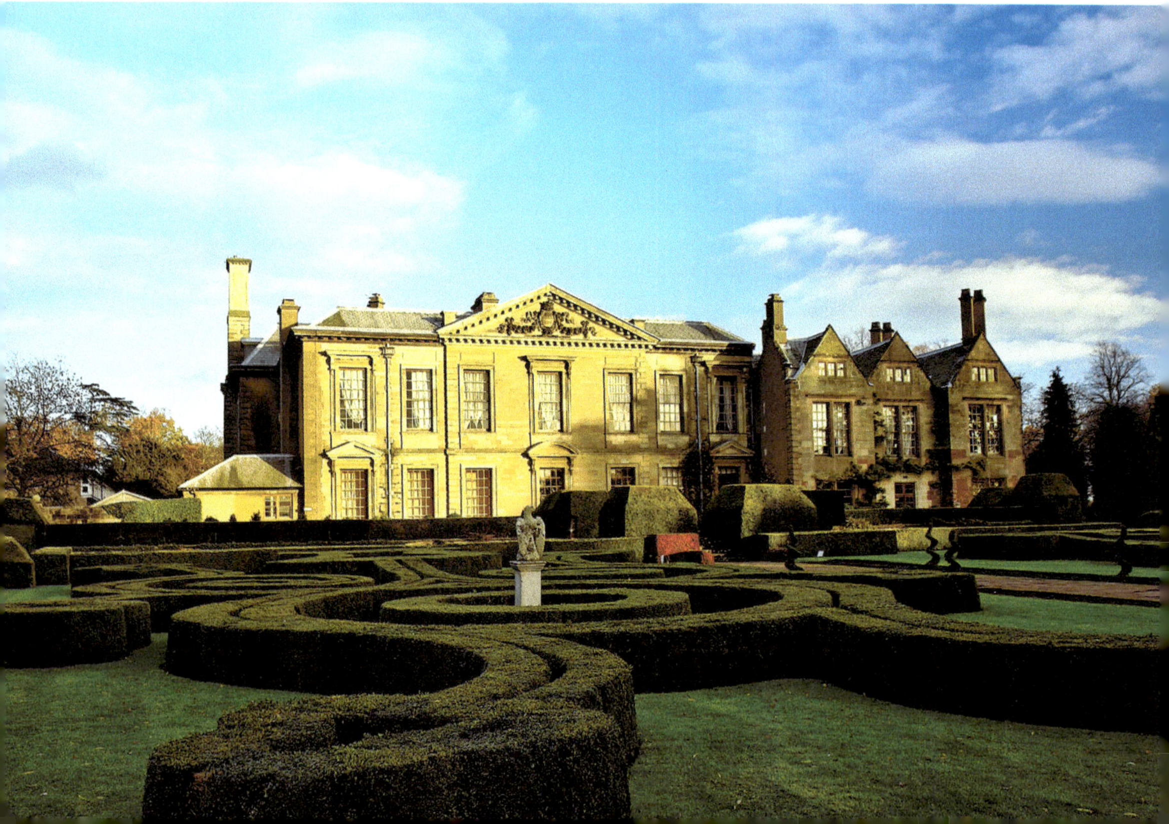

By 1332 it was given protection as a house of royal foundation since it was in distress through defective rule. William de Clinton and Robert de Stretford were brought in to turn it around, bringing more gifts from people such as John de Pulteney of London. In 1345 Abbot Geoffrey was murdered here and on 6 July Edward III issued letters patent to six of his justices, '*de inquirendo de morte abbatis de Combe*.' The inquiry was conducted with a jury from Northamptonshire. The details haven't survived, but to this day the ghost of Abbot Geoffrey makes his presence known.

The abbey was surrendered by Abbot Kynner, Oliver Adams, the ex-abbot, and twelve other monks on 21 January 1539. It passed on to the Duchess of Somerset, then to John Dudley, Duke of Northumberland, then to Court Surveyor Robert Kelway. Kelway died in 1581 and left it to his daughter Elizabeth, who with her husband John Harington of Exton, converted the main buildings and cloister into their home. In 1603 James I knighted Sir John and left his daughter, Princess Elizabeth, to be educated here at Sir John's expense, it nearly bankrupted him. In 1605 the Gunpowder Plot intended to take the princess from Coombe and set her up as a puppet monarch – it failed.

The abbey and its 650 acres of gardens and parkland was acquired by the Craven family in 1622; they enlarged the building and added a west wing. In 1771 the wife of the 6th Baron Craven hired Capability Brown to landscape the area. Brown planted the woodland and dammed up the Smite to create the great lake and probably designed the stable block. The 6th Baron became the 1st Lord Craven in 1801 and continued improving the house. Later in 1849 William Eden Nesfield was asked to make alterations in a Gothic Revival style. The result was the building of the east wing and parts of the north wing were demolished and rebuilt. After Lord Craven's death the estate with its houses and 6,000 acres was sold, then broken into smaller lots and resold in 1923.

The house and grounds were purchased by builder John Gray, who took up residence. He demolished parts and sold off fittings to recoup his money. During the war it was used by the Royal Artillery and in the 1950s by GEC apprentices. In 1964 it was acquired by the council who, in 1966, opened the attached 150 acres as a public park. The house itself, although externally in good condition, was internally declining until restored by a partnership between Coventry City Council and the No Ordinary Hotels Group in 1992. It was reopened as a quality hotel in 1995.

## 14. Council House

In 1911 a competition to design a new council house was won by Birmingham architects E. Garrett & H. W. Simister. Their design was to harmonise with St Mary's Hall and St Michael's. The foundation stone was laid in June 1913 by Mayor William Wyley. Despite the war, work continued and was completed in 1917. It wasn't officially opened until 11 June 1920 by the Duke of York, later George VI. The architect, E. Garrett, was killed in action.

The heraldic carvings were designed by the architects who, in 1913, consulted the council about their choice of twenty-four arms associated with the city. These were displayed in horizontal and vertical panels in the central bay carved in relief in the same stone as the building, Runcorn sandstone. Around the door are also a number of birds and animals. The first phase was completed by the opening of the council house and the Portland stone statues, the second phase, were created shortly afterwards. The designer/artist Henry Wilson was commissioned in 1924 to create the figures. Wilson had previously created the beautiful benches and canopies in the council chamber in 1920. This work reflects the Forest of Arden; the benches are covered with beautiful birds and mammals.

On the front of the Council House the first two figures, Godiva and Justice (9 feet 6 inches and 2.75 tons), were ordered in 1924 but not completed before the smaller figures of Edward the Confessor, the Black Prince, Ranulf, Earl of Chester, and the large figure of Leofric. Justice and Godiva were in place by August 1925. The Council House had all its windows smashed on 14 November 1940 and was peppered with shrapnel holes. These have all been repaired over the years and the building is back to its original condition. It has recently undergone changes, being landscaped outside and the basement has been converted into conference suites.

The Council House in Earl Street, looking good after recent landscaping.

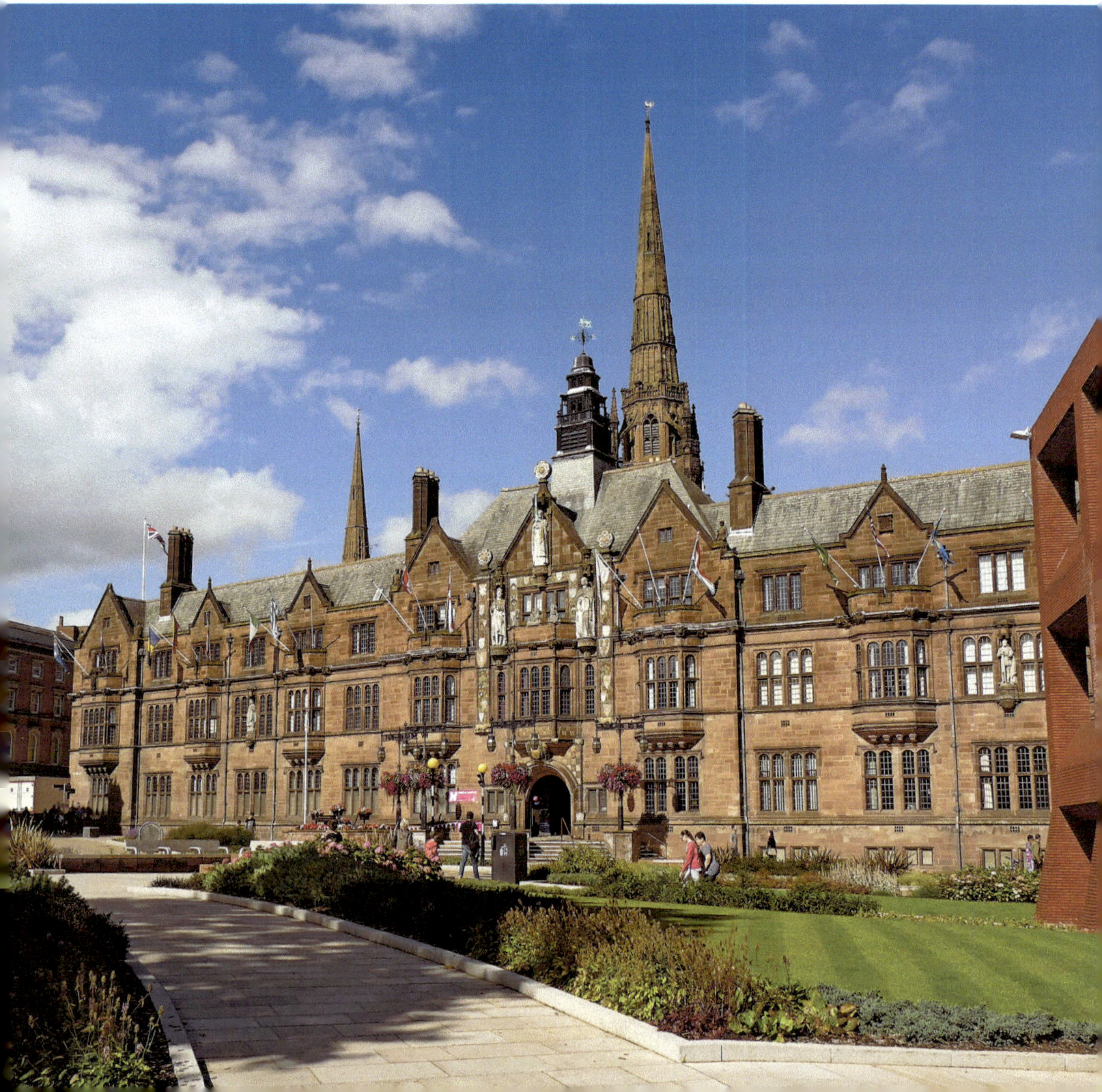

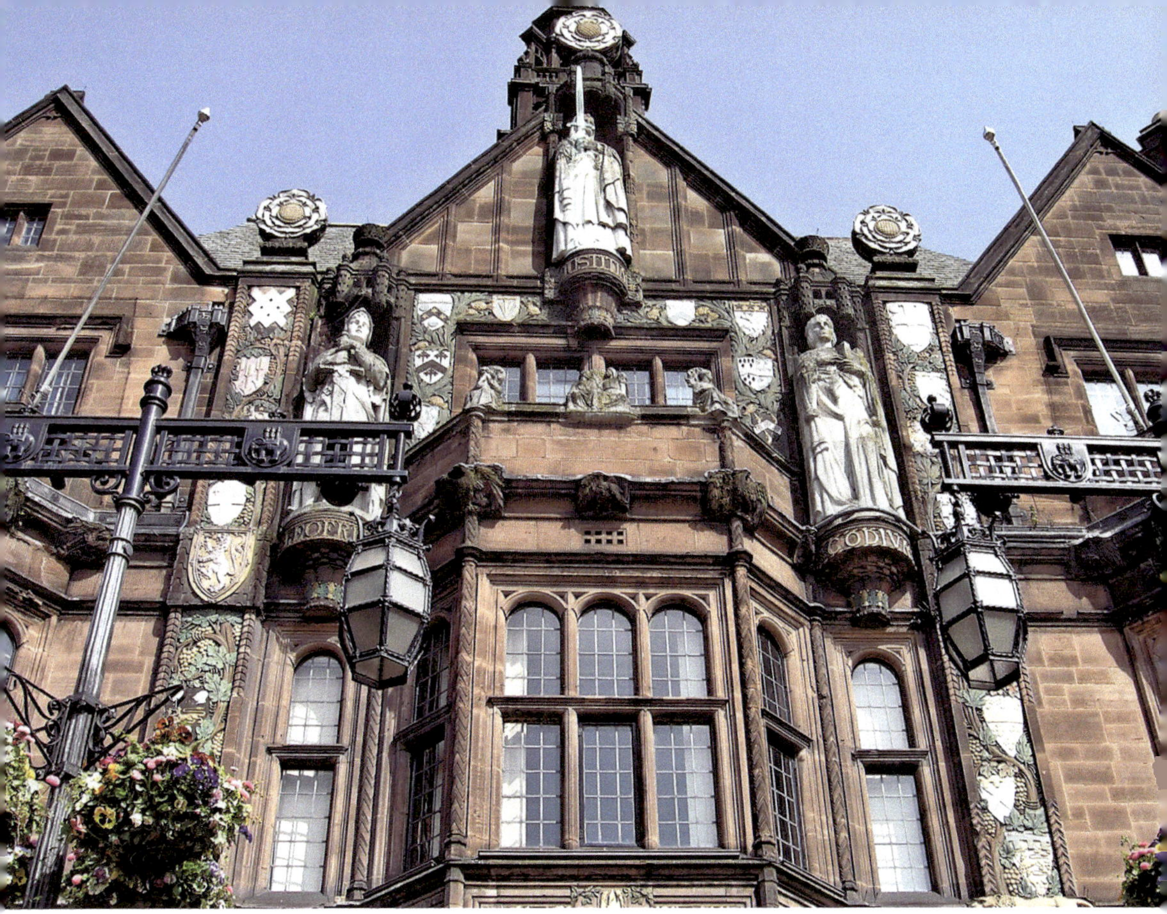

*Above*: The frontage of the building is a history of Coventry in stone.

*Right*: A detail showing the beautiful clock on the 100-foot clock tower.

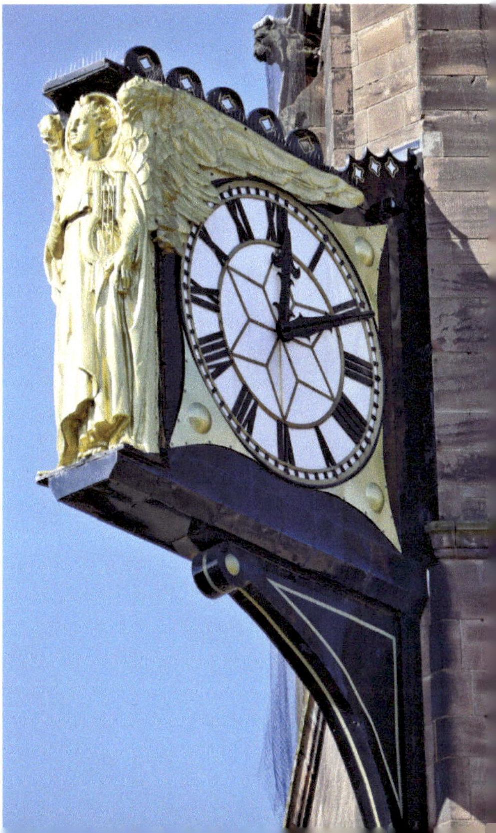

## 15. Coundon Hall, Tamworth Road

Said to have been built on the site of a medieval farmhouse, Coundon Hall is the last surviving large Georgian hall outside the city centre. It was built around 1800 and its owner in 1821 was John Hopkin; he died without issue. Thomas Isherwood was the owner into the 1860s.

The building was for sale in 1883 and described as standing in:

> Well laid out lawns, pleasure grounds and shrubberies, planted with trees and shrubs of mature growth, and about 52 acres of superior park-like lands, studded with fine elm, oak, and other trees, and divided into convenient enclosures of permanent iron fencing ... and bounded by belts of plantation. The stabling and offices are ample, and include stalls for 5 horses, four loose boxes, carriage house, and other suitable offices, and cottage for a coachman groom. There is also another prettily situated cottage residence, with garden and spinney, let to Mr F. W. King Hall and nearly all the lands were late in the occupation of Mr J. R. Winn...

Coundon Hall as seen today from Coundon Park. A better view was impossible as the building was surrounded by a 20-feet-high pile of mud and a 12-feet fence.

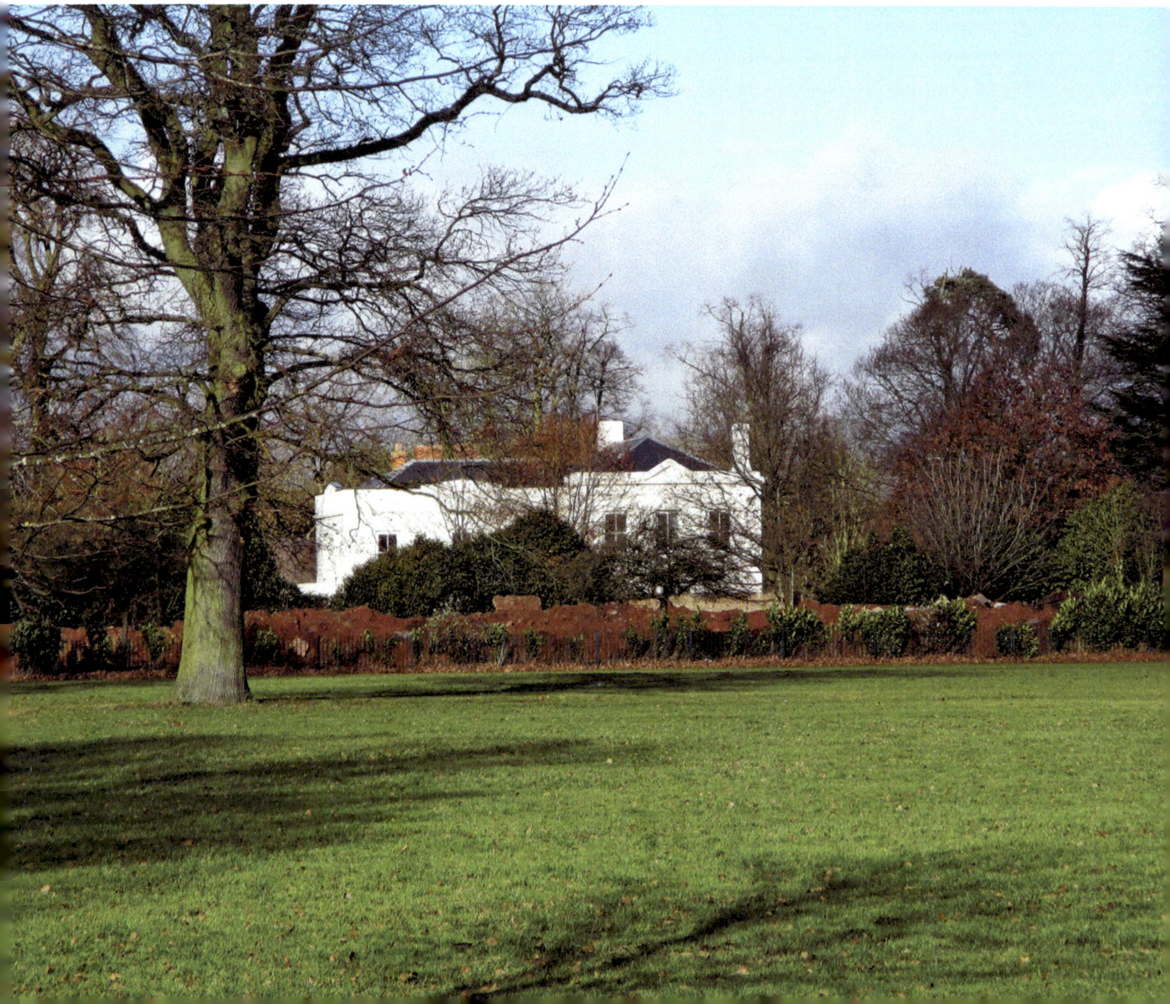

The cottage was Coundon Hall Farm, Winn a stud breeder of shire horses and rare breed cattle.

In 1891 Richard Alexander Rotherham of the watch making family is given as the owner and in 1896 Colonel Richard Caldicott was occupying the hall. A childless widower, he died the same year. Rotherham himself was in residence after the colonel's death. From 1898 to 1945 it was the home of Edgar Turrell, a magistrate with connections to the cycle and textile industry. All of the owners of the hall continued its tradition of keeping cattle, Herefords, White Parks and longhorns.

After Turrell's death the hall passed through many hands, becoming the Old Hall Hotel in 1947, then in the late 1960s it was a Beefeater House before its many reincarnations as a pub and eating house. Between various tenancies the hall was wrecked and set fire to by vandals until 2011 when Howl Associates put forward a new plan to turn the building into a hotel and spa. The initial plans were rejected but later modified plans were accepted. The building is due to reopen at the time of writing.

## 16. County Hall, The Establishment

County Hall is the only eighteenth-century public building in Coventry to survive. It was built next to the gaol in 1783–84 and opened in March 1785. It was designed by Samuel Eglinton in a classical style with a frontage of grey stone, rusticated at ground level with Roman Doric columns and pediments above.

The building functioned as the assizes court for the old county and city of Coventry, which was abolished in 1842 and afterwards it came under Warwickshire. Adjoining County Hall, facing Pepper Lane, is the former prison governor's house. The whole prison was rebuilt and enlarged in 1772–73 and the governor's house dates from this period.

The main courtroom rises through both storeys of the building; the windows are in the upper level. The fittings, which include a gallery with cast-iron railings, date mostly from the 1840s when it was improved for use as an assize court. Below are old cells but they have been blocked off as unstable.

Before its refitting by architects Steadman & Whitewell in 1824, the courtroom was always packed full of standing people. Those involved in trials mixed with the spectators. Some witnesses were deliberately held back and were dragged out by officers. Evidence was given from the front of the crowd and not always heard. The accused stood within a large square spiked box in the centre of the room with steps down to the cells; these can still be seen as can the box. It reopened in January 1825 and sessions held included the petty session judged by local magistrates and quarter session, which could range from theft to murder, judged by circuit judges of the Crown.

Those who left to be hanged went via the Lodge Gate, right of the present entrance. The cart carrying the condemned pulled up outside the present entrance and they climbed aboard with a clergyman and sat on their own coffin, which trundled off to Whitley Common to the gallows. The last was Mary Ann Higgins in 1831. Mary Ball left via the same door in 1849 but was hung from a drop gallows 15 feet to the right. Her execution was attended by 30,000 people.

The courtroom was used for numerous meetings. In 1825 a meeting was held to discuss how to stop slavery. In February 1842 a large number of Coventry Chartists met here;

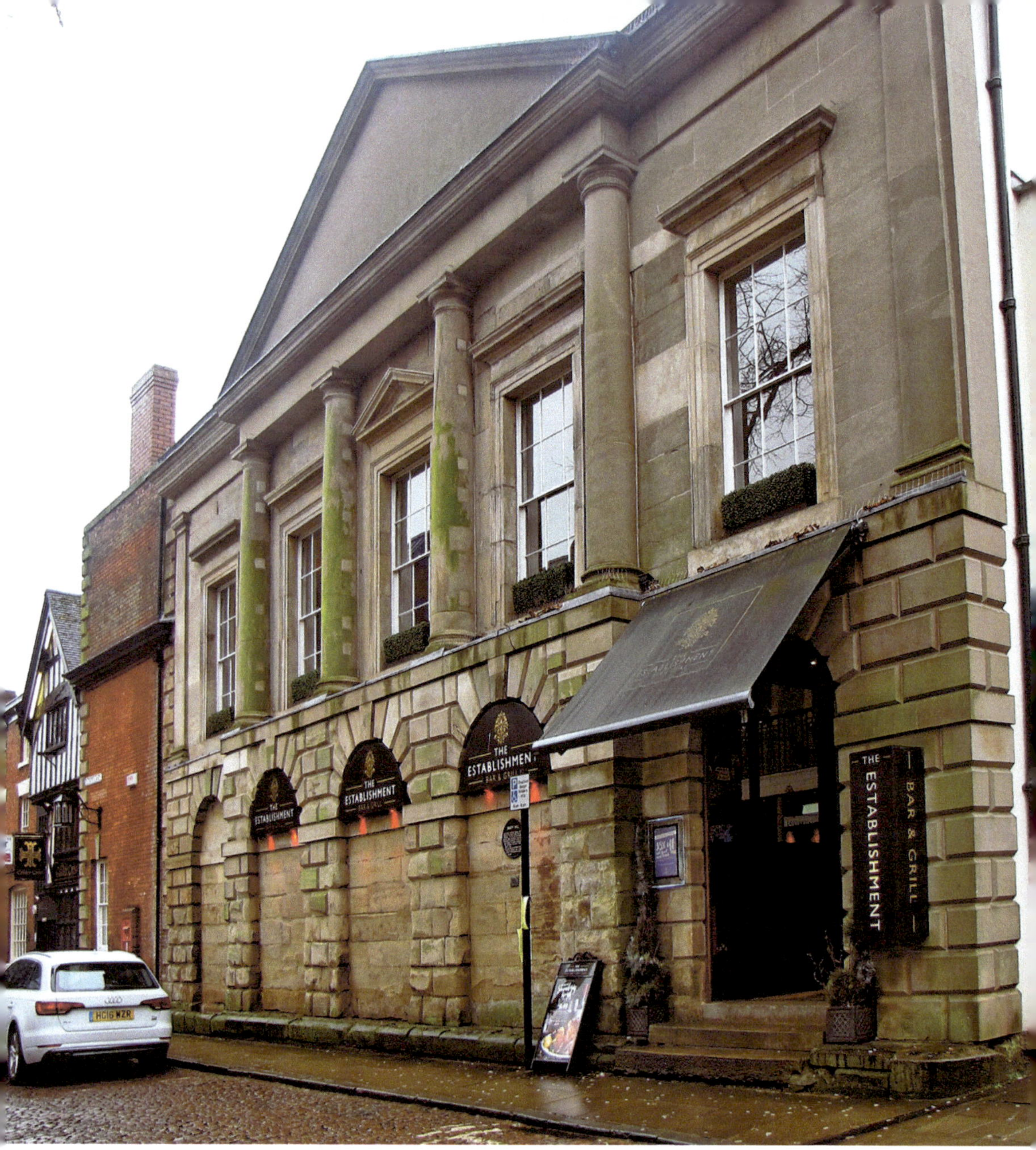


County Hall, now the Establishment in Cuckoo Lane. It went tough times but thankfully survived and sells Coventry Bitter.

the meeting, chaired by the mayor, discussed among other things the use of violence to make political points. It was also a meeting place for the city freemen. In 1936 the council acquired the hall and planned to demolish it under Gibson's plan and in 1988 the courts were moved into Much Park Street. County Hall stood empty for many years – a home to pigeons – but thankfully it survived and is now a bar/restaurant called The Establishment. It was suggested that the eighteenth-century prison governor's house become visitor accommodation – it is set to become student accommodation.

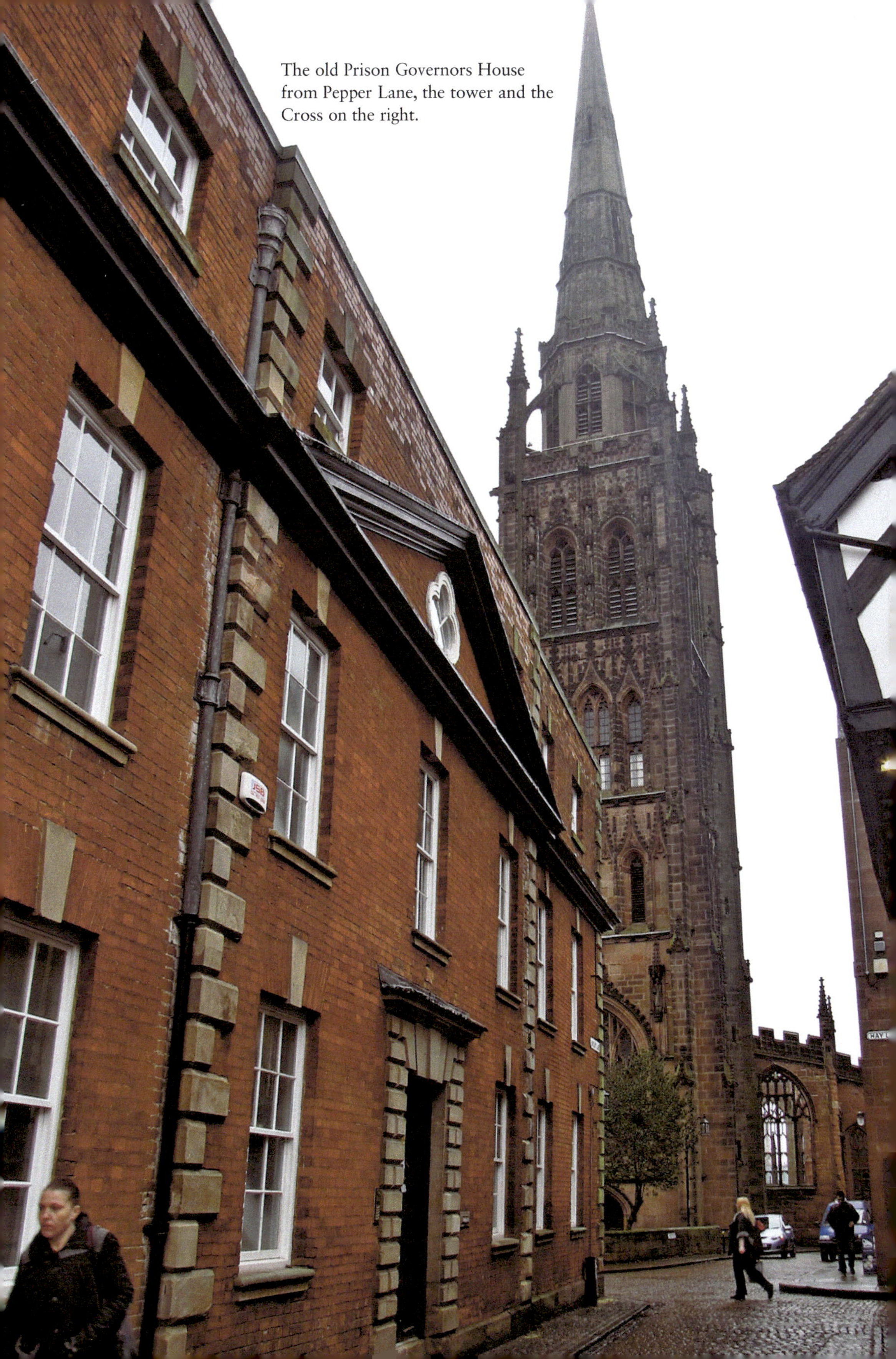

The old Prison Governors House from Pepper Lane, the tower and the Cross on the right.

## 17. Daimler Buildings

The site off Sandy Lane in Radford is the birthplace of the British motor industry. The old cotton mill, later known as Motor Mills, was acquired by the Great Horseless Carriage Co. and Daimler Co. to manufacture motorcars in 1896. Francis Baron, works manager of the GHCC, wrote, 'In 1897 at the Motor Mills, Coventry I built the first "petrol" motor cars in England…' One of the first of the cars went to Lord Iveagh for the Duke of York, later George V. This vehicle was completed at least one or two months before the first Daimler came off the production line. By the 1920s the GHCC had moved on and Daimler filled the entire site down to the canal.

Daimler occupied Motor Mills until 1937. Up until 1940 the old site was used as an air ministry store. Both sites received direct hits during the Blitz and there was a great deal of damage, except for on the office block and the Powerhouse. The Powerhouse stands alongside the canal. The Daimler offices, built in 1903 and which face Sandy Lane, are the only visible reminder of the famed company and are still in use.

The old Daimler offices as they appear today in Sandy Lane.

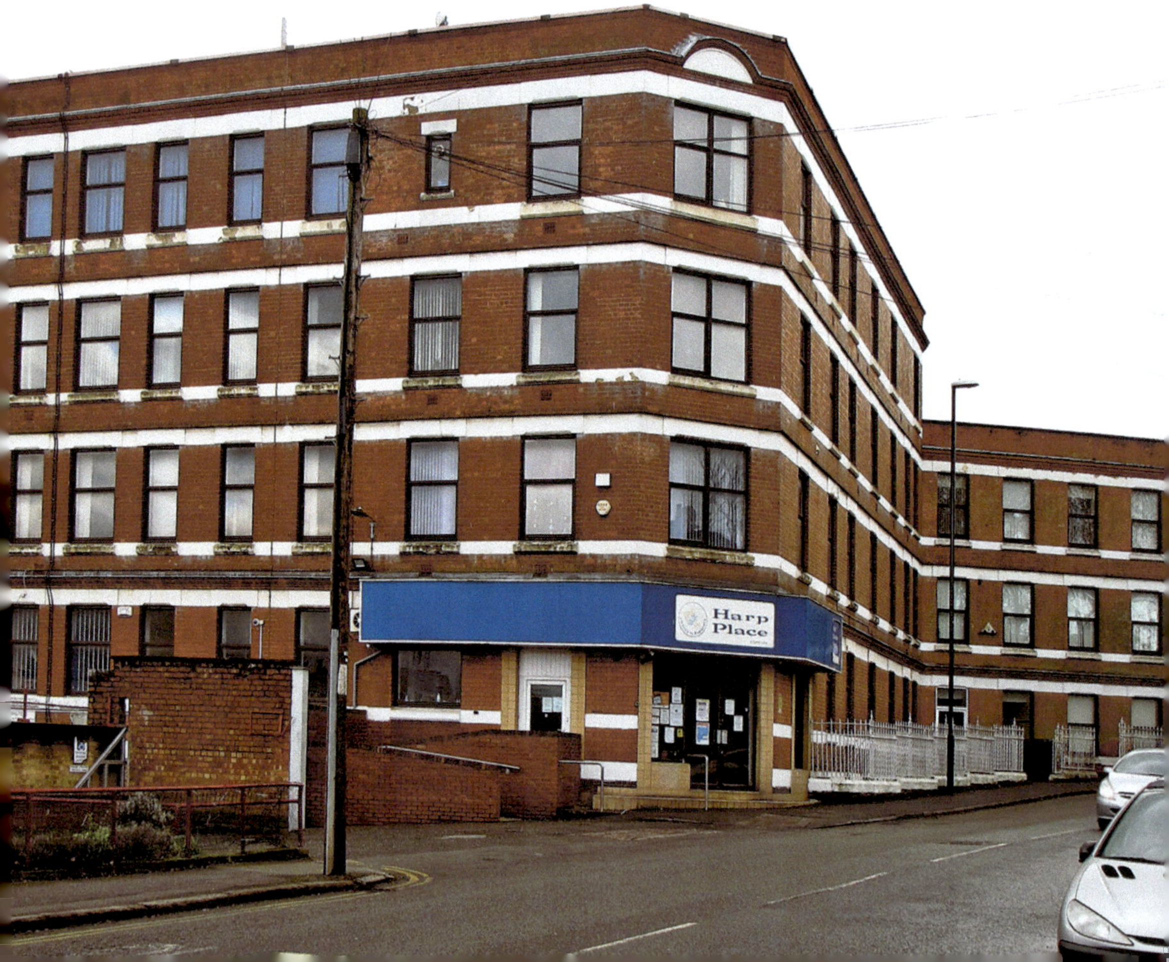

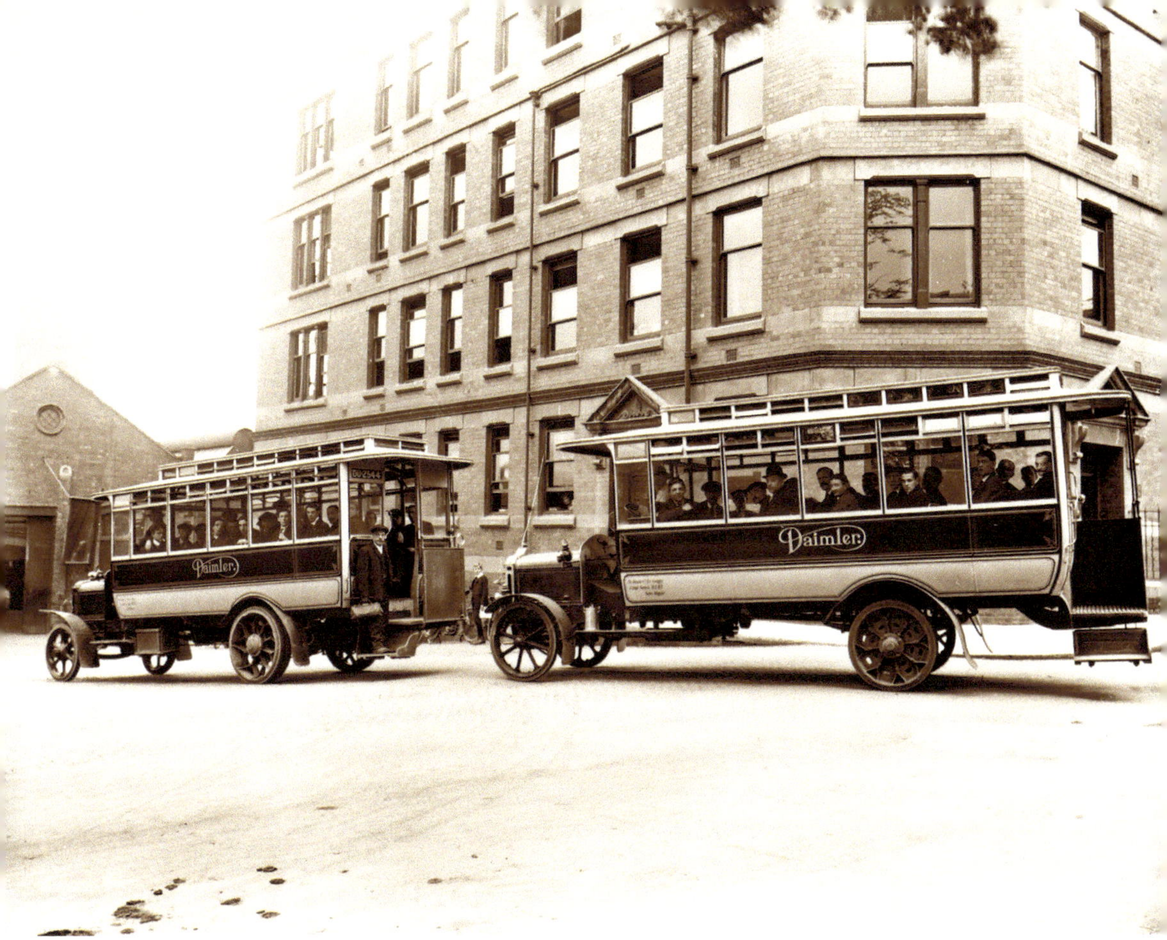


The old offices as they were in 1909, with Daimler buses passing by.

## 18. Drapers' Hall

Drapers' Hall was home to the Drapers' Co., once one of the city's most powerful companies. In 1424 it was enacted that no person sell cloth except at 'The Draperie'. At the end of the seventeenth century, the cloth trade began to decline and continued to do so throughout the eighteenth century when silk weaving become dominant. The first Drapers' Hall erected by the company in 1637 was a repository and place of business. Described as a dark and gloomy structure, it was taken down in 1775 and a classic building with Tuscan pilasters was erected in its place. Unfortunately this building had dry rot and was condemned in 1829.

Before its demolition the drapers engaged architects T. Rickman and H. W. Hutchinson's to design a Greek Revival building with Ionic columns. This new hall's opening was celebrated with a ball on 8 November 1832. The building had no windows and relied on skylights to bring in light. More light was added in 1890 when architect E. Burgess removed the two right-hand columns of the portico and inserted a window. The brick section was added around 1890. The hall's most interesting room is its ballroom with a painted musician's gallery, gilded mirrors and coved, sky-lighted ceiling with decorative moulding in the Greek style.

The hall was used as a lecture room and for the city's most prestigious balls. It had close association with the Coventry races; balls were held here to start and end the racing season. It was also used for public meetings, dinners, plays and musical entertainments. The theatre set up in the previous building was known for its connection to acting royalty the Kemble's and the famed Sarah Siddons.

In October 1939 the Draper's Co. and council were talking of demolishing Draper's for a new gallery and museum. It was said that, 'despite sentimental feelings respecting the old Hall, it cannot be allowed to stand in the way of modern progress...' That same month its cellar became a public air-raid shelter – wartime posters still exist down there.

It would seem that Drapers' Hall has been uncared for since the 1960s. Private groups have put forward schemes but nothing happens. This included the Coventry Society, who campaigned for over ten years to bring it back to use as a community centre and cloth museum only to be turned down. Recent plans to turn it into a music/arts venue didn't materialised. The hall has since been acquired by the Freemasons, who will continue to allow the Drapers' Co. use of it.

Draper's Hall from Bayley Lane. Note the new section added in 1890 on the right.

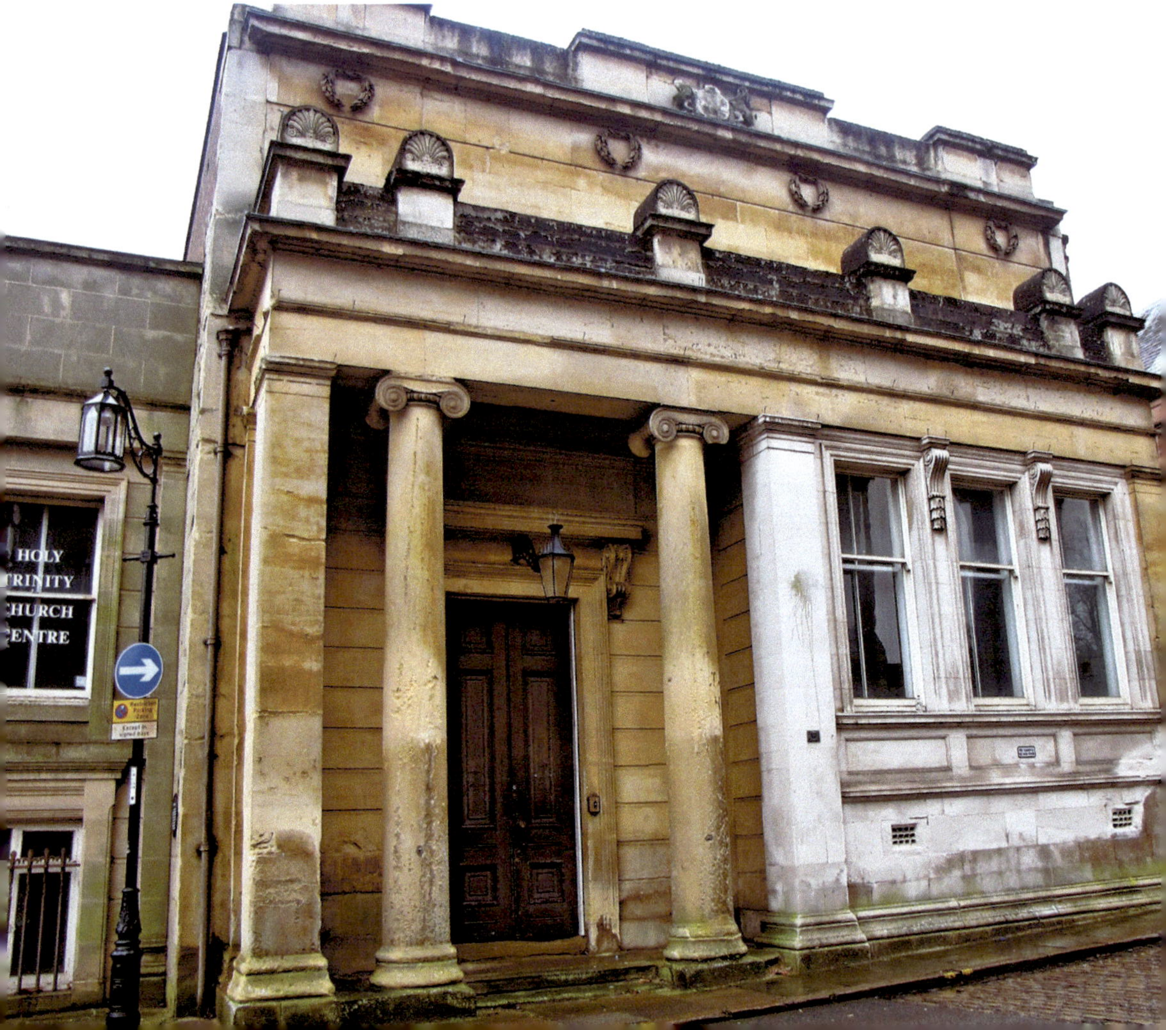

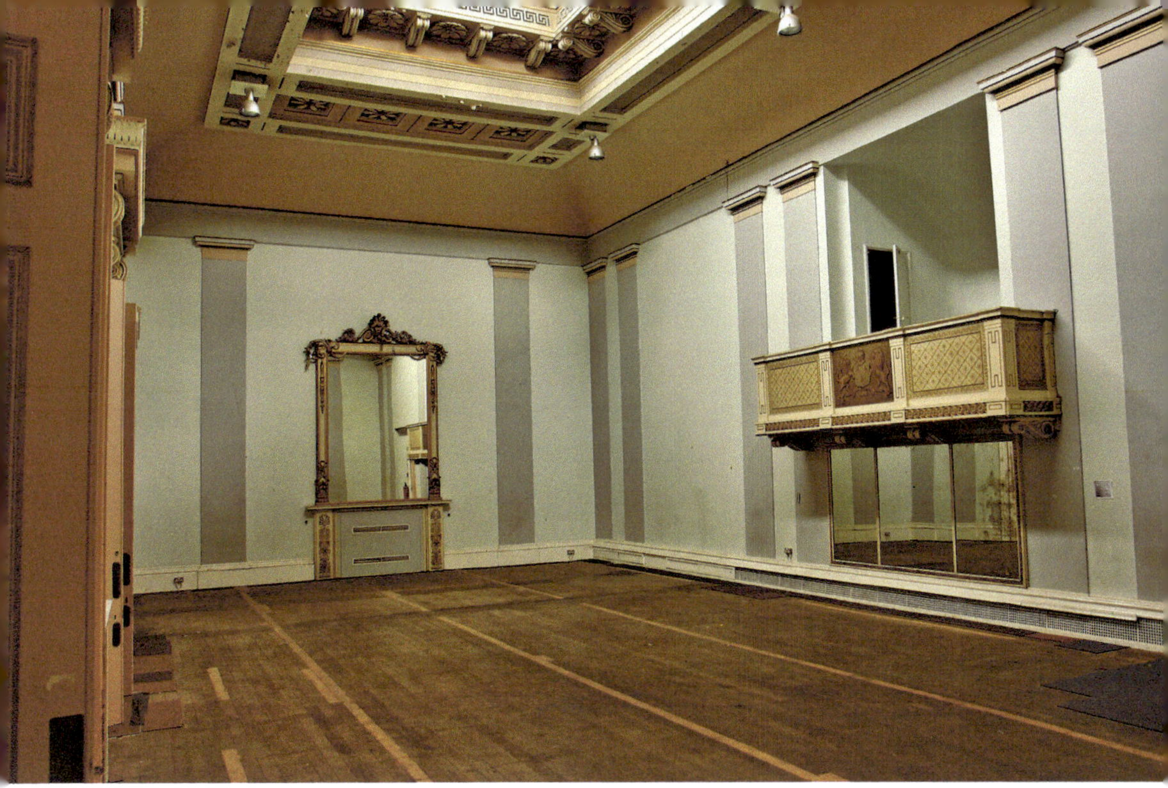

*Above*: The Ball Room in Drapers, once home to the city's most prestigious balls, awaiting a better future.

*Right*: The skylight in the ballroom is a thing of beauty.

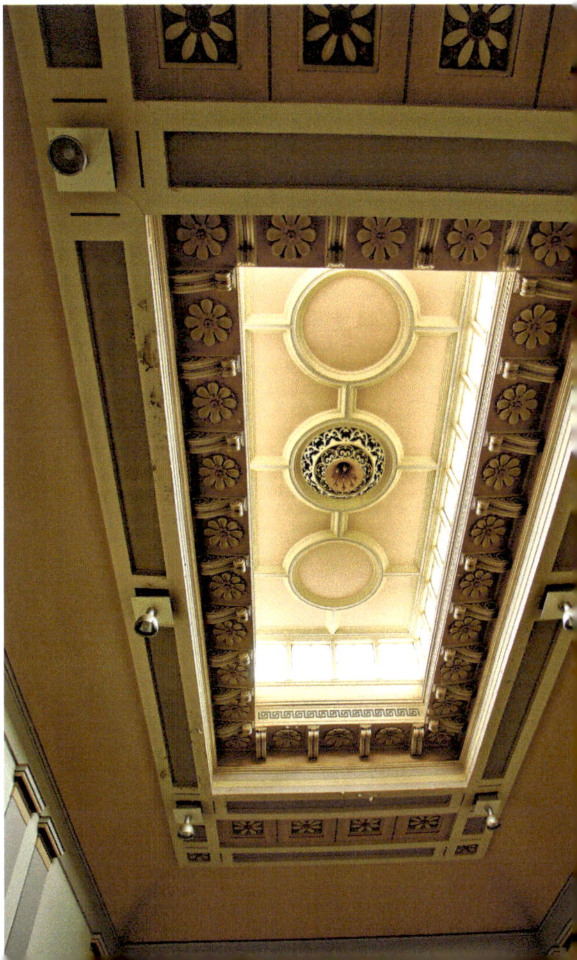

## 19. Fire Station

The old fire station was designed by city engineer Joseph. E. Swindlehurst and opened in Hales Street in 1902. It consisted of three bays with a 70-feet hose-drying tower. Three firemen's cottages stood left of the building. These were demolished in 1933–34 and three more identical bays were added. Attached were stables for the horses, and the first motorised engine was purchased in 1913.

The first firemen were volunteers, they became professional in 1934. During the raid of 14–15 November 1940, 500 tons of high explosives, 30,000 incendiaries and fifty parachute mines were dropped on the city. In the first hour, 240 fires were plotted. The fire station was hit at 8 p.m. Two firemen were on the top of the hose tower when it was hit from a high-explosive bomb halfway up. Neither was hurt, but the first man, in the haze of smoke and dust, mistook the hole made by the bomb for the floor and stepped out into space. He fell 20 feet and fractured bones in both heels. The second man came down safely. Fifty-seven firemen were killed during Coventry's Blitz.

The station was closed in 1976 and stood empty for many years; later a temporary market was here, then a youth centre. The Midland Fire Engine Society, who had a number of historic engines, wanted the building for a museum. Their secretary stated, 'If the city council is concerned with the tourist industry in Coventry then our group must be allowed to show what it can do.' Nothing happened. It continued empty and in a worsening state until 2003 when it was converted into a bar and restaurant. This closed in 2015 and in 2016 Sprinkles Gelato ice-cream parlour opened in the building.

The fire station as it appears today in Hales Street.

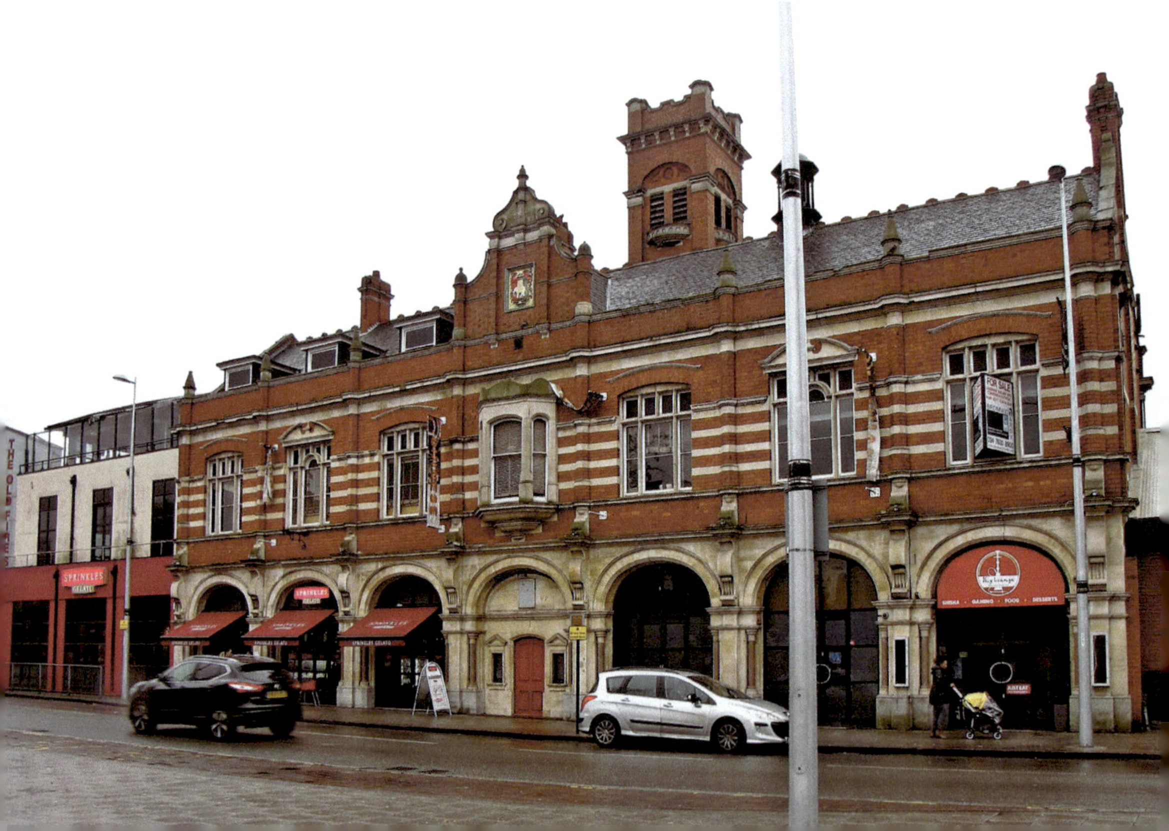

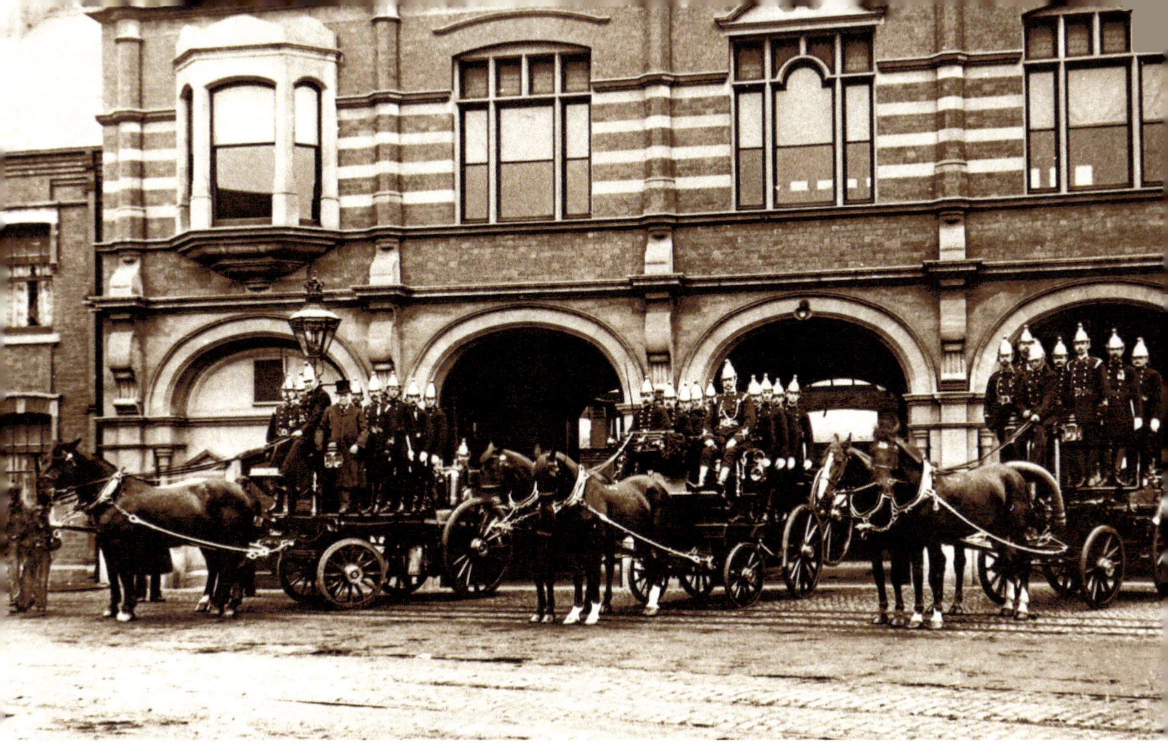

The station in Hales Street as it appeared in 1912 with its fine horse-drawn fire appliances.

## 20. Flying Standard

The Flying Standard building, which started in 1938, was originally called the Priory Gate, taken from the fact that it stands on the site of the original priory gate. It was built to reflect nearby Lychgate Cottages; it has a steel girder frame but much of the building is English oak. It is covered with ornamental woodwork and bargeboards, spiral and diamond chimneys created from handmade bricks. Few rooms are square, and the walls join at acute or obtuse angles. This came from the peculiar shape of the site and the need for economy of space. There is a balcony with balustrades and carved camber beams above the balcony and the diamond-paned glass was made in the Tudor style.

The French woodcarver Louis Havard and his son were employed by the contractor W. H. Jones & Son to carve the barge boards, bannister rails and doors. Charles Lofthouse of Lichfield created the oak finials that ornament the building. The Tudor-style barge boards were Louis Havard's own design and based on those at Windsor Castle. The building was constructed to accommodate five retail units with ground, first and second floors. In September 1939 Timothy White's (the chemist) occupied much of the right-hand ground floor and part of the first floor. In December 1939 Noel Fashions of Richmond moved in, selling exclusive made-to-measure designs. By June 1941 H. Samuel the jeweller moved in. After the war Owen Owen bombed out of their store found some refuge here, taking three floors. They sold corsets to soft furnishing and had a library. At Christmas toys were sold in the Toy Cave on the second floor.

Owen Owen moved out and the store continued under Timothy Whites, Samuel's and later a Wimpey Bar. The entire building is now part of the popular Wetherspoon pub chain. Historically, The Flying Standard has nothing to do with Standard Motors and so it should

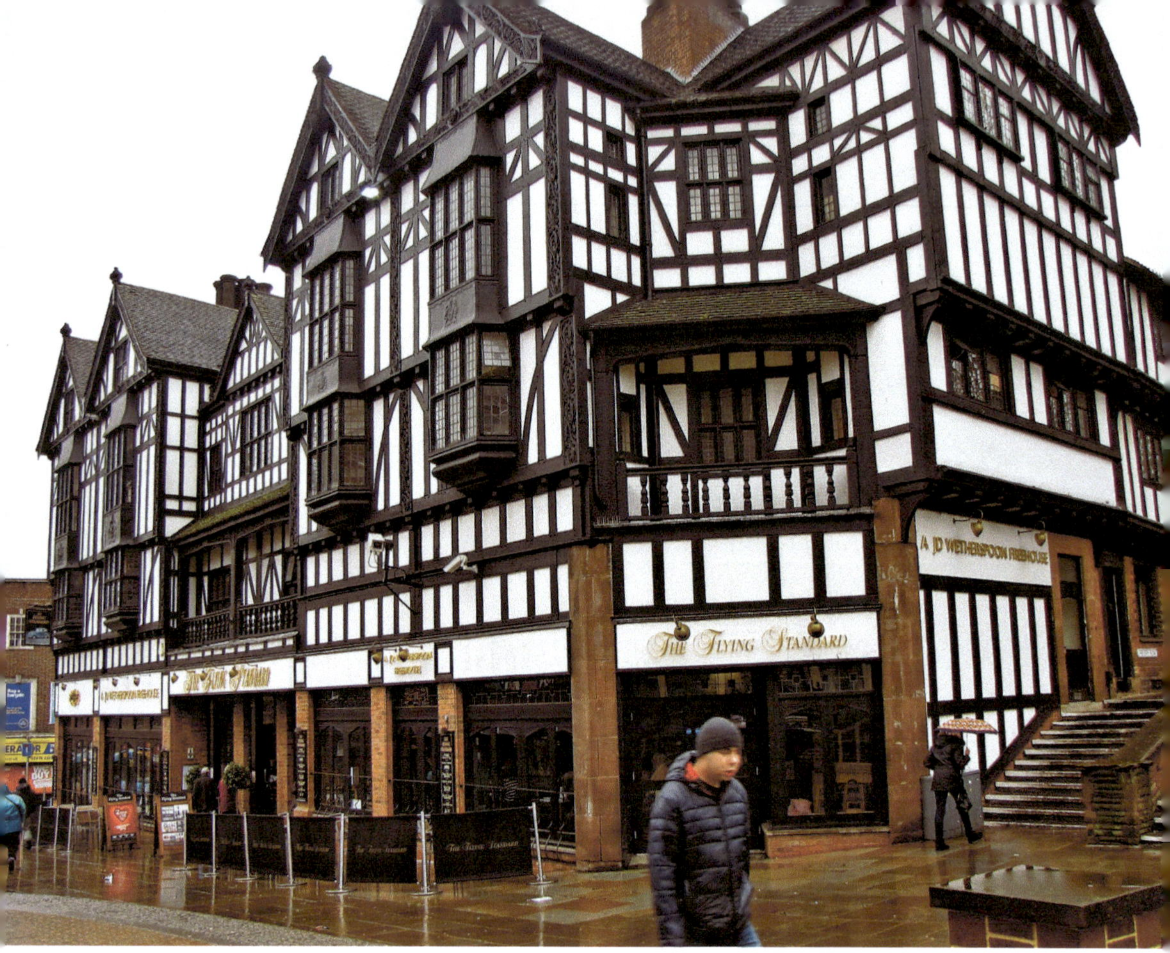


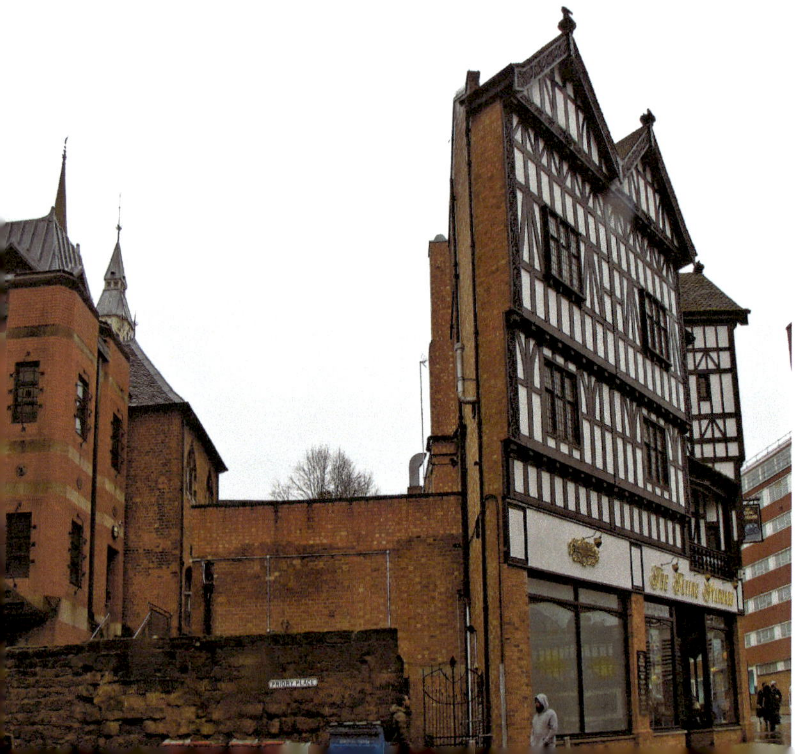


*Above*: The Flying Standard in Trinity Street, a Wetherspoon pub. Twentieth-century Tudor at its best.

*Left*: Where's the back gone? Incredibly, from the north, the building comes to a narrow section ending about 4 feet wide. Not something often seen on buildings.

have been called the Priory Gate since many kings have walked through the middle of this building – Henry IV, Henry V, Edward IV, Henry VI, Richard III, Henry VII and Henry VIII to name a few. Can any other pub compete with this?

## 21. Fords Hospital

Ford's Hospital was described by John Carter, the eminent nineteenth-century antiquarian, as the finest structure in England – it was so fine he said that it ought to be placed beneath a glass case. The famous architect Pugin featured its bargeboards in his book, *Ornamental Gables*. Ford's, also known as Greyfriars Hospital, was founded in 1509 as an almshouse for five men, with one woman to care for them under the will of William Ford, a Coventry merchant. These individuals would receive 5*d* a week forever. His executor William Pisford enlarged the endowment in 1517 for six poor men and their wives. Later, the amount was increased to 7½*d* per week for aged couples. In the eighteenth century and for most of its modern history it provided a home exclusively for fifteen elderly women. The building originally had a chapel over the entrance and a chaplain who had his own room. He was paid £6 a year and said mass in this chapel for the soul of Pisford.

Ford's received a direct hit on 14 October 1940; the section near the front was partly wrecked and it was here that most of the inmates were trapped. Eight died and nine were injured. The courtyard, which had been admired for centuries, escaped the most serious damage. The heavy oak timbering took much of the shock. At the time it was said that

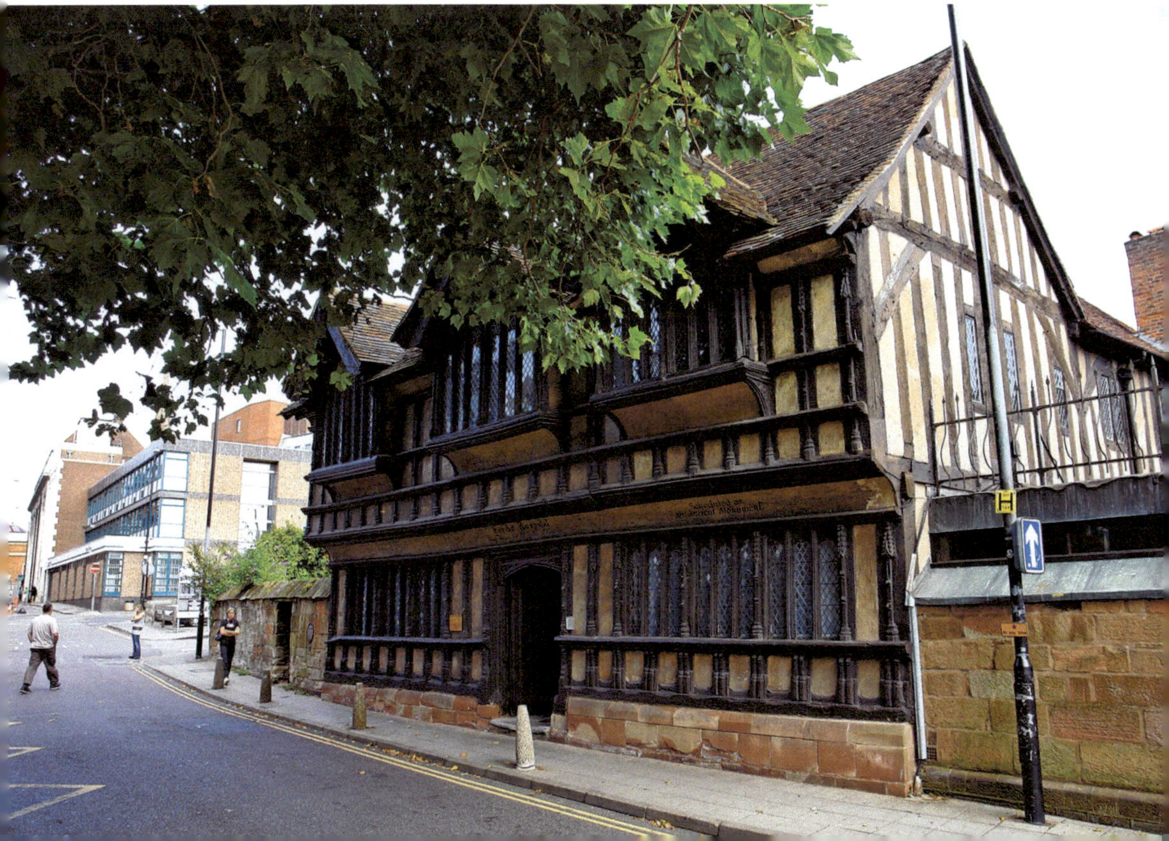

Ford's Hospital from Greyfriar's Lane, once used for a Shakespeare episode of *Doctor Who*.

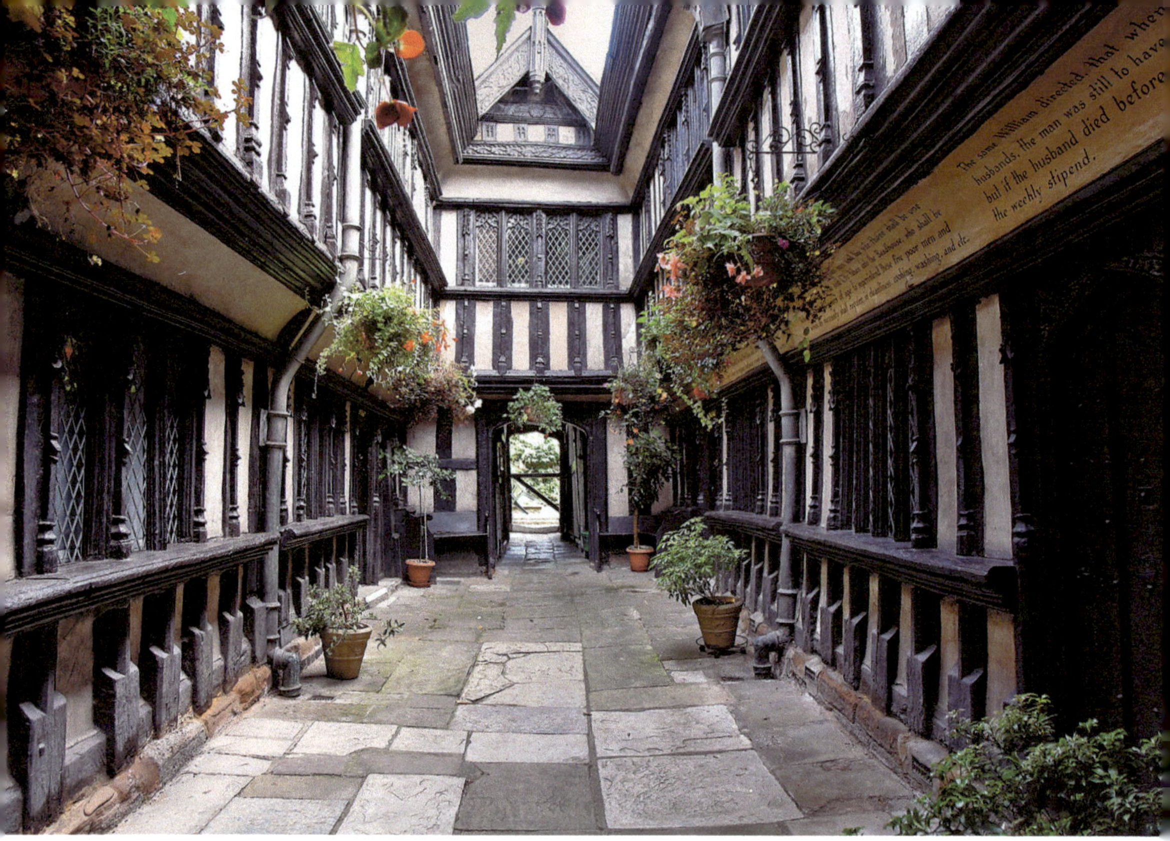


The beautiful courtyard was open for well over four and a half centuries; it is now gated due to youths. This is a gem.

whereas a modern building would have simply collapsed, apart from having its frontage pushed forward, this medieval craftsmanship appeared to have suffered comparatively little.

The building was made weatherproof for the duration and the carvings and other parts that survived were put into storage. In 1941 it was proposed to dismantle it and move it elsewhere to fit in with Gibson's plan. Ford's remained and the council and trustees restored and reopened it in 1953.

## 22. Frederick Lancaster Library

Known as the Castle, this striking £19-million building designed by Short & Associates houses the university library and was completed in 2001. It is the largest deep-plan naturally ventilated building in Europe. It was named after Coventry-based Frederick Lancaster, who designed one of the first British petrol-driven cars and invented many parts of the modern car. It has numerous study zones based over five floors and central study and resource space for staff and students. It houses over 350 computers, books, journals, and electronic resources and numerous study areas.

It was built for sustainable energy use and all floors have moveable partitions. The light is carried through the building by five 6.5-metre square light wells, which carry natural light through the building. The light well also doubles as a conduit to carry natural air to ventilate the building. This makes it entirely naturally ventilated, except the computer area, which needs air conditioning.

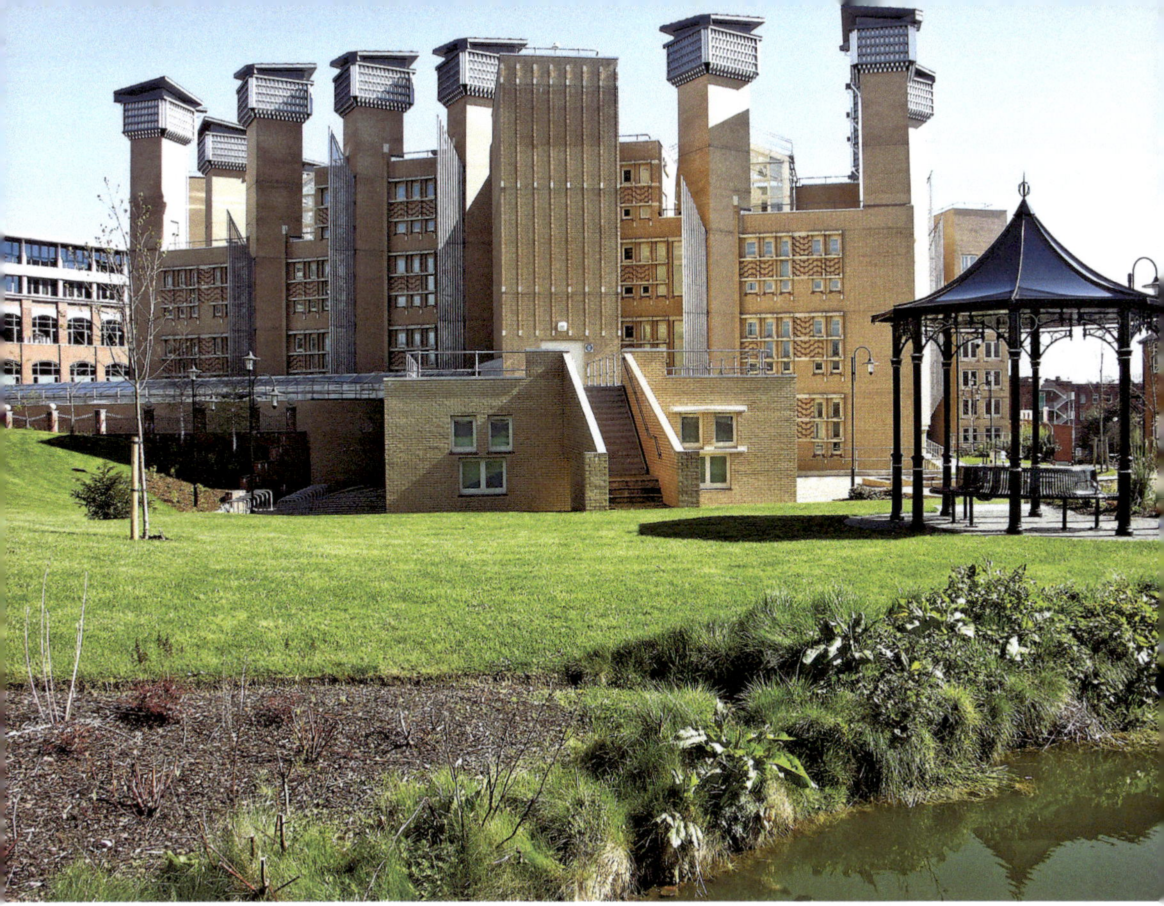

The university library: an interesting building that is called the Castle because of its turrets.

Air is drawn into the building through vents on all elevations into a plenum beneath the ground floor. This feeds air into the light wells that is then fed onto the floors by vents at the foot of each. They open and close in response to sensors around the building, checking on temperature and air quality. Air exhausts out through vents in the perimeter walls to the towers. These are the most eye-catching feature of the building. Air also exhausts into the central light well so there are four inlet light wells and one exhaust light well.

The metal constructions on the tops of the towers also have a function. Air rises through the building as long as it can leave freely out of these towers. High winds can hamper the convection effect. The metal structures are designed to deflect winds of all strengths to ensure the building breathes. The building monitors its own environment and stores heat to be released at the appropriate time. At night the building sends cool air around itself, so in the morning it will start at a comfortable temperature and with all this the building runs at reduced energy cost, costing half of what a similar conventional building would cost.

## 23. Golden Cross

Edward IV opened a mint in Coventry on 6 July 1465, during his great national recoinage. There is nothing that tells us where it stood, only a tradition that says it was on the site of the Golden Cross. The only chronicler who mentions it was Leland, who said, 'There was

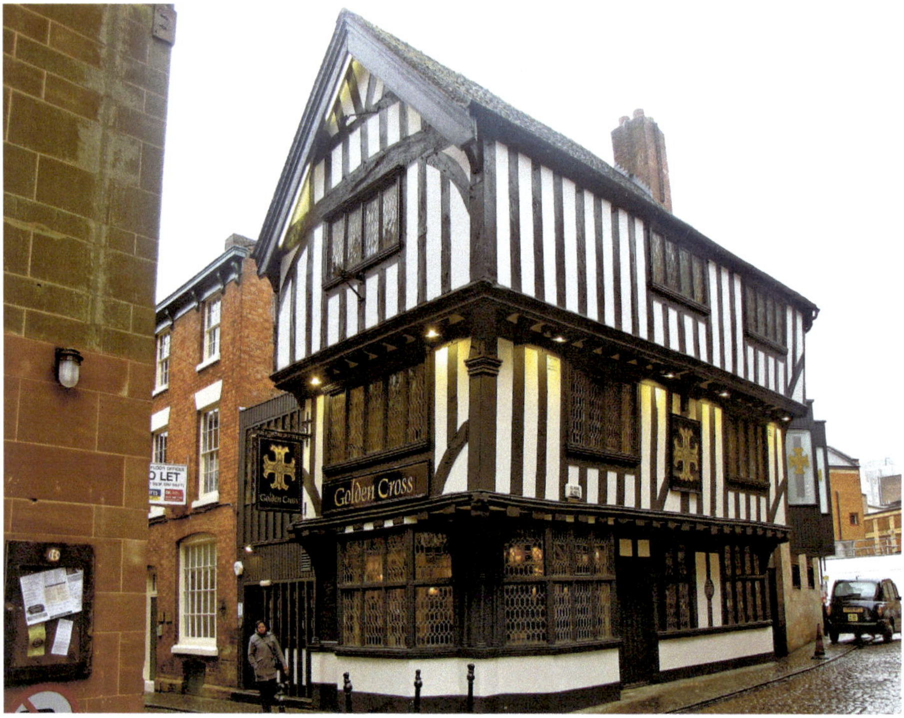


*Above*: The Golden Cross on the corner of Hay and Pepper Lane, a fine looking building, with sloping floor upstairs.

*Below*: Inside the Cross today, note the fine ceiling.

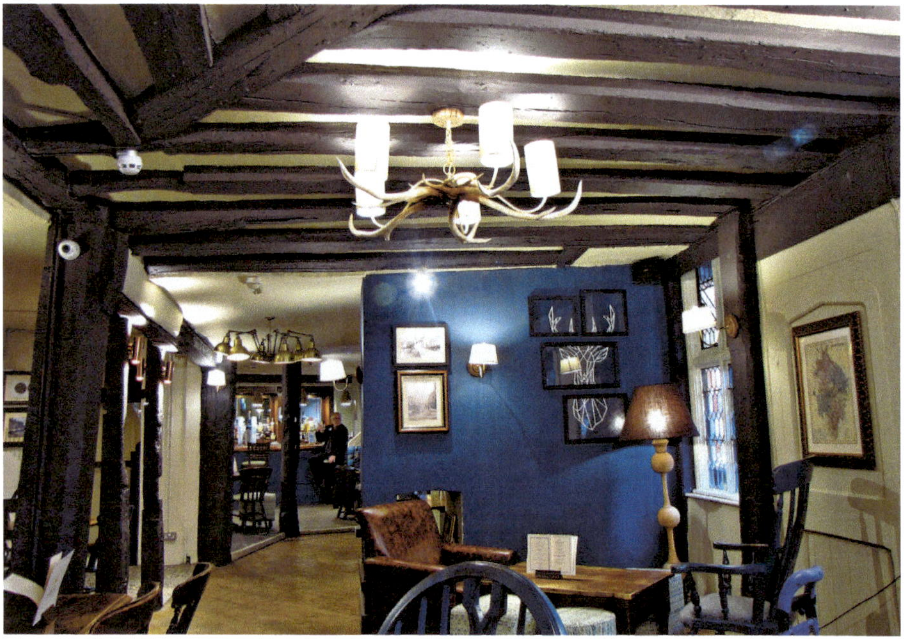

a Parliament and a Mint of coynage at Coventry.' Thomas Sharp the Coventry historian wrote in 1806 that he had not discovered a trace of this mint in any other document. 'But for the existence of the coins,' he said, 'we should be utterly ignorant that Coventry ever possessed the privilege of coining.' This is true for there are gold and silver coins from the reign of Edward IV bearing the 'C' of the Coventry mint under the king's head and the words, 'CIVITAS COVENTRE'.

The tradition that the Cross was the site of the mint dates from the beginning of the nineteenth century. The inn's original name wasn't the Golden Cross; it is likely to have been the Royal Exchange that was mentioned in March 1693, although that could have stood on the opposite corner. Its existence, however, could have left us with the connection as the Royal Exchange is associated with money.

The building was later the Dog & Duck mentioned by Hewitt in 1756 as a billet for soldiers. In 1770 Thomas Higgins changed the name to the Cross Guns and in 1773 he took the name with him. Sometime after the name Golden Cross appears. So is the name based on a memory of the Royal Exchange? I think the answer lies here, for a decree of Edward IV dated 16 September 1465 states that Hugh Boyce will control the king's 'Mints and Exchanges' in Bristol, Norwich and Coventry. Mints could also house exchanges!

The earliest mention I can find of the Golden Cross name is when Richard Farmer was the landlord in 1818. In April 1825, Thomas Smith left a horse in its stables and tried to sell it to a butcher in Jordan Well for £5. It seemed the horse didn't belong to him as he was tried at the County Hall next door and received the death sentence. In 1865, we know from another trial that the Cross still had its stables for an ostler worked here named Henry Sly. In 1867 it is described as an old established house.

The pub was restored in the 1880s using timber taken out of the roof and bell frame of St Michael's during its simultaneous restoration. Through most of the twentieth century it was a regular watering hole for the barristers of the County Hall. Its opening hours have been sketchy in recent years and little had been done to it; however in January 2017, after a refurb the Golden Cross, possibly the oldest pub in Coventry, reopened its doors.

## 24. Greyfriars (Christchurch)

Saint Francis of Assisi was the founder of this order, which arrived in Coventry in 1234. The Greyfriars were a popular order and lived wholly on charity. They walked in pairs with wallets on their shoulders, to receive alms. Greyfriars was built on land given by Ranulf Blundeville, Earl of Chester. Richard II gave them shingles from Kenilworth to roof their oratory. Edward, the Black Prince, gave them stone from his quarry in the Great Park. The Hastings family of Allesley and Fillongley castles were benefactors and were buried in the church's Hastings Chapel. Other chapels were Saint Anne's and the Rood Chapel. The body of the Sir Roger Mortimer, Marcher Lord and lover of Queen Isabella, was brought here after his execution in 1330. A license was later given to move him but no record exists of his removal. It was said that to be buried in the robes of a Greyfriar would ensure entrance into heaven, and many nobles subsequently were buried in this fashion.

These friars were emissaries to the pope and enjoyed considerable privileges; they were subject to no diocesan control. But as their influence waned, so did their income,

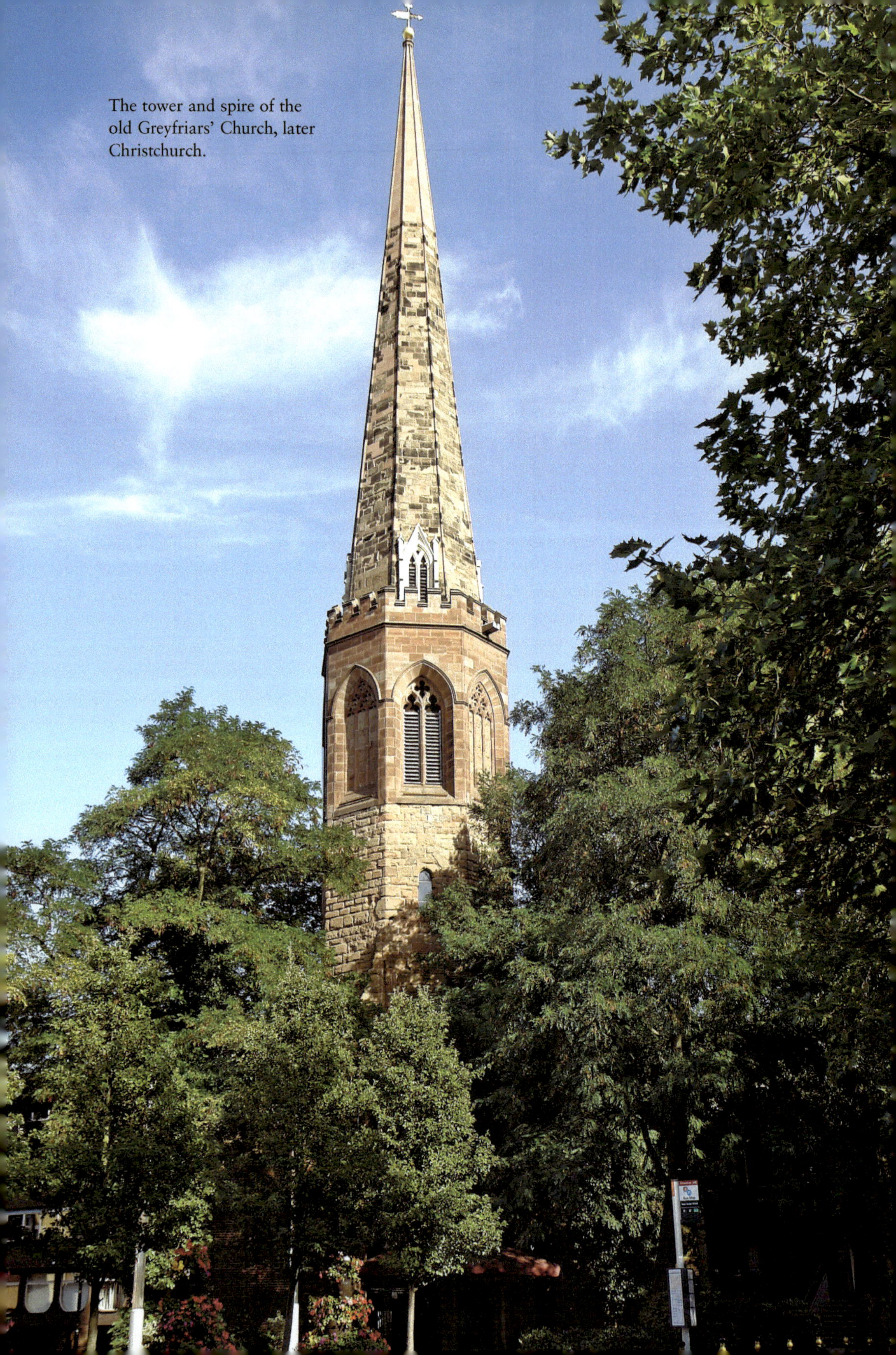

The tower and spire of the old Greyfriars' Church, later Christchurch.

and in 1534 (shortly before the Dissolution of the Monasteries) church commissioners reported, 'The hole howse besides the churche ys in moch ruyne.' The order had no land or tenements and eleven friars signed the suppression order giving their house to the king. The building and site was granted to the mayor, bailiffs and commonalty of Coventry. The church was demolished leaving its 210-feet tower and spire alone in an orchard. The steeple was blown down and repaired many times. Greyfriars' spire is the smallest of Coventry's three spires and rises from an octagon tower – its beauty lies in its simplicity. The moulded arches were bricked up but those on the east and north sides were open. It was used in the past by a Mr Seagar as a pigsty, who boasted that he had the tallest pigsty in the kingdom.

The plan to rebuild it originated with William Bunney, who started a subscription in 1819. His scheme came to nothing and before his death he bequeathed 200 guineas to the project. In 1826 a public meeting was called and the Commission of Parliamentary Grants for Building Churches said that if the inhabitants would raise half of the amount required, they would furnish the rest. The sum was procured.

The new smaller church was designed by a Mr Rickman, architect, and the contractor was Mr Walthew of Birmingham. The erection of the building now called Christchurch commenced

An early twentieth-century photograph of the inside of the church. The altar in the later church was under the tower, the original was cruciform.

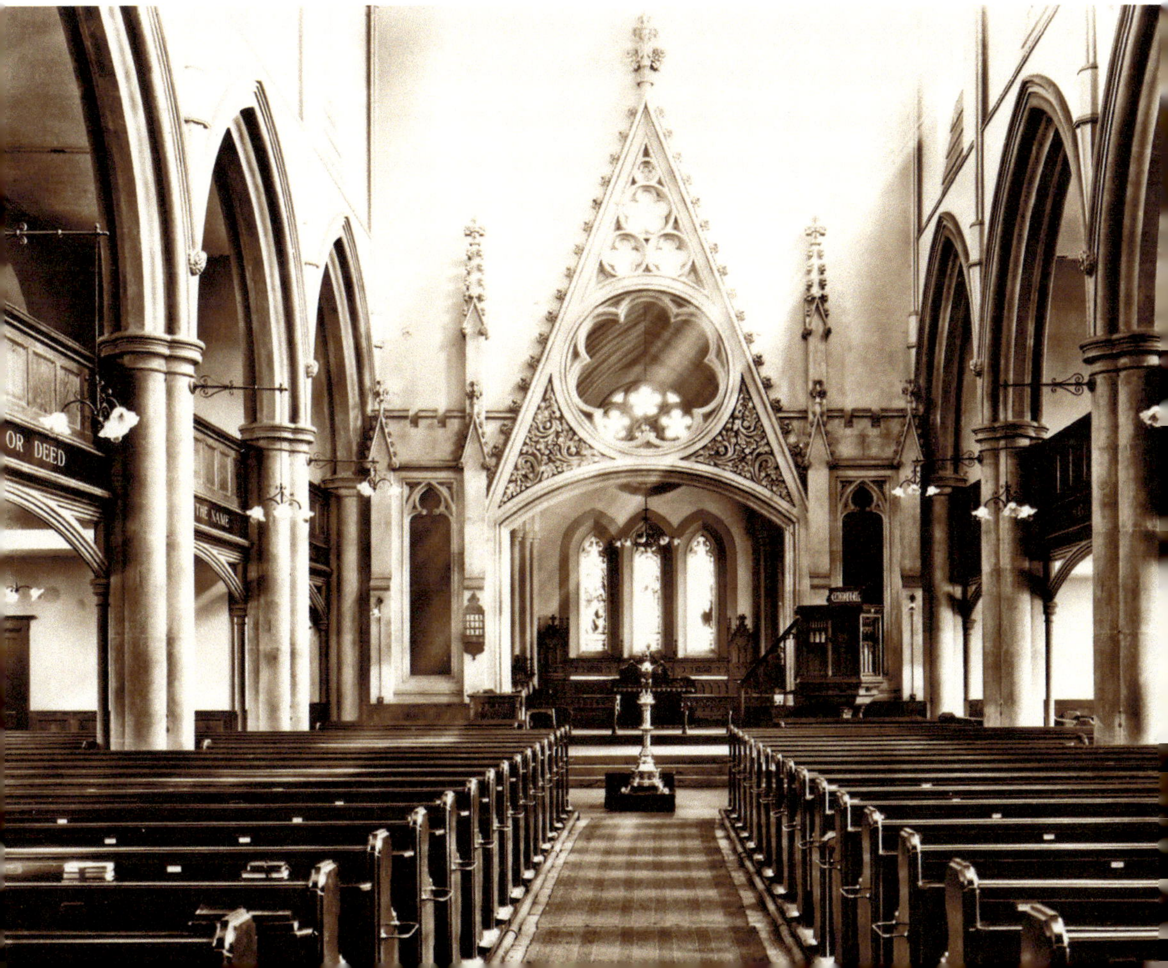

in 1829 and was completed and consecrated on 3 August 1832. The inside was elegantly simple, measuring 101 feet in length, with side aisles and six Perpendicular windows on each side. The chancel was lighted with stained-glass windows and there was a circular window over the altar. This second church was destroyed by bombs on 8 April 1941, once again leaving the tower and spire standing alone. It is now a café – probably the tallest in the kingdom!

## 25. Herbert Art Gallery & Museum

Known these days simply as the Herbert, this was the first post-war museum and art gallery built in Britain. It was originally intended to stand on the opposite side of Bayley Lane, using a £100,000 gift from Sir Alfred Herbert for its construction, but the first stage of the museum was stopped by the war. Its base became a public toilet and that now forms the basement of Draper's Bar. When a larger area became available due to bombing and clearance, new plans were drawn up in 1952 by the architects Albert Herbert & Son (Sir Alfred's cousin). In May 1954 the foundation stone was laid by Sir Alfred Herbert, who donated a further £100,000 to the project. Sir Alfred died in May 1957 and the museum and art gallery that bears his name was opened on 9 March 1960.

The glass extension of the Herbert off Bayley Lane.

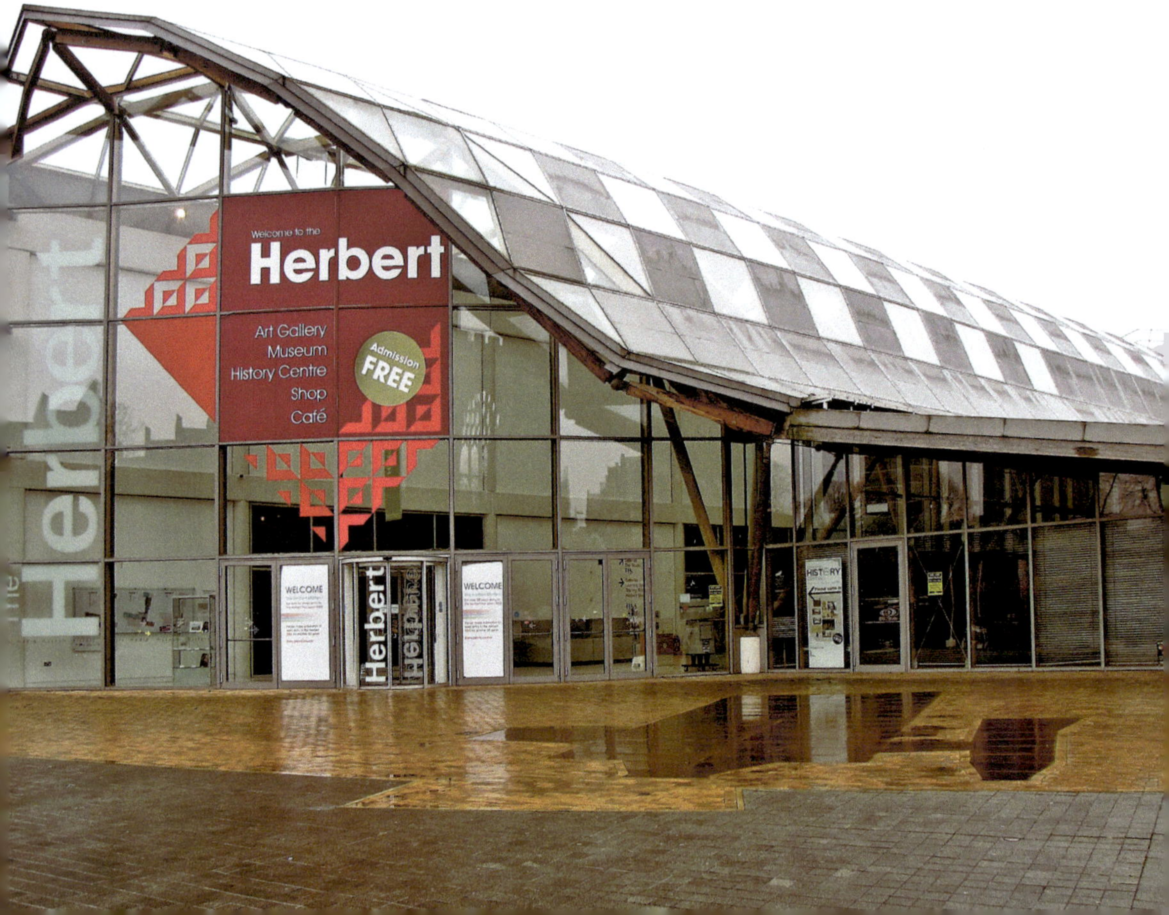

In 2008 it reopened as the Herbert after a £14-million council-led refurbishment with an extension designed by Pringles, Richards and Sharratt, which houses the archives and local studies sections. The most striking part of the extension is the glass gallery, described as an, 'exposed Glulam gridshell,' it was inspired by the roof structure of Spence's cathedral opposite. This trust-led building now has limited opening.

## 26. Holy Trinity

Holy Trinity Church was originally attached to Coventry Priory, used by tenants of the priory to free up the cathedral church to the bishop, prior and monks – and later the pilgrims who brought financial benefits to the order. It is usually stated that Holy Trinity began sometime between 1101 and 1113. The church itself is first documented in 1139.

Trinity may have begun life as a Saxon minster. There are many things to back this up such as being cruciform, which shows it is high status. Also the nearby cathedral of St Mary was built according to papal deeds in the parish of Holy Trinity. The proximity of nearby chapels in the twelfth century such as the chapels of Our Lady on the Mount and Holy Cross are suggestive of the presence of a minster church. This would also make it the mother church of the city. Another important event, the ringing of the curfew bell from Trinity is associated with the mother church. Fair days were also fixed on the day of the main church's dedication; Coventry's Great Fair Day was fixed in 1218 on the festival of the Holy Trinity. Lastly, many early charters, when referring to the city's churches, refer to St Mary's, St Michael's and 'the parish church'. This can only be Holy Trinity. This is all suggestive that Trinity was originally a Saxon minster and the mother church of Coventry.

It is said that in 1257 much of the early church was destroyed by fire and so rebuilding began. However, the original chancel survived, for in 1391 it was written that the chancel is, 'ruinated and decayed.' This could not have belonged to the church built in the previous century, so was more likely to constitute part of an older building. Trinity's surviving thirteenth-century fabric shows it always had a cruciform shape. The building we see today stands 194 feet long with a tower and a spire reaching 237 feet, making it one of the largest parish churches in England.

In the late fourteenth century, guilds started to establish chapels. In 1392 the merchant Corpus Christi Guild paid a priest to sing mass five times a day for its members, King Richard and Queen Anne in the chapel of Our Lady, on the left of the high altar. In 1517 the butchers founded a chapel, followed by the dyers and tanners. This was followed by the founding of chantry chapels, the first being Cellet's or Jesus Chapel in the south transept over the Jesus Passage, which carried the footpath through the churchyard and was blocked in 1833. The blocked passage arch can be seen outside.

In 1349, William Cospston and Peter Percy founded Percye's Chantry for two priests to sing mass for their parents until the world ends. Other chantries include the Holy Cross, Lodynton's and Allesley Chantry. The Marler Chapel with its two green men was the last addition to the church in 1526 by the will of Richard Marler, a grocer and one of the wealthiest merchants in England. Beneath this chapel is an untouched charnel house. By 1522 Trinity had eleven priests, two chantry priests and a vicar. In addition to the high

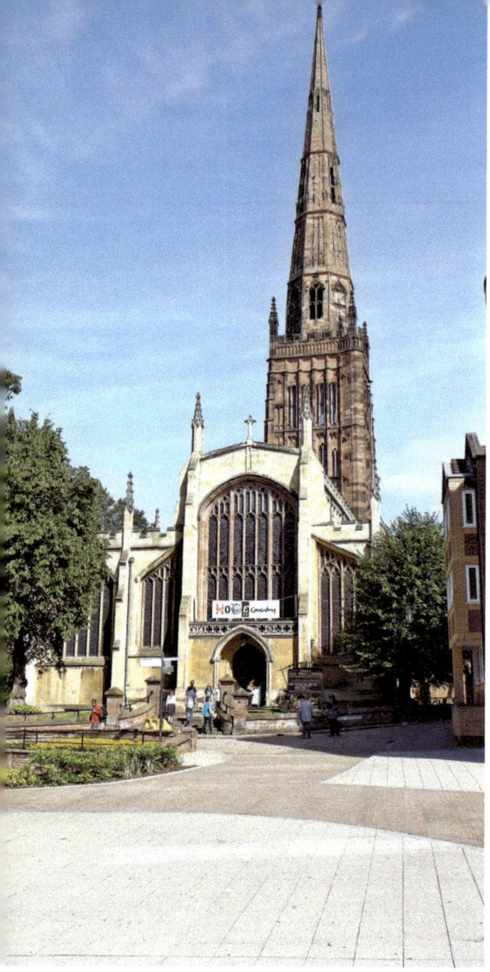

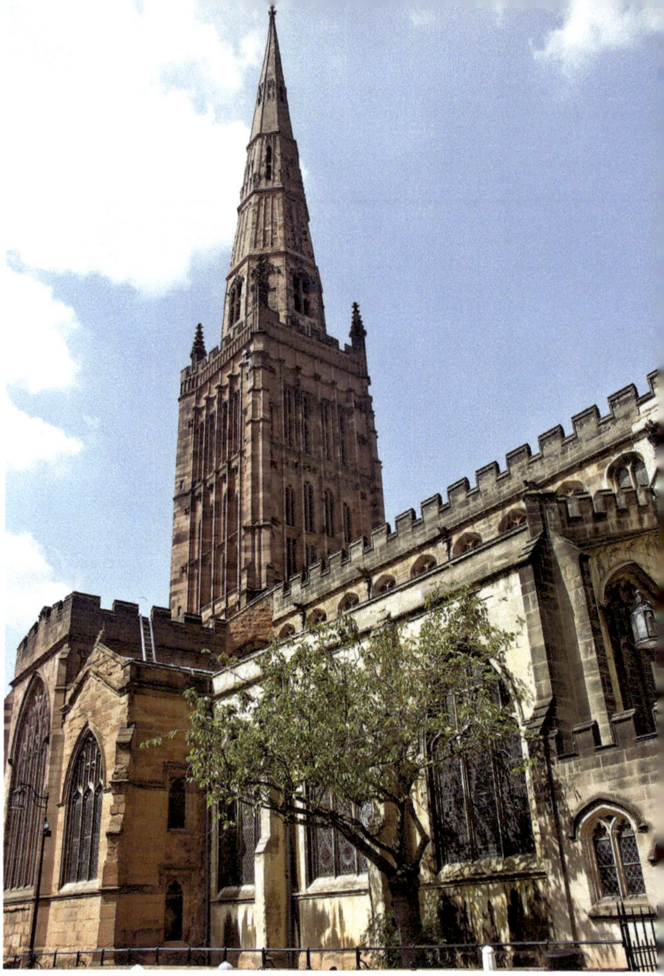

*Above left*: The front of Holy Trinity from Broadgate.

*Above right*: The south side of Trinity, the chapel on this side was the Jesus Chapel.

altar, there were at least eight further altars in the building. This changed in 1539 with the Dissolution, when Coventry lost its cathedral and Trinity lost eight priests. By 1560 the rood screen and high altar were removed and the first Protestant communion table was brought in and Trinity became the church we see today.

The *Doom* painting covering the chancel arch depicts the Day of Judgement. It was created between 1435 and 1460, probably prompted by an earthquake – a portent of the end of the world. It shows the dead rising from their graves and being judged by Christ. On one side souls await St Peter at the gates of Heaven and on the other a mouth to Hell, where the evil doers, including clergymen, are seen being cast down by demons. The *Doom* hadn't been in existence for much more than a 125 years before reformers whitewashed it out. Its existence was noted in the late eighteenth century and in 1831. Shortly afterwards local artist David Gee was paid £25 to restore it. He protected it with a coating of meglip. Meglip contained asphaltum and bitumen, which, over time, goes black and destabilises paintwork. Add to this the smoke from oil lamps, and it is unsurprising that the image began to disappear in the 1860s. In 2002 work began on its recovery; cleaning took a year, done inch by inch with cotton buds! The restoration of

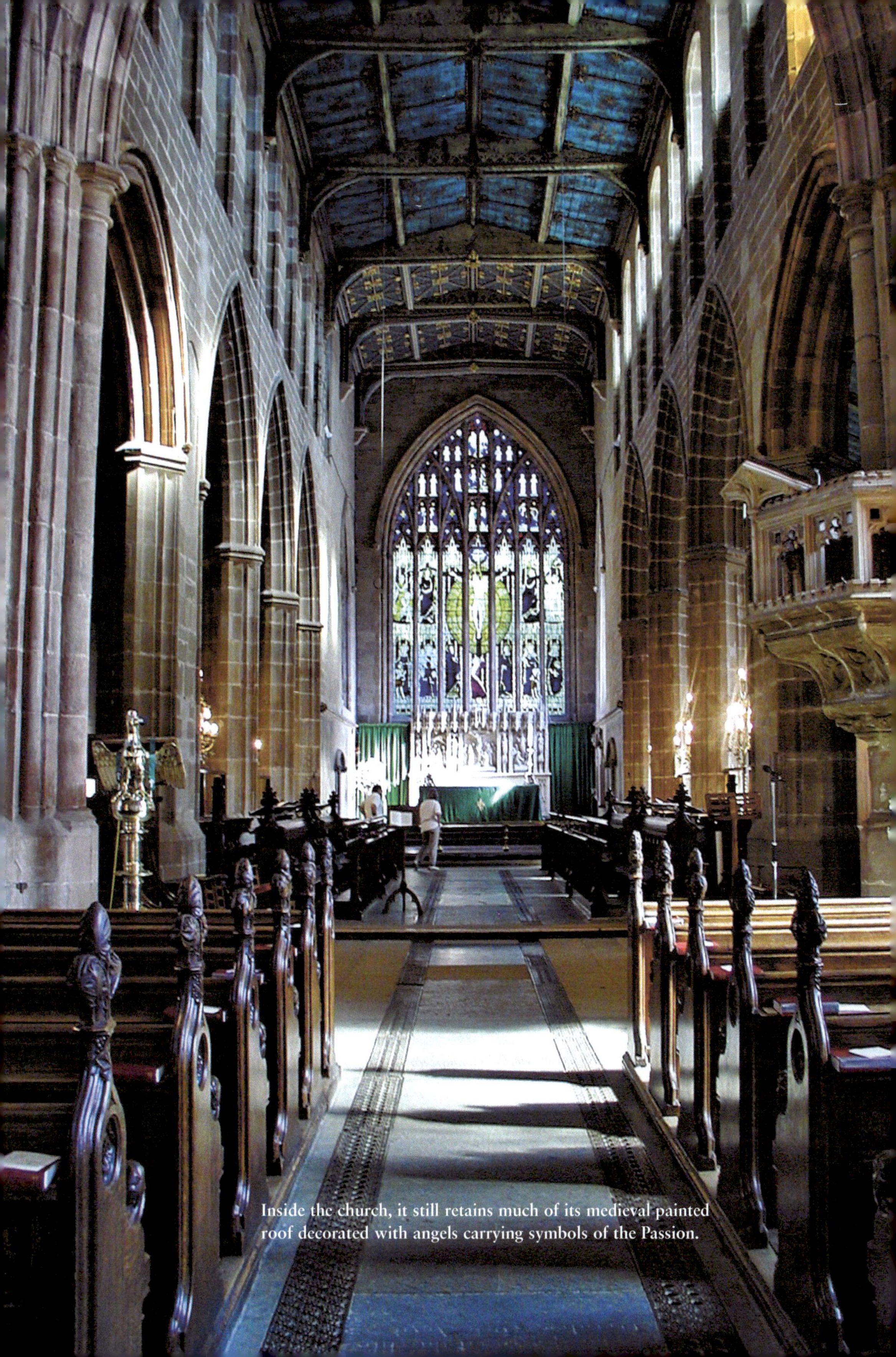

Inside the church, it still retains much of its medieval painted roof decorated with angels carrying symbols of the Passion.

the *Doom* not only raised the national profile of Holy Trinity Church, and it also gave Coventry and the nation a new treasure.

Trinity is highly decorated and like many churches received restoration during the nineteenth century. Its tower and spire, noted as being shell-like, has received many restorations, starting with the first recorded in 1667 after it collapsed, killing a passing boy. Up until 1914 the spire was repaired twelve times. Its last restoration was in 2001. The Archdeacon's Court was originally a chapel and once used for the Ecclesiastical Court. The monuments were moved here during the 1854–56 restoration. One is to Doctor Philemon Holland the 'Translator General', who transcribed many of the classics into English. Another is to Revd Joseph Rann, Trinity's vicar who in 1776 published four editions of the works of Shakespeare with copious notes. It was during Rann's time in 1773 that Sarah Siddons married in the church. Rann chose not to perform the ceremony for 'common players', which is ironic as Sarah Siddons became the greatest Shakespearean actress of her time. George Eliot also attended this church.

A noted time in the church's history was under Revd G. W. Clitheroe who, during the many raids on the city, manned the church roof with his small team, protecting it from incendiary bombs. On recalling the night of 14 November 1940, he recalled watching the city burn and likened it to Dante's *Inferno*. But for the bravery of Clitheroe and his team, Trinity would have burned. Clitheroe's message of defiance and faith hung across the west window on massive banners during the war years, it read, 'It all depends on me, and I depend on God.'

## 27. Kirby House, No. 16 Little Park Street

All that is left of Kirby House is its façade and remains of some internal walls at the front. The actual façade may have been added in 1700 and appears to have been remodelled in 1735. It is likely that it was added on to a building dating from the sixteenth or seventeenth century. Inside, Jacobean panelling and a staircase back this up. It takes its name from Thomas Hulston Kirby, a solicitor who acquired the building in 1874. In 1959 it was the office of another solicitor who, after being quoted £10,000 for the building's restoration, notified the council of its intent to demolish. The council immediately put a preservation order on the building. In 1964 the council acquired the building as a possible new mayor's parlour but after having it surveyed they found its restoration too costly and requested the removal of the preservation order.

Four years later the building was in a dangerous condition and was held up by scaffolding. Councillors continued arguing whether to save or demolish it. In December 1969 they applied for its demolition. This led to a public enquiry and after three years the Department of the Environment refused the order. Over the following eight years the building rotted. It was during this period that the Coventry Society was founded to fight to save what was left of it. Finally the council sold it on to a developer, who then sold it on to builder W. A. Blackburn who, with architects Crouch Butler & Savage and historic consultants R. S. Melville, began restoration in 1980. Salvaging what little was left and using original photographs to restore and reproduce the inside, they restored the ancient panelling and brought this fine building back to life. The building has since been used by Sun Life, a solicitor, and now houses the Citizens Advice Bureau.

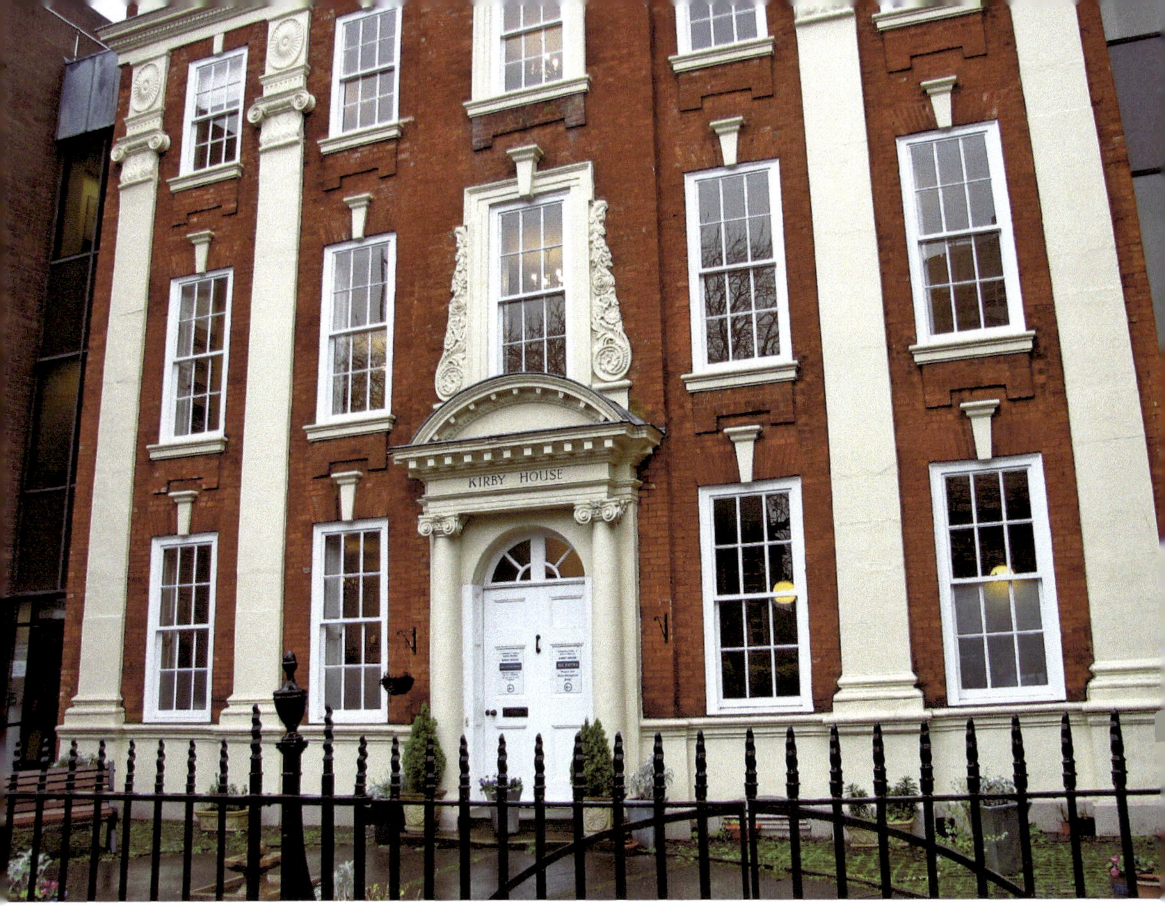


Kirby House as seen from Little Park Street.

## 28. Lych Gate Cottages, Priory Row

A modern plaque on Lych Gate Cottages states they were built in the spring of 1415 and were part of the forecourt of Coventry Priory. Coventry's late archaeologist Margaret Rylatt believed this to be wrong and I agreed with her. The building is known to have been built from reused timbers and this dating is based on six test samples. There are problems with this theory. The three-storeyed building range stands on brick barrel-vaulted cellars that appear to date to the seventeenth century. In addition, the building stands 4 metres higher than the level of the priory forecourt. It also stands on the edge of the west tower, which was demolished in 1648, and to have domestic houses on the forecourt makes little sense as the area was walled with its own gate, creating a secure area.

A drawing by Smyth in 1576 shows the west towers of St Mary's Priory still standing. One small section can still be seen today. A great portion of these ruins was removed and cottages were built on part of this, along with a house upon the spot where the transepts met beneath the great central tower and gardens formed between them. The Trinity Deeds of 1650 make it clear when and who built them, and says:

> Whereas the west part of the ruins of the Cathedral Church of St Mary, in this city, that was demolished in the reign of Henry VIII had been made use of by butchers to keep

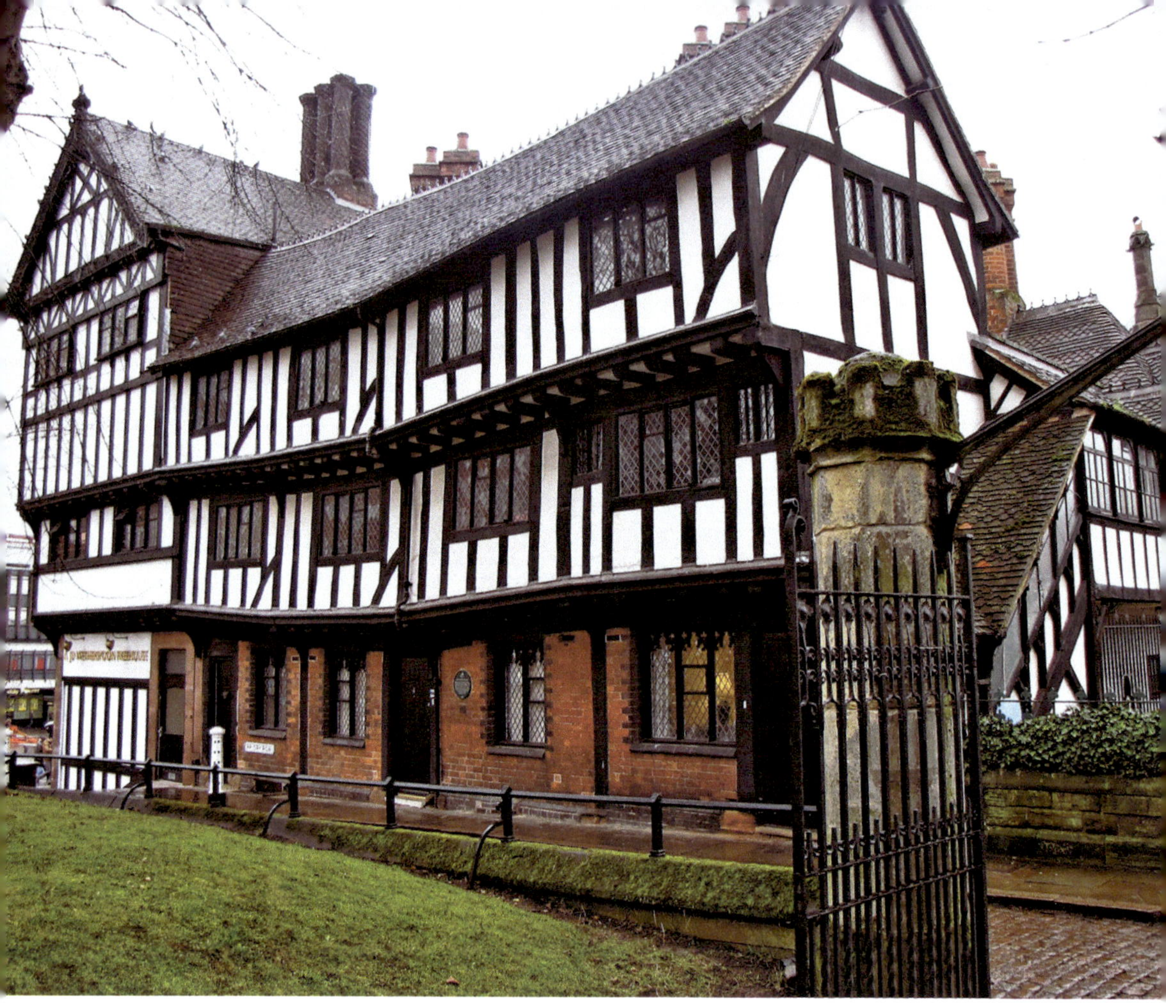

Lych Gate Cottages with cobbled Priory Row in the foreground.

> hogs in, the city this year gave to Mr John Bryan, Vicar of Trinity, a grant thereof from the City, and built a dwelling House [for himself called Tower House] over against the Lane, between the two Churchyards, where formerly a steeple stood belonging to the said Cathedral, the Cross Iles going over there. He also made dwelling Houses on the Bottom of the two steeples that were on both sides of the Entrance into the Priory, from the Butcherow, and cleansed the ground of the ruins, and converted it to Gardens.

Bryan seemed to have used old timbers for these buildings, mainly from the churchyard for the Holy Trinity Churchwardens Account for 1644 proves they were there. It reads, 'Payments for taking downe diverse houses and buildings without Bishop's gate and Spon gate ... and bringing the tiles and Timber into Trinitie Church.' These items were for reuse and no doubt some came from a building dated 1415. Records show some houses dismantled outside the gates were rebuilt in nearby New Buildings, like in the Spon Street townscape. Many timbered buildings literally had their beams numbered so the carpenters could see where they fitted. The cottages were private residences up until 1937 when the council acquired them. In 1997–98 they were restored, and in 2016 they were given to the Historic Coventry Trust.

## 29. National Westminster Bank

Designed by F. C. R. Palmer & W. F. C. Holden and built in 1929, this is the only original building to survive pre-war Broadgate. Amazingly, it, Lloyds bank, the old Post Office, and Ford's Hospital were threatened with demolition in 1941 as Gibson planned a new road from Broadgate to the station. Built initially as the National Provincial Bank, it consists of a banking hall, offices and shops. It has a grand Roman portico decorated with coins and with four Doric columns facing Broadgate and sweeps around the corner with Greek columns in Hertford Street. Built in red-brick Flemish bond and Portland stone, the lines of this building were ruined when Broadgate House was extended to it, blocking the original view.

The bank has stainless steel doors decorated with images of ancient Greek coins. The exceptions are the lion and crown taken from British coins, St George and the dragon and the hen and chicks from an Irish penny. The coins' designs are based on ones held in the British Museum. The doors were designed by W. F. C. Holden and were made by the Birmingham Guild, whose employee, Mr Pearson, hammered out all the designs by hand. Inside, the body of the banking hall remains relatively unchanged with its geometrically glazed large glass lantern and green-clad marble walls.

The NatWest Bank as it appeared in the mid-1930s, showing the full aspect of the building, which now is blocked.

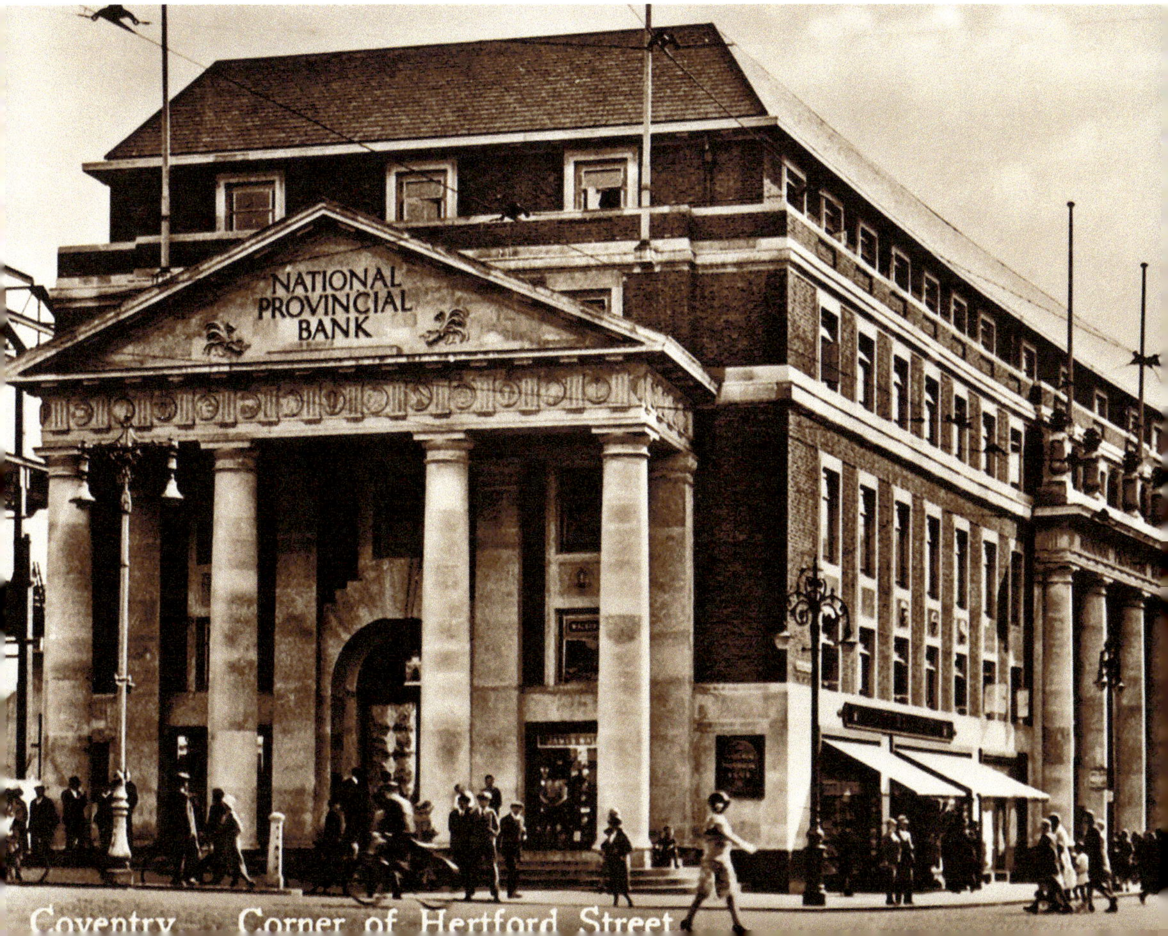

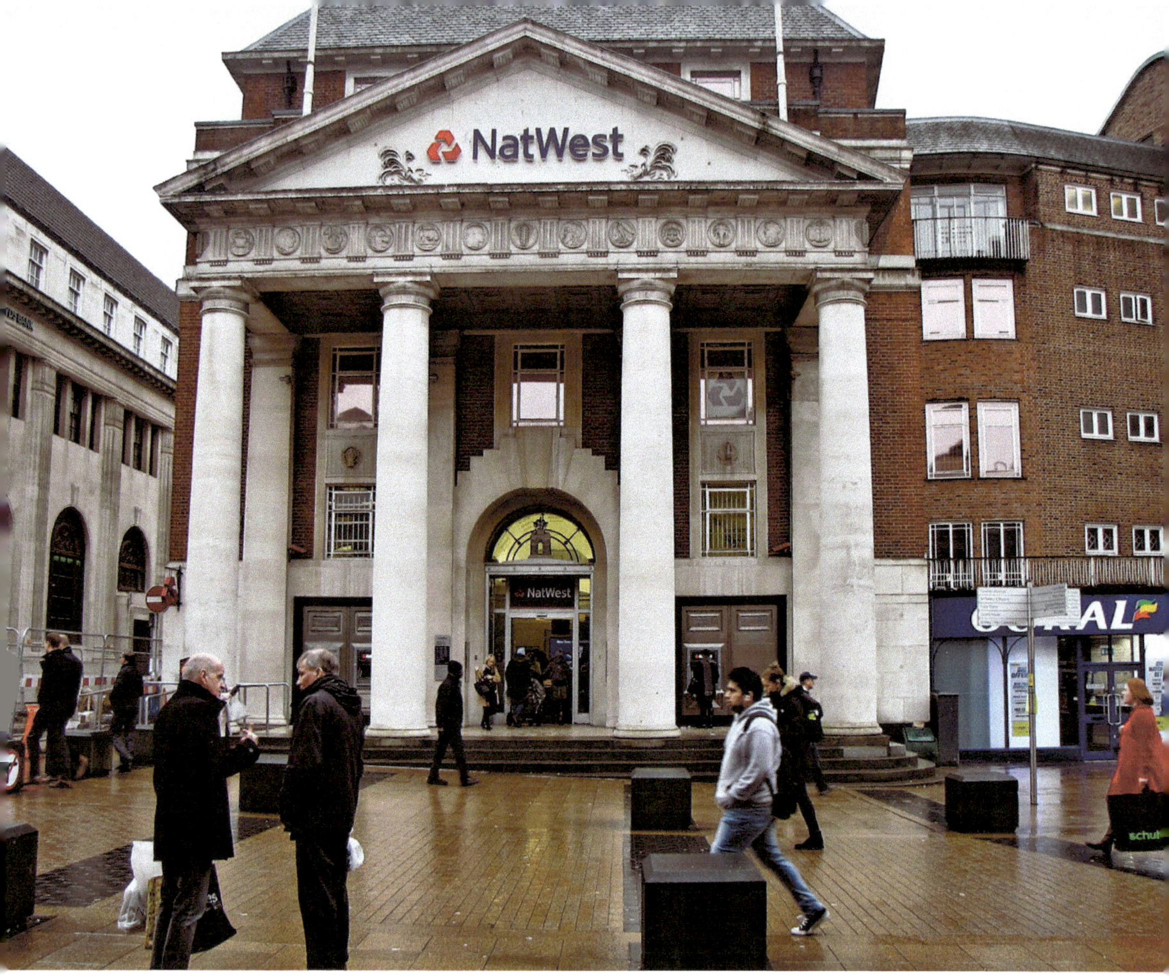


The main prospect of it today is its fine columned frontage. This used to be called, 'the top of the town.'

## 30. Old Grammar School, Hales Street

St John's Hospital as the Old Grammar School was originally known was said to have been founded around 1157 by the Benedictine Prior Laurence of St Mary's Priory. It is said he granted the land and that the hospital was constructed under the supervision of Edmund, archdeacon of Coventry, who pleaded with the prior for provision for aged and infirm travellers. Oddly this hospital-cum-church was under the supervision of the Knights Hospitaller, the military order from the Hospital of St John of Jerusalem. The order was founded in 1023 to care for sick and injured pilgrims in Jerusalem and after the First Crusade became a military order.

Strangely, at the time of the founding of St John's, the Hospitallers were not held in favour by the Benedictine Order. As the Hospitallers inherited the buildings and estates of the purged Knights Templar, it may be possible this building has a different origin that has itself been purged from history. Interestingly, the Templars were accused of summoning the devil and this building has a legend attached to it of the devil being summoned and appearing to the men within.

In 1522 it held three priests, three clerks and five sisters and maintained thirty beds. Most were allowed to stay two nights and two days, although this could vary. Part of the chancel and choir were reserved for religious purposes while the beds of the sick and infirm lined the walls of the rest of the chancel and nave. The present surviving building was the main part of that church. The infirmary, hall and lodgings are long gone. The whole complex is said to have been rebuilt in the early 1300s. The east window is particularly beautiful, with a possible French influence. It was surrendered in 1544 and in July 1546 the buildings and ground were granted by the Crown to John Hales, clerk of the Hanaper. Hales had been one the king's commissioners in the dissolution of Coventry's monastic houses. Although the hospital was valued at £95 13*s* in 1545, Hales paid the king £400.

Henry VIII stipulated that Hales should set up a grammar school in the city, although there was no written stipulation that he had to endow it. Hales did set up a school – in the choir of Whitefriars' Church – which he didn't own, and was forced to remove it. He moved it to St John's and with it Whitefriars' choir stalls. Fifty of them survived in 1862. The conversion of the hospital into a school with one classroom meant a number of structural changes. The height of the building was reduced by raising the floor and lowering the roof by constructing a wooden waggon-hood ceiling below the original open timber roof, which

The Old Grammar or Free School as it appeared in the early nineteenth century. The timbered section that stands over the site of Hales Street houses the library.

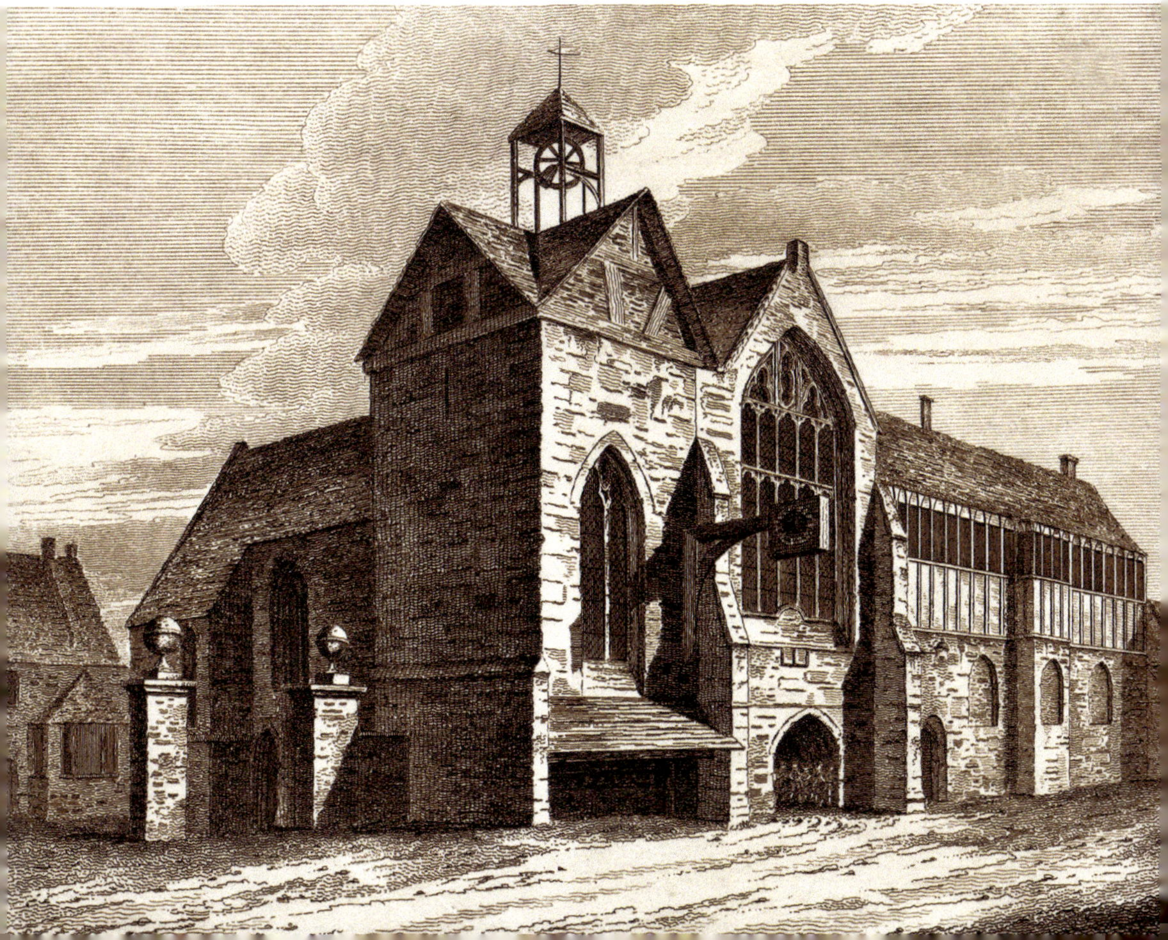

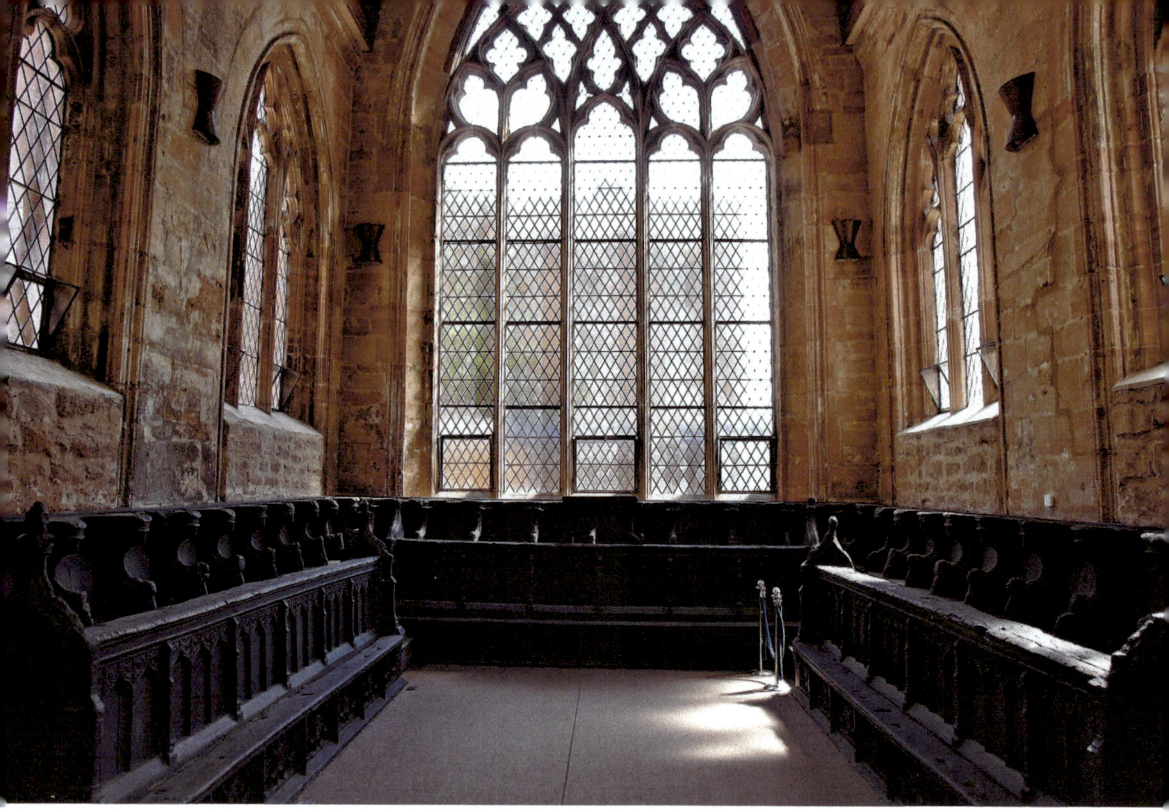

The east end of the original church still contains benches from Whitefriars put there when it was converted into a school.

remains hidden to this day. The south aisle was demolished and part of the north aisle, formerly St Katherine's Chapel, was changed into a classroom. The arches on both sides were walled in with stone.

In 1628 the first rules were made:

> This Schoole is a Free Grammar Schoole, for the teaching of grammar and musick unto the children of all the Free Inhabitants within this Citie and the inner liberties thereof, and to none other, whose children after their admission, shall be taught gratis. All other Fforyners coming thither shall compound with the Maister and the Usher for theire teaching.

In the early 1880s, when the new Henry VIII School was built, the grammar school was threatened with demolition. William Bennett wanted to clear it to build a theatre. The Catholic community wanted to turn it into a church or erect a new church on the site. In February 1884, Canon Beaumont wrote in *Holy Trinity Parish Magazine*,

> The erection of the new Grammar School has made it necessary that the old Free School should be sold. The building possesses the greatest Interest, historically and architecturally ... It is felt that it would be an act of vandalism to destroy such a relic of the past, but there is no prospect of it being saved unless it can be secured for some public purpose. A committee has therefore, been formed to take steps for its purchase ... An earnest appeal is made to all who, valuing the associations of the past, desire to preserve this building ... from certain destructional conversion to secular and commercial users.

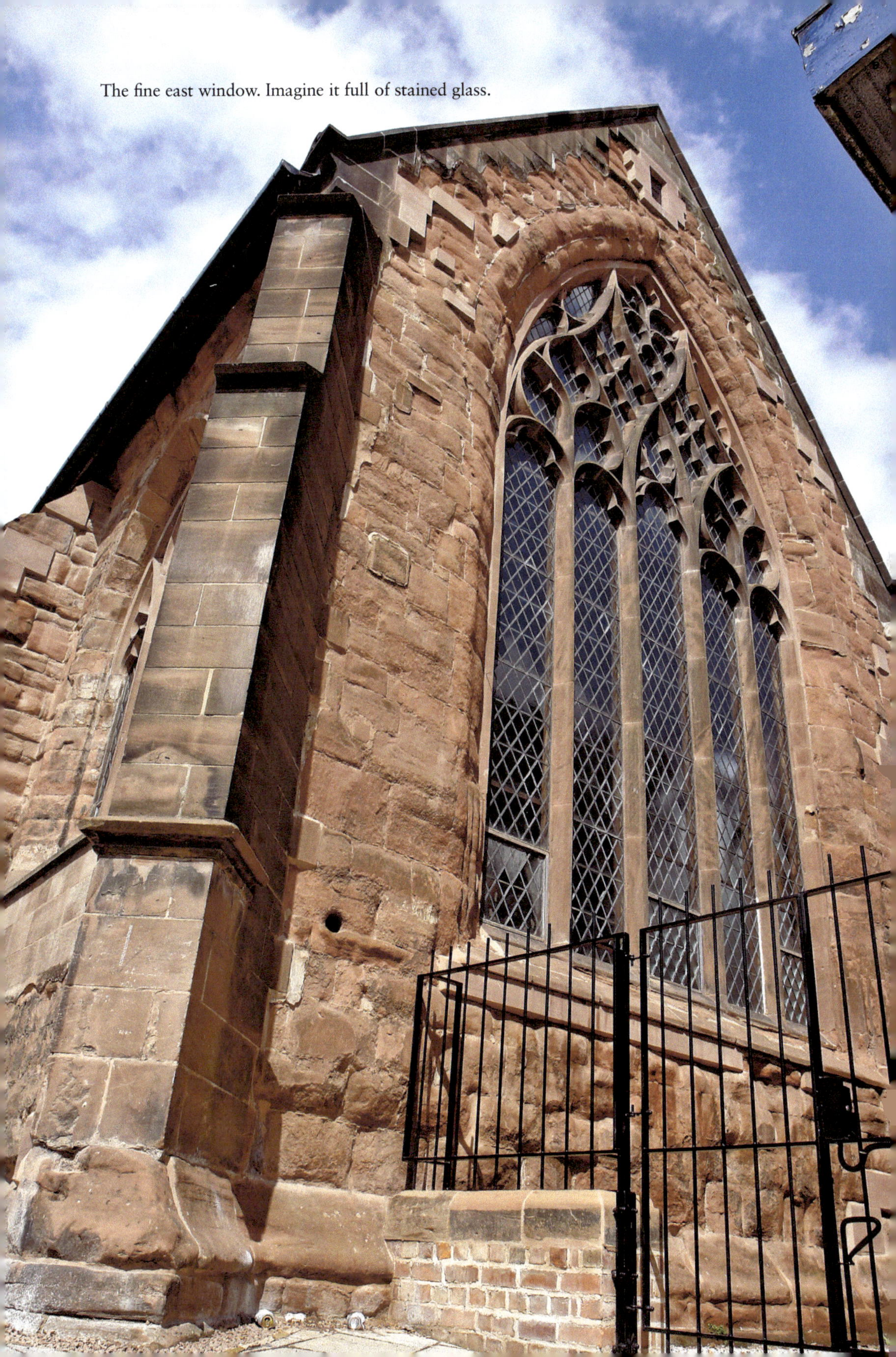

The fine east window. Imagine it full of stained glass.

In April 1885 Beaumont's committee had saved it, paying £1,400. Afterwards parochial meetings and services were held there and it had much community use. In 1941 it received minor bomb damage and in 1952 the council requested its demolition to widen Bishop Street, the Ministry of Works refused. It remained empty for years, just being used for jumble sales, and was put on the at-risk register. Trinity Church went into partnership with the Transport Museum and in 2013, as part of a lottery bid for the museum, it received £1.5-million funding for restoration. In 2013 the Transport Museum's executive said, 'This funding will allow us to save a unique and historically significant building, and tell our city's story in an innovative museum.' It was reported that the building would provide 'heritage, learning and community activities.' The Revd Mayhew of Trinity said, 'We are particularly excited that it will, once again, be used for educational purposes.' After much excellent restoration work it was relaunched to the public in July 2015. The hopes for the building never materialised and it is now a venue building for events such as live music, movies, meetings, conferences and weddings. Public access is limited mainly to heritage weekends.

## 31. Precinct

As the Precinct and Broadgate is made up of large blocks, not individual buildings, I've condensed them into one. The buildings that make up the Upper and Lower Precincts are significant as they make up the first pedestrian precinct in Europe. They were built in brick and stone in Festival of Britain style and designed by Donald Gibson – one could say they are neat, functional and not unattractive. The first building that forms the corner of the Upper Precinct, facing Broadgate, was Broadgate House (left Broadgate entrance). It opened in 1953, was built on council land, and cost £400,000. This still contains council offices and shops. The building also bridged Hertford Street, keeping an open flow and aspect from Broadgate – sadly this was filled-in many years ago.

The first piece of private building was Owen Owen (now Primark), built in 1953–54. It was designed by Hellberg & Harris of Coventry and was the first post-war store built in the city, replacing an earlier Owens that was bombed in 1940. The most distinctive store in Broadgate, it cost £940,000. Owens was followed by the Hotel Leofric, which opened in 1955 and was designed by Coventry architects Hattrells. It was the best hotel in the city centre and bookings had to be made a year in advance; it is now student accommodation. Building continued into the upper and lower two-tiered precincts, crossed by Smithford and Market Way. Gibson left in 1955 and building continued under Arthur Ling. Ling wanted to put more height into the plan and added blocks of flats.

The lines of Gibson's work were originally flowed more and took perspectives into account. Much of these lines have been destroyed by modern additions such as the escalator and ramp in the Upper Precinct, which totally, with Cathedral Lanes, destroy Gibson's original concept. Other areas such as Market Way, which had a curved sweep of shops, were ruined by the building of a concrete tower. Two of the most iconic buildings are perhaps the round market with its rooftop car park and the round café in the Lower Precinct. Unusual even in its time, the café, despite rumours, has never revolved.

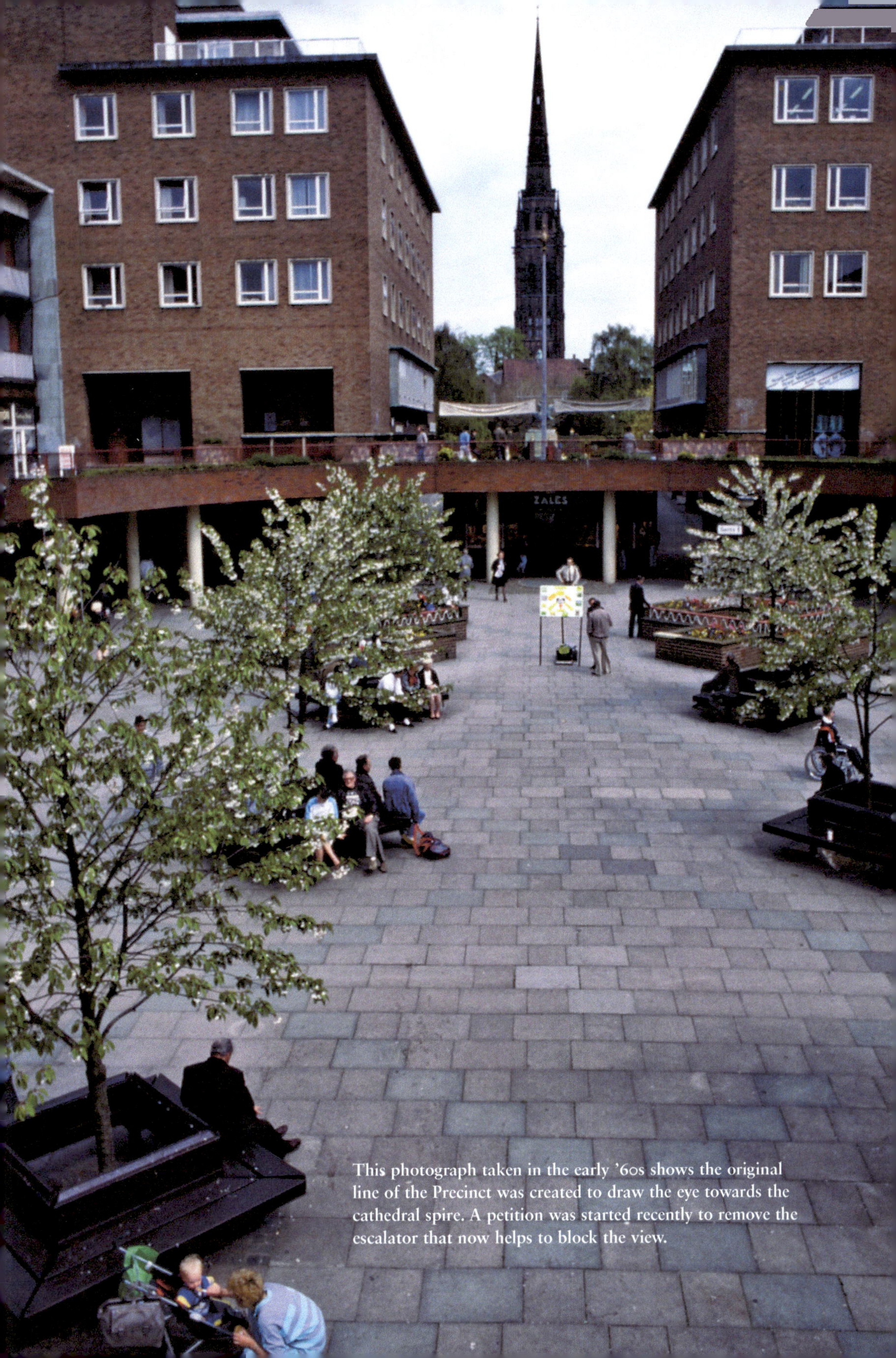


This photograph taken in the early '60s shows the original line of the Precinct was created to draw the eye towards the cathedral spire. A petition was started recently to remove the escalator that now helps to block the view.

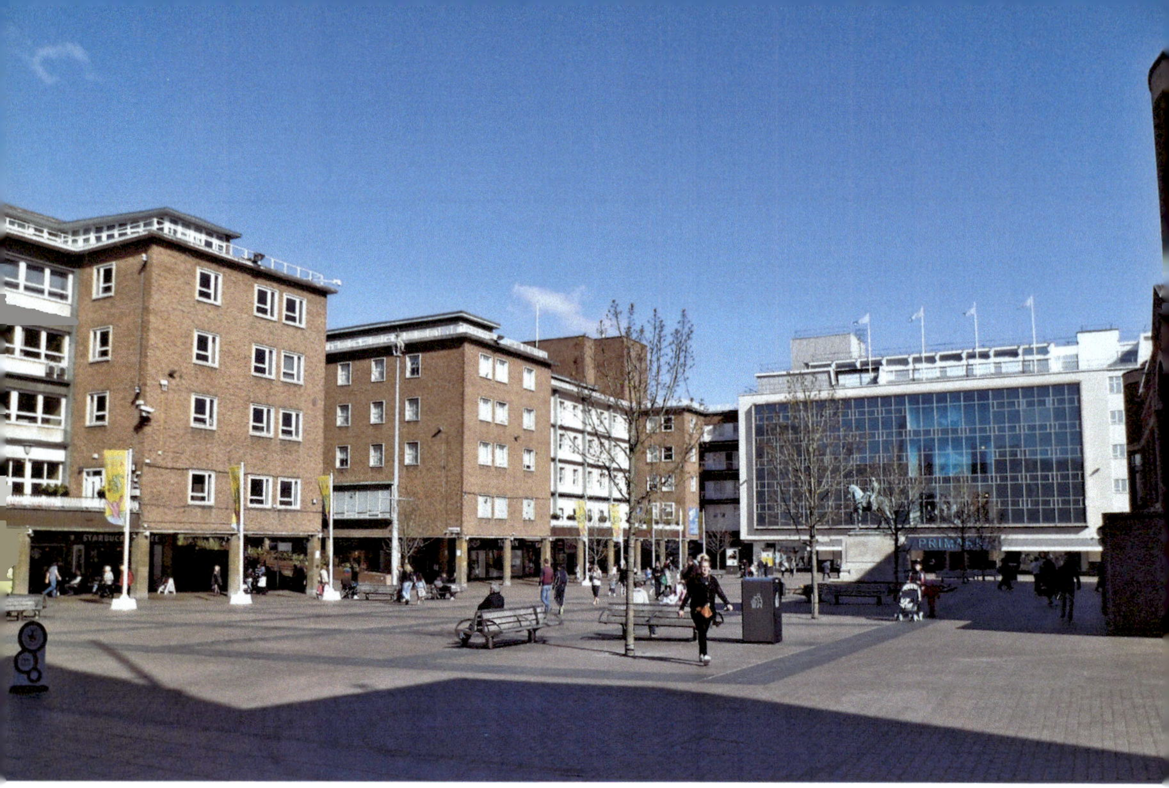

*Above*: Broadgate now entirely pedestrianised. Broadgate House left turns into the Upper Precinct as does the old Leofric (right). The old Owen Owen building is now Primark.

*Below*: Looking down the Upper Precinct today.

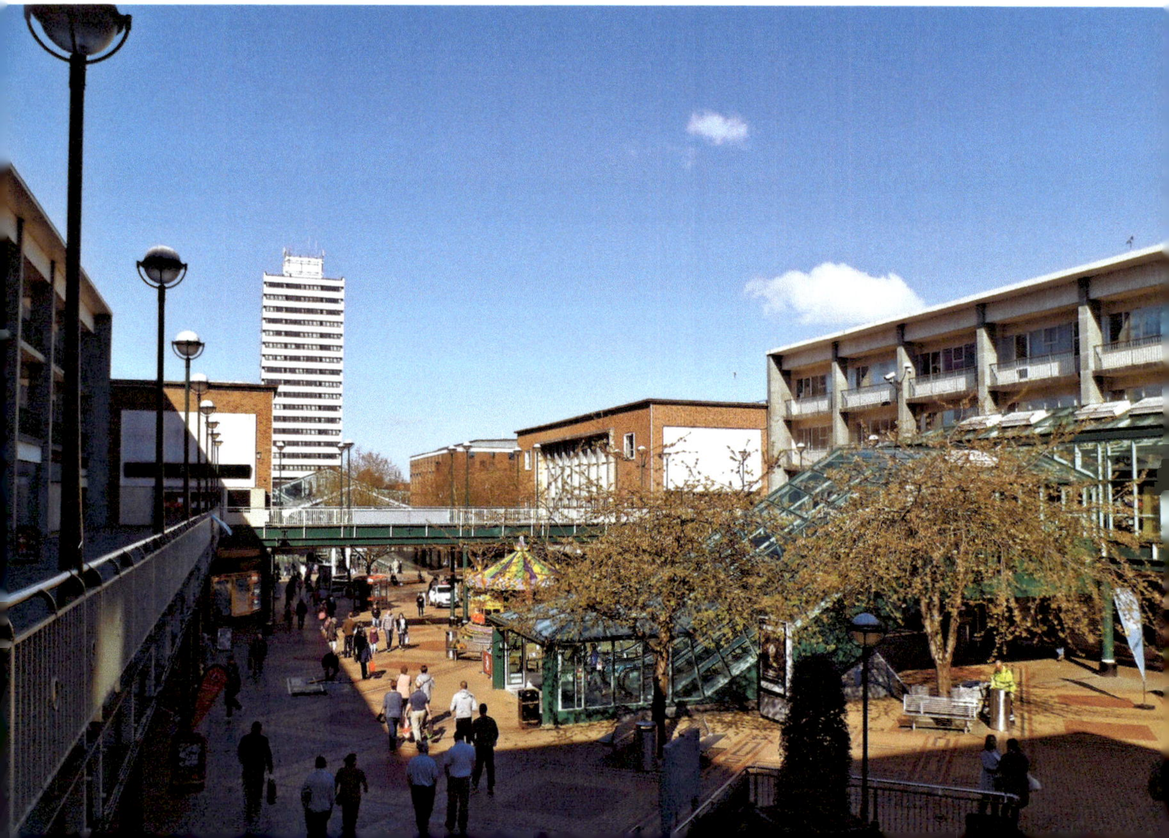

## 32. Premier Inn, The Butts

The Premier Inn located in The Butts was originally the Technical College – a fine building, looking more like a town hall. Work began in August 1933 and it was opened in September 1935. The building was designed by A. W. Hoare of Coventry and built by Garlicks Ltd. The Prince of Wales (Edward VIII) visited it while it was under construction in 1932. The 260-feet-long three-storey building has two wings, between which was the 115-feet-long Great Hall. The building is a steel-framed structure cased in brick.

The façade is of a classical design, clad in reconstituted Clipsham stone. The main façade is surmounted by four pairs of Doric columns, between which are carved panels showing the city's principal trades. Below, the portico bears the city's coat of arms. The building was officially opened on 19 December 1935 by the Duke of York, later George VI. During the Blitz it continued to educate adults and children and housed Coventry's homeless; it was hit by a number of bombs but received little damage. The college was closed in 2008 and moved to a new site. The Great Hall was originally a lecture theatre and was used after the war by the Midland Theatre Co. It continued up to 2009 as the Butts Theatre, which closed when developers acquired the site. The theatre seemed lost but with the help and support of the council, a twenty-five-year deal was made with the developers and the theatre reopened in 2013 as the Albany Theatre.

The Technical College, today a Premier Hotel.

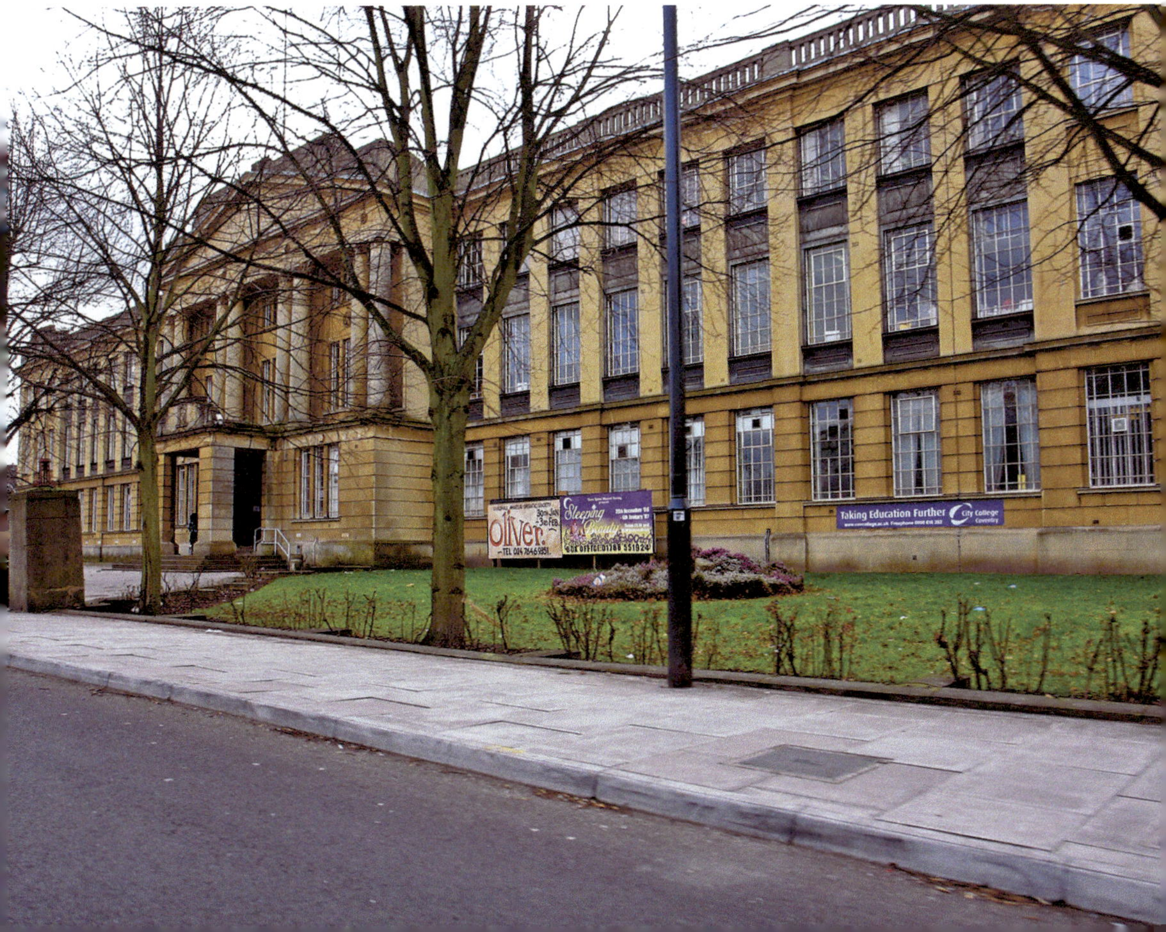

## 33. Ribbon Factory, New Buildings

The Ribbon Factory, built in 1849, is now the only remaining ribbon-weaving factory in the city centre. The manager's house was added in 1858. The factory consists of three floors; on the ground was the winding engine and on the two floors above were twenty-two rented looms.

Steam power was introduced from the 1830s and led to events like the Beck Riot of 1832, when Beck's factory nearby was fired by a mob. The New Buildings factory represents the change between home-produced silks on handlooms to factory-produced silks on steam looms. The weavers were paid employees here who paid rent to the owner for the loom. The factory ceased production in the late 1850s and in 1860 John Gulson gave part of the building rent-free to the ragged school, which was still operating into the 1930s. By 1873 the manager's house was called 'The Armoury', having become the armoury of the Rifle Volunteers Corps, who used part of the factory as their drill hall. In 1908 the Stevens Memorial Hall was built at the rear and was used by the ragged Sunday school among other things until its demolition in 1999. In modern times a dance school and local newspaper occupied the upper floors of the factory, with Exchange & Mart on street level. The factory was restored during the Phoenix Initiative in 2002.

The old Ribbon Factory in New Buildings showing the manager's house in the foreground.

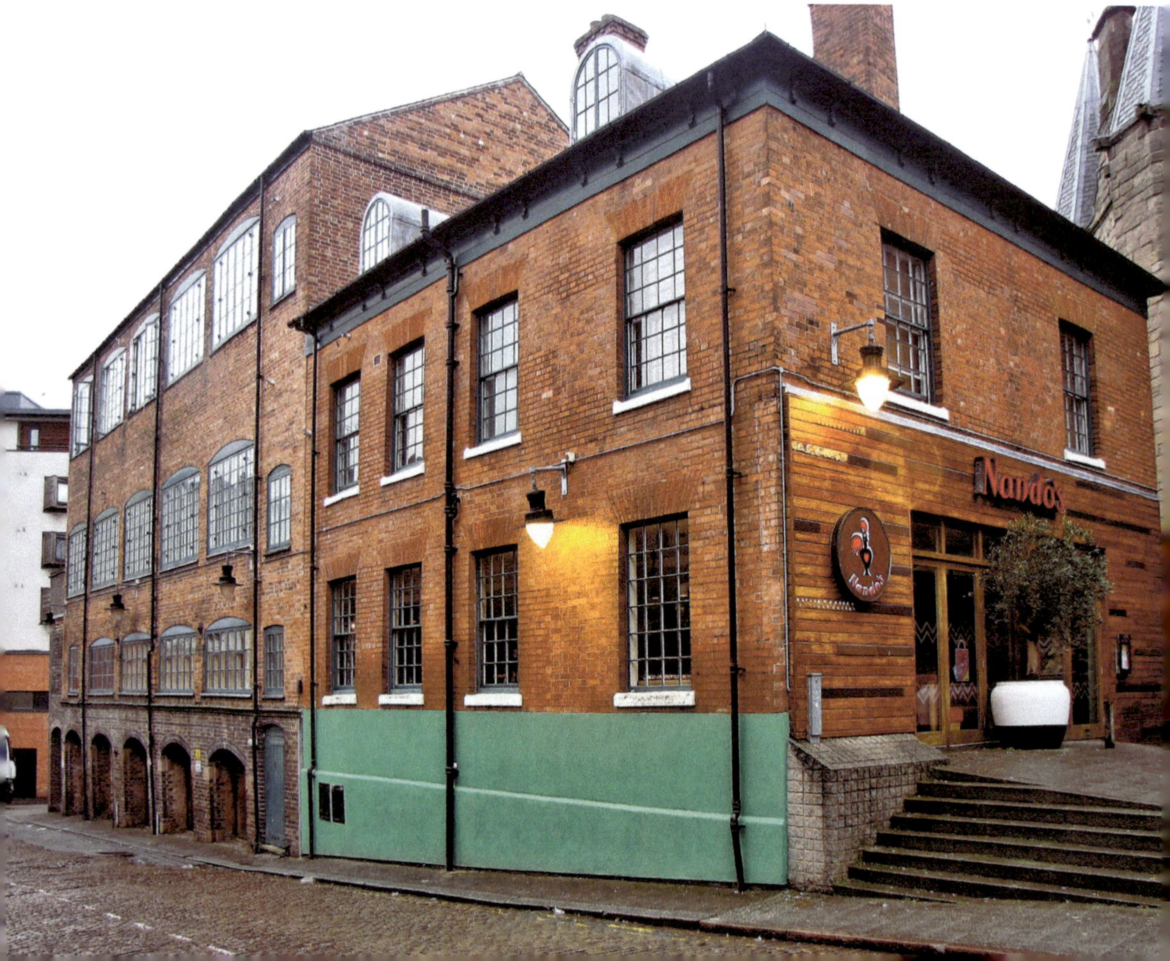

## 34. Rotherham House, Spon Street

Numbers 26, 27 and 28 are significant to Coventry's watch trade, in fact the central section – No. 27 – belonged to master watchmakers. The previous timbered building on this site belonged to William Jeliff, who died in 1681. In 1775 four-times-mayor Alderman Samuel Vale, a noted watch manufacturer, lived here. In the 1780s Vale demolished the old house and built the Georgian town house we see today. Behind it he added his workshops. The two outer sections – Nos 26 and 28 – were added in the late nineteenth century by the Rotherham's in the style of the original.

The firm became Vale, Howlette & Carr, then Vale, Howlette, Carr & Rotherham. These families were connected to each other through marriage and trade. The Rotherham connection is usually linked to Richard Kevitt Rotherham, who it is said was a former apprentice of the firm. There is no evidence for this and the first Rotherham we find is John Rotherham – he is recorded as a partner to Vale in 1810. He married Bridget Platts, née Kevitt, in St John's Church in 1789 and lived next door to Vale in the original No. 28. Richard Kevitt Rotherham was John's son and is recorded as a watch manufacturer in Spon Street in 1813. In 1812 he married Charlotte Carr, daughter of John Carr Snr. This

The Rotherham House in Spon Street, home to master watchmakers and a fine frontage to their factories.

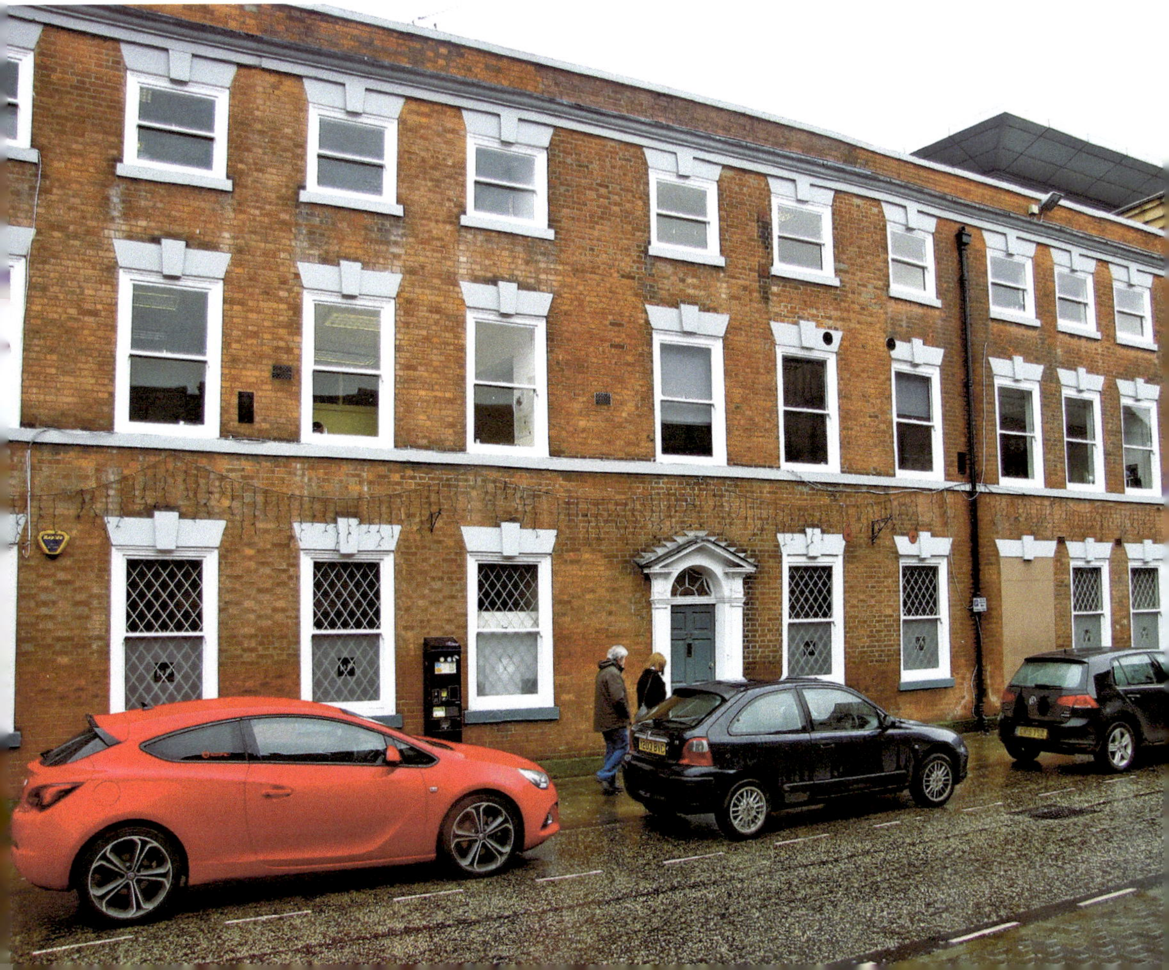

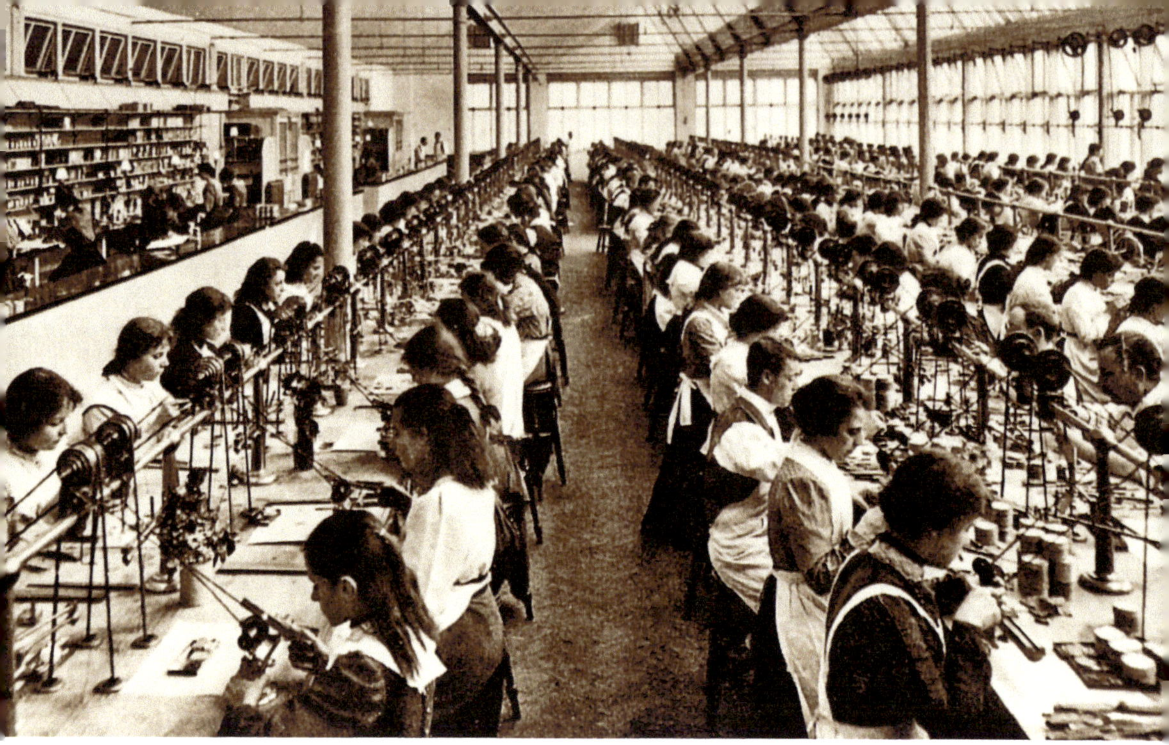

Girls working in the Rotherham factory behind the Georgian House taken in 1910.

marriage may have been the origin of Rotherham's eventual takeover of the company, which, in 1822, was Vale, Rotherham & Sons before becoming Rotherham & Sons. In 1841 Richard's address was given as No. 4 Spon Street (now demolished).

Sometime after, Rotherham took over the old Vale house and works. In 1884 his grandson John Rotherham turned the Vale workshops into a true factory, introducing power. At that time the firm employed over 500 people. By 1930 they had ceased watch production and produced instruments and timers for the military. They continued to produce clocks until 1964. The factory's most famous visitor was Charles Dickens, who came in 1858 and was presented with a Rotherham watch – he carried it until his death. In 1973 Rotherham was incorporated into Cornercroft Engineering. The building now houses the Ian Darby Partnership.

## 35. St Bartholomew's, Binley

The parish church at Binley was erected by William Baron Craven of Coombe Abbey for £5,000 and dedicated to St Bartholomew in 1773. It replaced a medieval church dedicated to St Swithin. The first sermon was read by his father, Revd John Craven. It was built in the Adams style, possibly by Adams himself, and houses the Craven family chapel. The entrance has Tuscan columns, arched windows and a bell turret with cupola. The ceiling is ornamented with plasterwork, including scriptural medallions. The late eighteenth-century east window was created by William Peckett of York. During services, which were well attended when the Cravens attended, the congregation entered through the main door and the Craven's through the north door, screened into their private chapel looking onto the semicircular apse.

Capel Bond, considered one of the most remarkable eighteenth-century composers, died in Coventry on 14 February 1790. He was buried at St Bartholomew's.

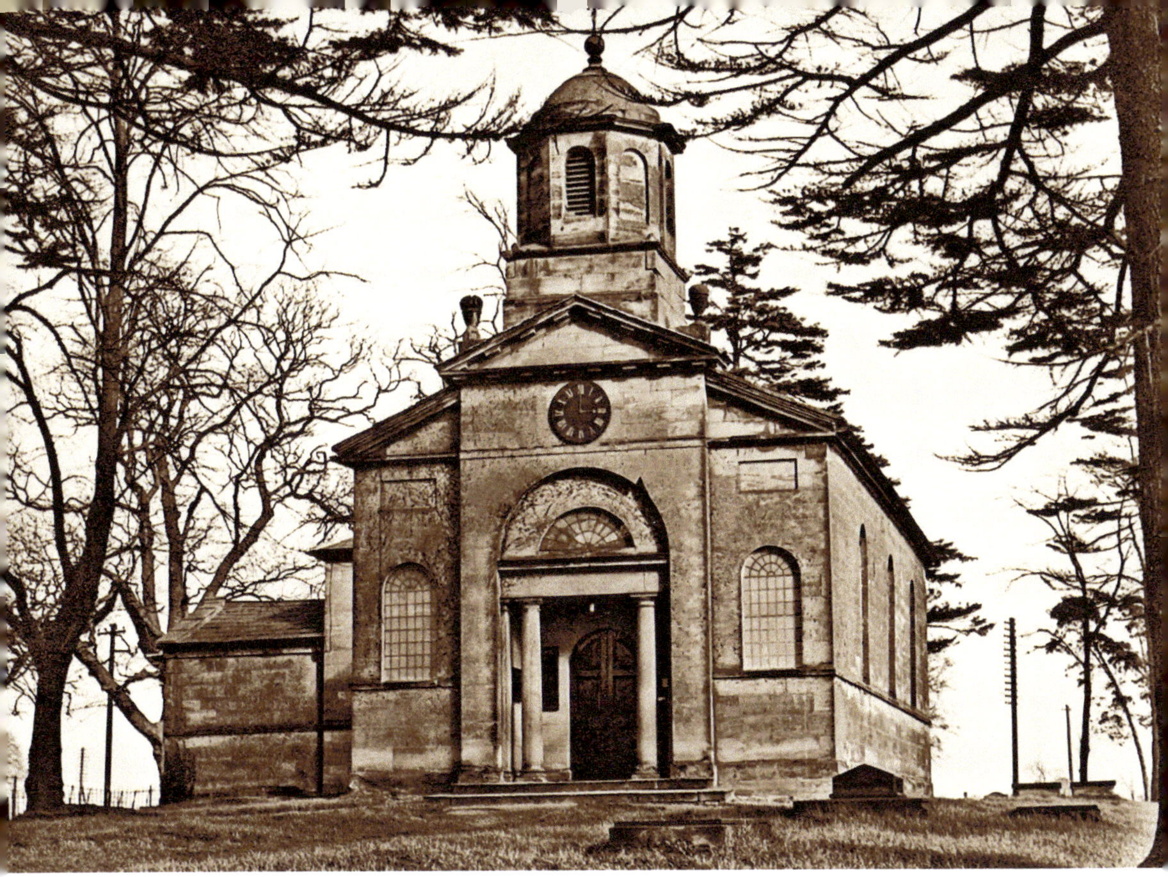

St Bartholomew's in Binley stylistically stands alone in Coventry.

## 36. St Catherine's Well

St Catherine's Well, or Conduit Knob, our smallest and most unusually placed building, is in the curve of a row of 1930s houses in Beaumont Crescent, Coundon. It is an ancient spring covered by an early fifteenth-century 10-feet sandstone kennel chapel that stood atop a grassy knoll, or knob – hence the alternative name. The earliest mention of it appears to be in the Pittanancer's Rental, showing it stood on Coventry Priory land in 1410. The spring in 1847 supplied 100,000 gallons a day to Spon End's water supply.

Clues point to the well having an ancient origin. The name St Catherine is attached to many wells dedicated to the sun, the saint's wheel being the sun symbol. There was also a belief that the well led down into underground tunnels, guarded by a giant cockerel. It was quite a common story attached to pagan wells that once the water was passed through you would enter the underworld; the cockerel was thought of as a pagan guardian. As the well later stood on priory land, it is likely they built the structure over it and rededicated it.

The well was tidied up in 1935, previously it had stood on a grassy knoll. I don't know if the grass covered the supporting structure and steps, but it is quite likely it did and therefore the work in 1935 would have exposed and restored what was already there. Coventrians still followed well lore into the early twentieth century. Newborns were washed in Radford Spring, which it was believed would cure various problems.

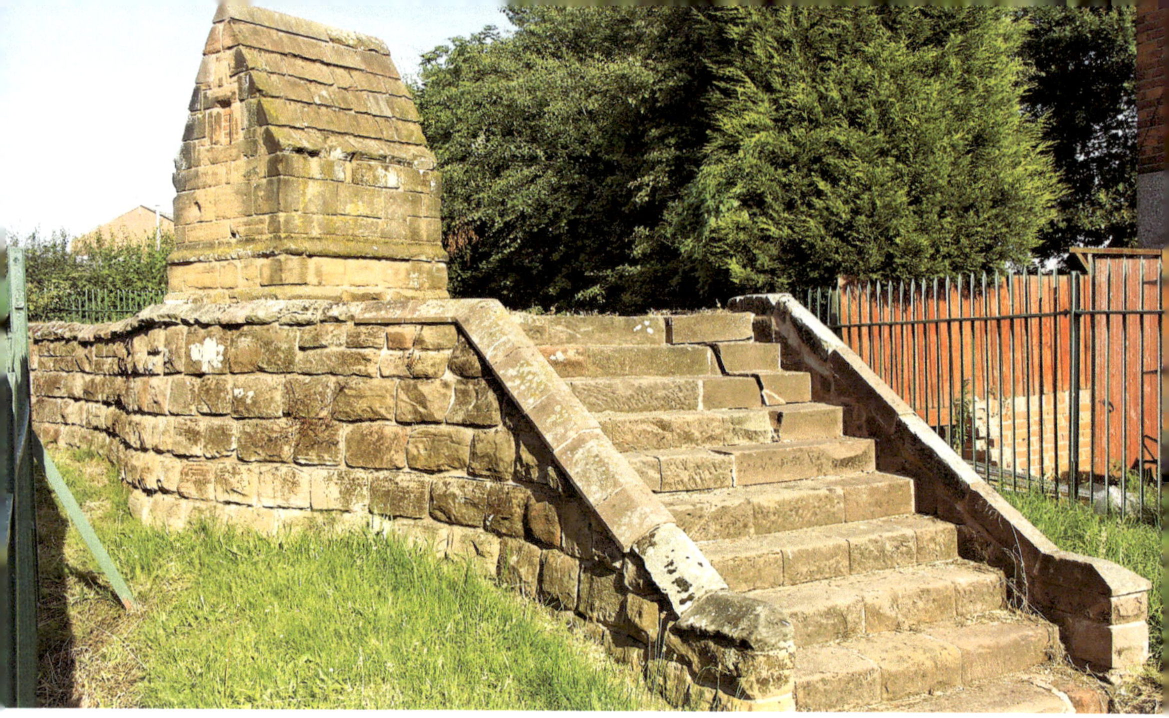

St Catherine's Well – a medieval anomaly in a 1930s street.

## 37. St John the Baptist

Built on oak piles driven into the old lake bed (the Babbu Lacu), St John's stands around 14 inches above the water in the appropriately named Fleet Street – named from the old English *fleot*, meaning 'to float'. It was built on ground given by Queen Isabella in 1344 to the Guild of St John to build a chapel so priests could pray for her soul and the soul of her murdered husband, Edward II. In 1357 it was served by two priests – one was Robert de Whoream, who lived in a hermitage attached to it. As the building grew it took in more priests: first six, then nine, then, in 1461, twelve.

The church was used and maintained by the United Guild of the Holy Trinity based in St Mary's Hall. In their day there were five altars: the high altar and altars dedicated to St John the Baptist, the Virgin Mary, St Catherine and the Holy Trinity. These were the four guilds that formed the Trinity Guild. In 1546 the commission preparing for the guilds' dissolution reported that Bablake employed nine priests who celebrated divine service daily and had their own rooms within the college precincts. The college took up the area of the present quadrangle. Attached to this college was also a school maintained by the Trinity Guild.

In December 1547 an act was passed for the suppression of all colleges, chapels, chantries and guilds. Holy Trinity Guild was suppressed, and their church (St John's) and its contents were granted to the Corporation for a penny a year. It was put to various uses, and from 1607 occasional lectures and services continued. It was used as a prison for Scottish prisoners during the Second Civil War. It was also used as a market, stretch house and other unsavoury uses until it became derelict. In 1734 it became the parochial church of the new parish of St John. The church was restored in 1841 and again in 1868–76. During this period the exterior of grey sandstone was clad with local red sandstone, completely changing the look of the building.

The tale about St John's being the origin of the phrase 'sent to Coventry' only dates from the 1930s.

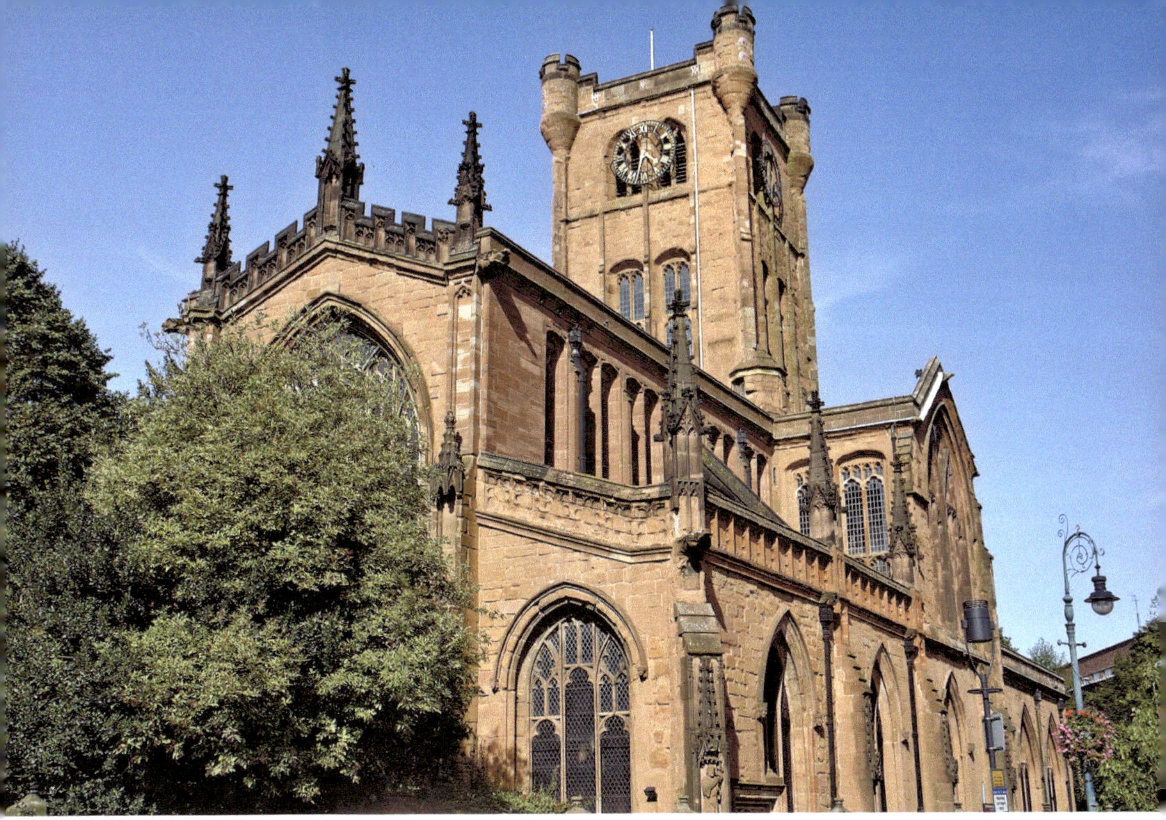

*Above*: St John's Church in Fleet Street – an unusual embattled church.

*Right*: Inside St John's – the altar holds a small compartment that contains a bone of St Valentine.

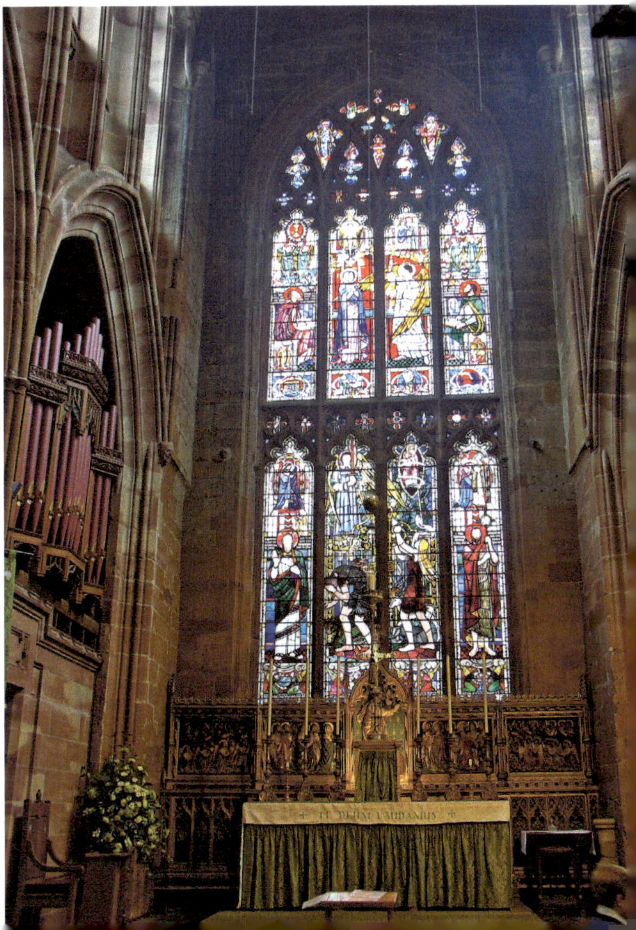

## 38. St Mary's Guildhall, Bayley Lane

Work began on the hall in 1340, the first half-timbered stage was built by the merchant guild of St Mary as a meeting place and banqueting hall. This first guild amalgamated with the guilds of St John, St Catherine and Holy Trinity and became the united guild of the Holy Trinity. Greatly enriched, they began the second phase of building. Work began in 1394 by extending the hall to Bayley Lane and ended in 1414, leaving the hall as we see it today.

The Trinity Guild traded across Europe to the Baltics and many rich merchants became members, including the famous Dick Whittington. Others included Henry V, Henry VI and Henry VII. There were also 2,000 female members. In 1345 Coventry received its Charter of Incorporation and the most powerful men formed the first council and chose its first mayor. Most of these men where guild members, so the guildhall also became the council house, a role that ended in the late nineteenth century. As for the Trinity Guild, it was dissolved in December 1547. The only guild now associated with the building are the Freemen.

The hall has a stunning history. It was rebuilt from the remains of Coventry Castle and has been a meeting place for kings, queens, the rich and the poor. The castle's entrance tower, Caesar's Tower, was bombed and after being mostly rebuilt now stands at the rear. The medieval mystery plays were rehearsed here. Shakespeare played here on numerous

*Below left*: The fine entrance to the Guildhall has a Green Man in the centre.

*Below right*: The beautiful ceiling contains nearly 200 fourteenth- and fifteenth-century bosses.

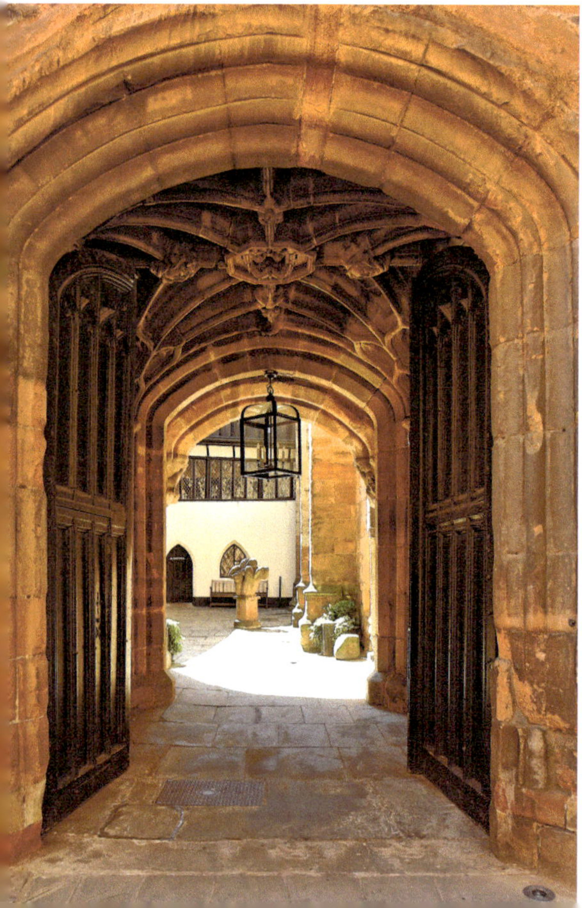

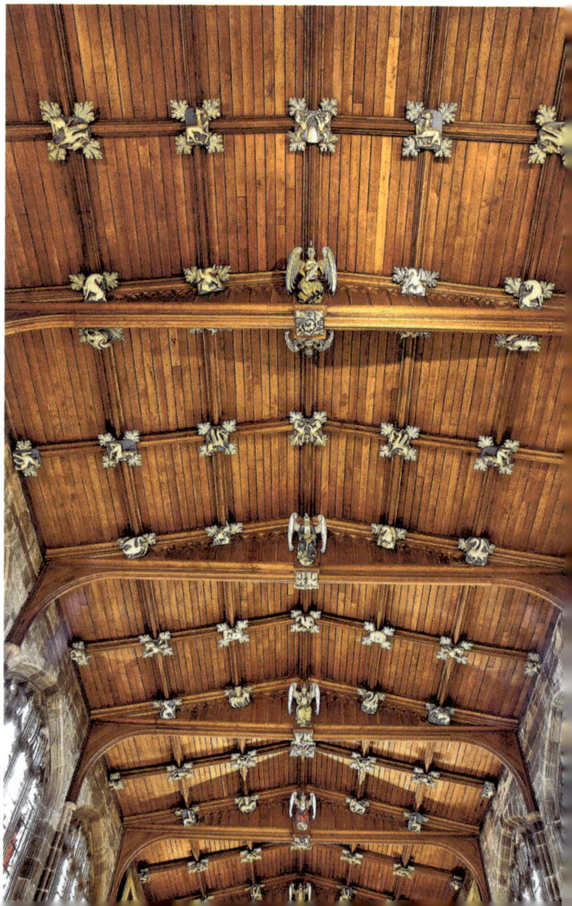

occasions as did the great Georgian actress Sarah Siddons. During the seventeenth, eighteenth and nineteenth centuries the great hall was used as a courtroom. Many were condemned here, transported or imprisoned. One who mentions this was the novelist George Eliot, a frequent visitor. In her novel *Adam Bede*, the hall is the courtroom in the trial of Hetty Sorrell. Other writers to visit include Jane Austen and Charles Dickens.

In 1829 Charles Perkins and John Bates were sentenced to death here for stealing a lamb. On the same day Edwin Horsefall was sentenced to death for stealing a sheep. In January 1852 Ann Smith was tried for attempting to steal a pocket watch from Richard Bradnick. Richard had been in the Greyhound (demolished recently) in Much Park Street and as he left, the young lady lifted his watch. Unfortunately for Ann, Richard (my great-great-uncle) was the County Bailiff (Sheriff) of Coventry and arrested her – she got four months!

Notable visitors include Henry V, who feasted here with his queen after Agincourt. His son Henry VI moved the royal court to the city during the Wars of the Roses and was a regular visitor. He is commemorated all over the building. Henry VII visited and feasted here. James I dined here, as did James II – the table collapsed on him and covered him in Corporation Custard. The medieval kitchen that supplied this food is the oldest in England and is still used today; its restoration has been a matter of discussion for 150 years.

The hall holds many treasures, including a huge number of medieval roof bosses, which were taken down for safety after the April air raids in 1941 and restored into a new roof in 1952–53.

Looking from the Minstrels' Gallery into the Great Hall. The Coventry Tapestry can be seen under the North Window.

*Inset*: Looking towards the Minstrels' Gallery in 1863, Victorian tourists enjoy the hall.

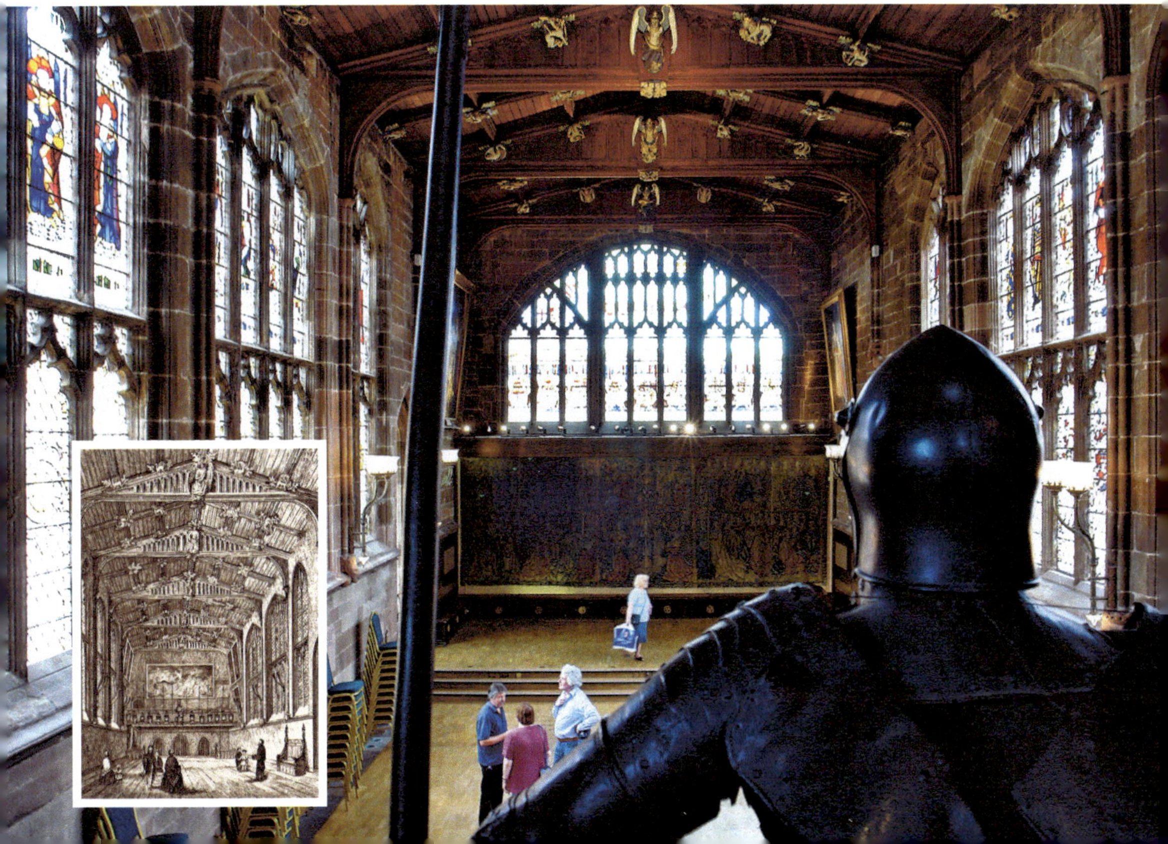

Portraits in glass adorn the windows, including some of the best stained glass of the twentieth century. The north window, dating around 1492, venerates Henry VI and his ancestors. The hall's greatest treasure is the unique Coventry Tapestry, made for this wall between 1495 and 1500. The tapestry and stained glass above represent the last major surviving relic of the cult of Henry VI in England. It depicts 'Saint' Henry and is the second most venerated image in Tudor England after the Virgin. Over 300 miracles were attributed to the dead king but his sainthood failed because of Henry VII's tight purse. It commemorates Coventry's greatest moment when it became the centre of the royal court and home to a saint. The hall considered the finest in England has been open to visitors for over 250 years. Up until the Second World War it was open all year around, and since then just six months a year. Protection of one of England's greatest guildhall has long interested the council and in 1893 all but civic events were banned. Gradually this has changed. The hall is the third most visited building in the city centre.

## 39. St Michael's Cathedral

Coventry's new cathedral wasn't welcomed by all: in 1944 one newspaper reader wrote,

> The plans for the proposed new Cathedral have now been before the public for some little time, but on the whole they do not appear to have aroused very much enthusiasm. Most of the support for the plans seems to come from the clerical circle, whereas old Coventrians and former worshippers at the Cathedral evince few signs of satisfaction. The reason for this is undoubtedly the very great disappointment felt at the fact that it was not proposed to restore the old Cathedral to Its former state. This was what most Coventry folk were expecting, and the publication of the plans proved something of a bombshell…

Objections continued, and Sir Alfred Herbert offered to pay towards the old cathedral's restoration. The original design put forward by Giles Gilbert Scott was a truly impressive building, being effectively a massive Norman-style cathedral with cloisters attached to the end of the ruins, keeping half of the ruins and tower as a cloister and entrance. The apse was to be incorporated into the massive Norman-style tower.

Scott was pressured from the new bishop to design a modern building and the Royal Fine Arts Commission to design a medieval building. His compromise was to blend the two; unable to reconcile this, he resigned in 1947. His remarkable design is now generally forgotten. Thereafter a competition was held, it had 219 entries and was won by a relatively unknown Basil Spence. Spence's new design had a mixed reception, he said, 'I received 700 letters about my design. Eighty percent of them were rude ---- the rest very rude.' The provost said, 'We see the cathedral as a great laboratory of experiment. We feel we have been given a licence to do experimental and probably controversial work.' Controversial it certainly was, and still is with tourists and Coventrians – some love it, some hate it. Time, however, makes a modern building less controversial, and in 1999 it was voted Britain's best-loved building.

Work began in June 1954, and in March 1956 the queen laid the foundation stone; by 1962 the building was completed, and in May it was consecrated. Attached to the old cathedral by a porch, it has sheer massive walls inspired by Norman cathedrals. As you approach the steps, you see the striking bronze figures of Christ and the Devil by Jacob Epstein, beyond them is John Hutton's fabulous glass West Screen decorated with saints, angels and Apostles

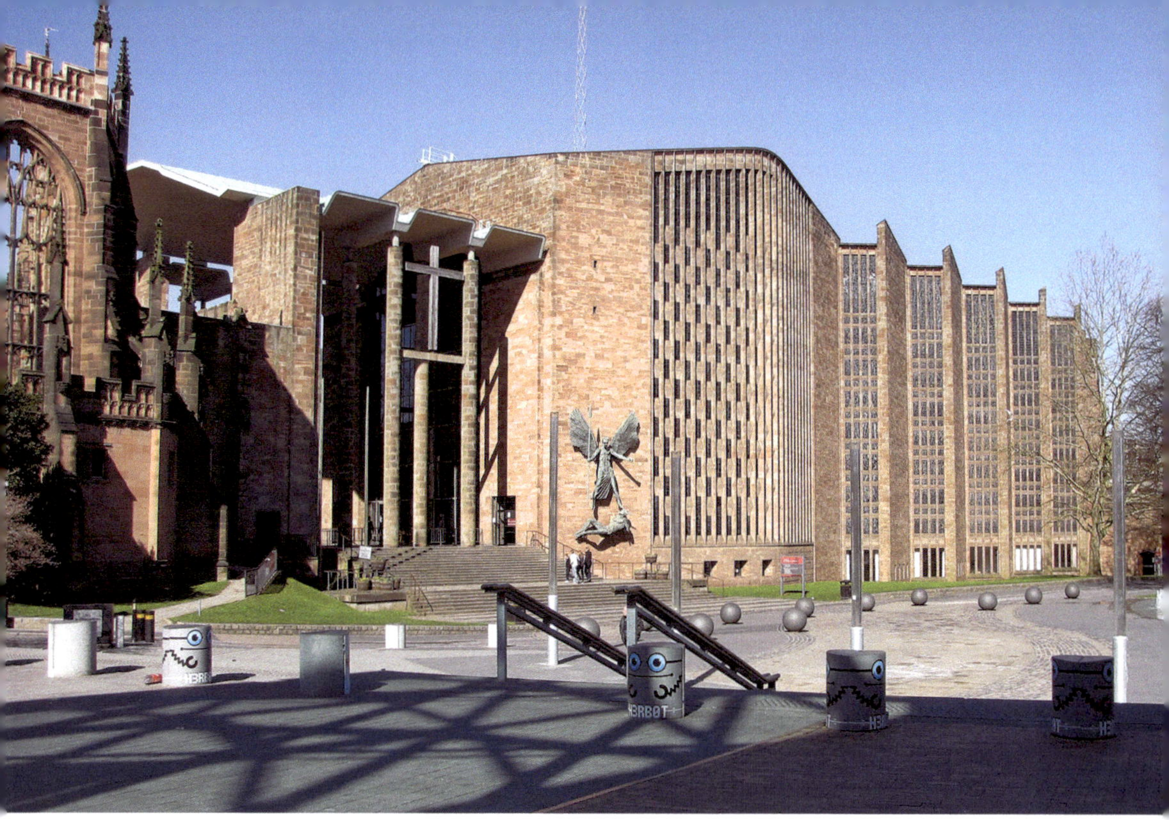

*Above*: Coventry's new cathedral in Priory Street attached to the old, showing its Norman-style walls and St Michael and the Devil.

*Right*: The world's second-largest tapestry hangs behind the altar, which unusually faces north.

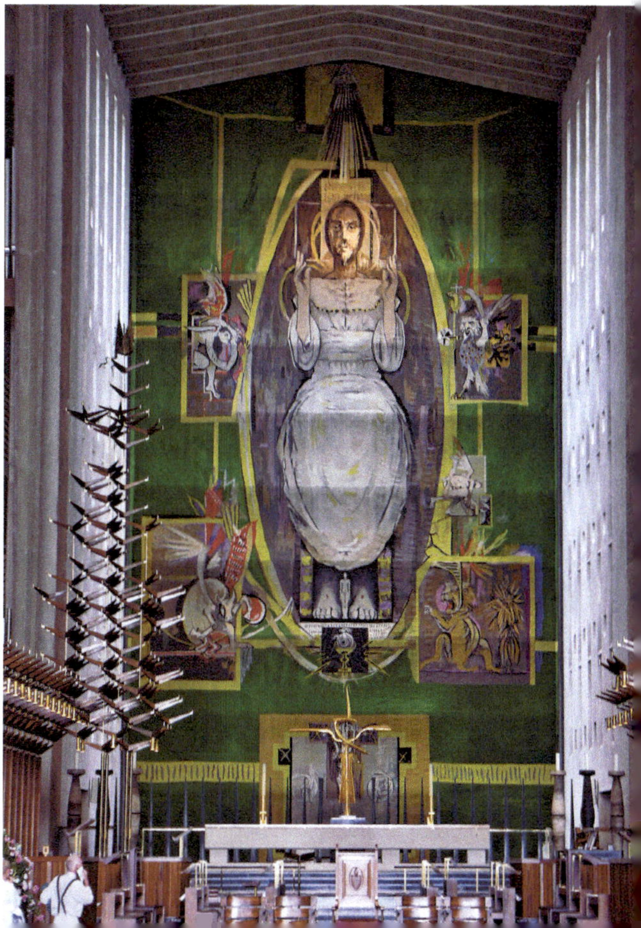

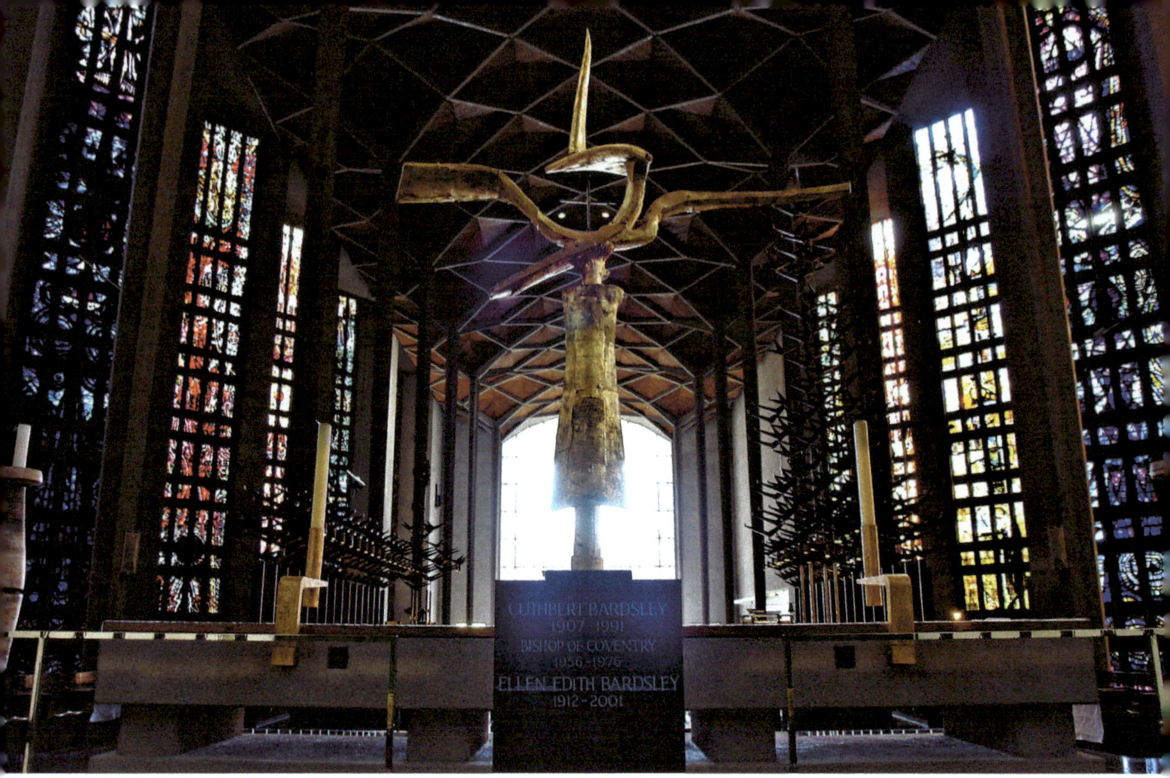


Looking back through the main body of the cathedral.

cut by Hutton using a small hand tool. This remarkable work, or the glass dust from it, aided his passing and Hutton's ashes are buried at its base. As you enter the building, beyond the slender columns and impressive medieval-style vaulted ceiling is Graham Sutherland's 92-feet-high tapestry of Christ in Majesty – the second largest in the world. To the right is the baptistery window, standing 81 feet high and holding 195 panels of stained glass. Designed by John Piper and made by Patrick Reyntiens, this stunning piece of abstract art depicts the light of God sweeping through the darkness. The building is full of details of interest, including magnificent medieval stained glass by the famed John Thornton in the undercroft.

## 40. St Michael & All Saints

The first mention of a church here was a chapel dedicated to St Michael. It was built by Ranulf Gernon, Earl of Chester, and given to the monks of Coventry Priory in 1135. The Langley Cartulary in the early 1200s refers to it as 'Saint Michael in the Bailey'. This, of course, refers to the fact it was sited within the bailey of the earl's castle. Foundations have been found opposite St Mary's Hall and the south porch once contained some mouldings from this period. East of the south porch, 'massive foundations' were uncovered in the past, probably a curtain wall edging along the castle's northern ditch, which ran through the centre of the ruins.

By the thirteenth century, the Norman chapel had been replaced by a larger early English church in the Decorated style. In 1248 the bishop got the prior to provide monks, priests and ministers to serve in the chapels attached to this church, including the Chapel on the Mount and the Chapel of the Cross. Practically nothing survives of this smaller thirteenth-century church, except for a decorated doorway in the south porch.

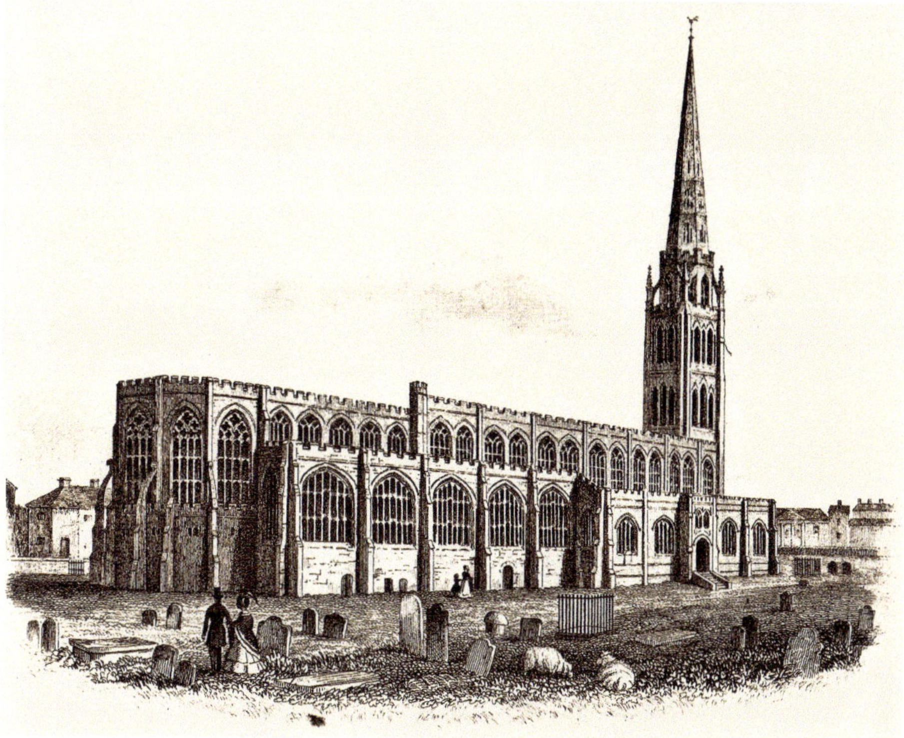

An engraving from the 1830s shows the details of the buildings architecture.

The building we see today dates mainly from the fourteenth century. In 1324 Merynton's Chantry was founded and others soon followed, all had priests who sang daily mass for the souls of the donors. Later in 1373 the church's tower was commenced. It is said that it took twenty-two years to build, with construction ending in 1394. The spire itself wasn't added until 1432.

Coventry merchants and brothers William and Adam Botoner are said to have expended £100 annually building it. The spire was paid for by their sisters Ann and Mary. The tower with its octagon and spire is the third tallest in England and was declared a masterpiece by Sir Christopher Wren. What makes it unique, unlike its rivals Salisbury and Norwich, is that it is the highest tower/spire in the land, built from the ground up and not springing from the centre of the church. The tower is 130 feet 8.5 inches high and is heavily decorated, being adorned with forty-two kings, saints, confessors and benefactors. The spire is around 126 feet high and 17 inches thick at the base, and leans by 4.5 degrees. The tower, octagon and spire as a whole measured 295 feet 9.5 inches, but after the restoration of 1880 it was shortened slightly, making it 294 feet and almost bringing it into line with the church, which measures 293 feet 9 inches.

The choir and body of the church were erected around the same time as the tower, again paid for by Ann and Mary Botoner. In 1451 Henry VI heard mass here. In 1617 James I visited, and in 1687 James II touched 200 people here for the King's Evil. In 1730 a massive dragon weather vane was placed at the top of the spire but its weight caused damage; a new weathercock and globe of copper, weighing 20 pounds, replaced it and still graces the spire today. The interior was renovated in 1849, and another restoration took place between

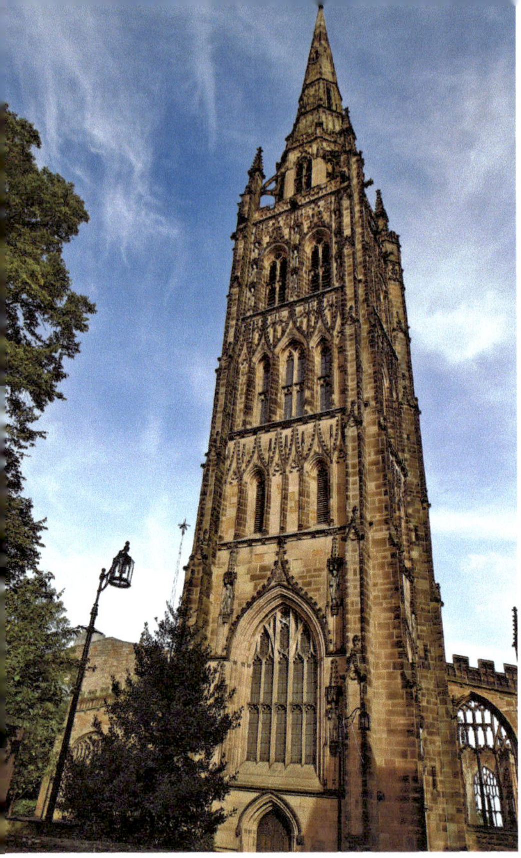

*Left*: The tower, octagon and spire – considered a masterpiece of medieval art.

*Below*: Inside the ruins looking down the nave and chancel.

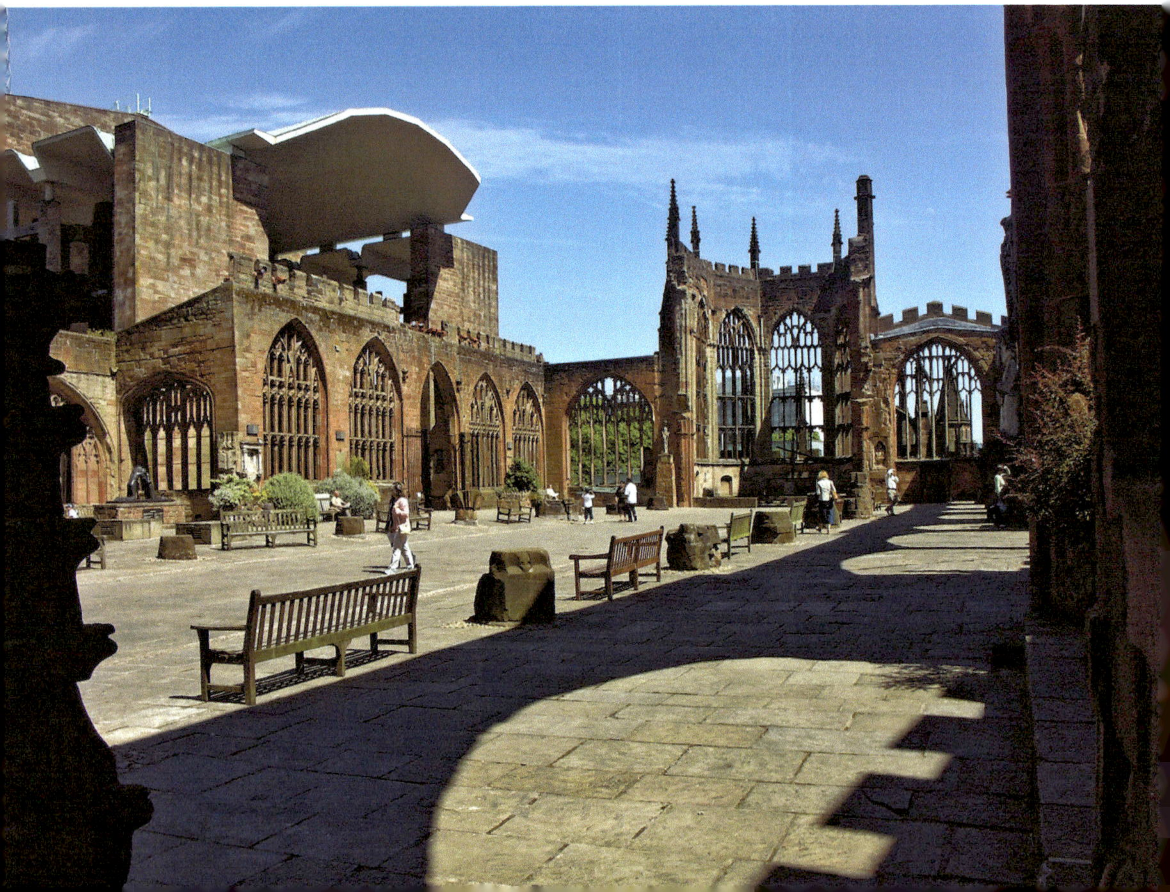

1885 and 1900, which cost nearly £40,000 reaching all parts. The Collegiate Church of St Michael was made a cathedral in 1918. On the night of 14 November 1940, the cathedral was destroyed by incendiary bombs. The day after, its stone mason, Jock Forbes, picked up two burned roof timbers, wired them together into the form of a cross and stood them in the rubble by the altar. When the church was semi-cleared, it was placed on a new altar with the words 'Father Forgive' carved behind. This and the cross of nails became symbols of the cathedral's international Ministry of Forgiveness and Reconciliation.

A recent £1-million restoration scheme to stabilise the crumbling ruins was funded mainly by the World Monuments Fund after the building was listed as threatened in 2012. This good work has been put under threat recently by using the building for 'events' such as a house music gig that vibrated the building for nine hours – the tower's best-known resident, a rare peregrine falcon, left for a week!

Large numbers of graves lie below the floor, my own three-times great-granddad and grandmother lie in the chancel; he was churchwarden in the eighteenth century. The cathedral's website states, 'Today the ruins of the old Cathedral are preserved as a memorial and sacred space for the City.' More events are planned in the future.

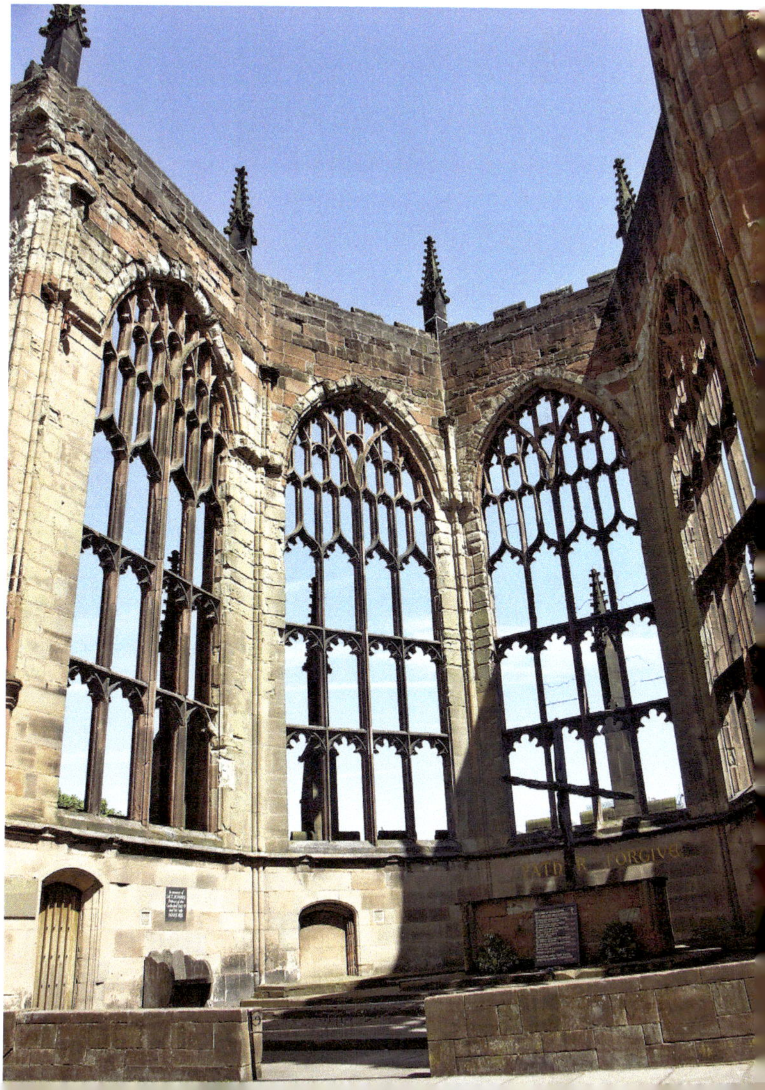

The apse of the church with a copy of the original charred cross. A weekly service is still held here.

## 41. St Michael's House

Number 11 Priory Row is traditionally said to be one of the three buildings built by three brothers who bet that they could build the best house, the winners house would be paid for by the losers. The other buildings were Kirby House and the Castle Grounds. If this story is true, it is impossible to say. What we can say for sure is that in 1721 David Wells purchased the site off Humphrey Burton. Wells demolished the existing building to construct his own town house. This grand house called 'The Priory' was completed by 1741. David Wells was a wine cooper and the ironwork grape vines outside reflect his trade. He was also a church warden in St Michael's and Holy Trinity.

Wells took an interest in the priory remains and unearthed then incorporated them into his garden; these including the head of a king and a nun. In 1826 Wells' house was purchased by Nathaniel Troughton, a surgeon and artist who created many wonderful drawings of Coventry, which survive in the archives. Troughton lived there until his death in 1868, leaving his wife Elizabeth and daughter Fanny in residence – the house was left to his daughter. Miss Troughton left to live in Berkshire and let it to Mrs Bathe. In 1878 she sold the cellars below to a Mr Graham of Collin's Wine Merchants. This company expanded from the cellars of now demolished Nos 12 and 13 Priory Row all the way up to the corner of Hill Top. In 1940 the building was gutted by firebombs and was at serious risk of being demolished but luckily it was restored to its former beauty.

St Michael's House off Priory Lane, a fine looking building.

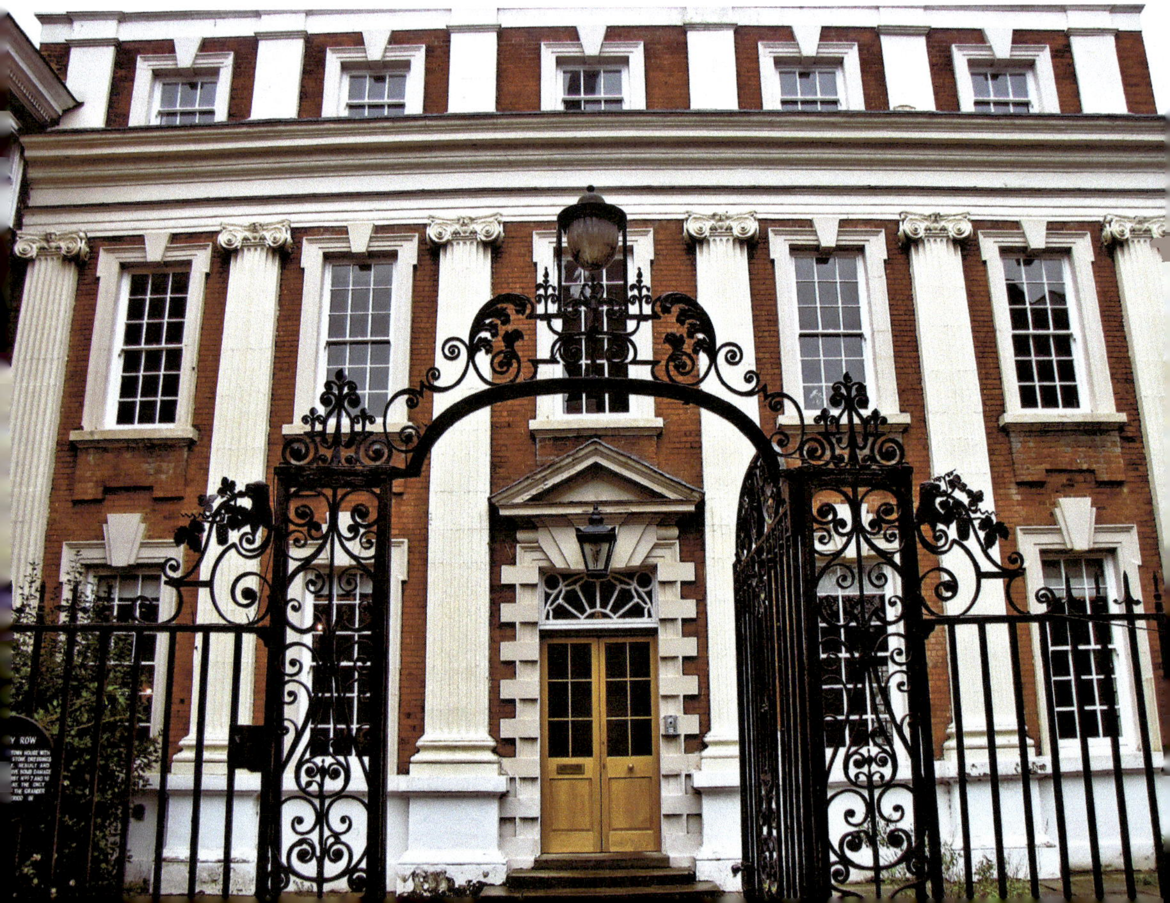

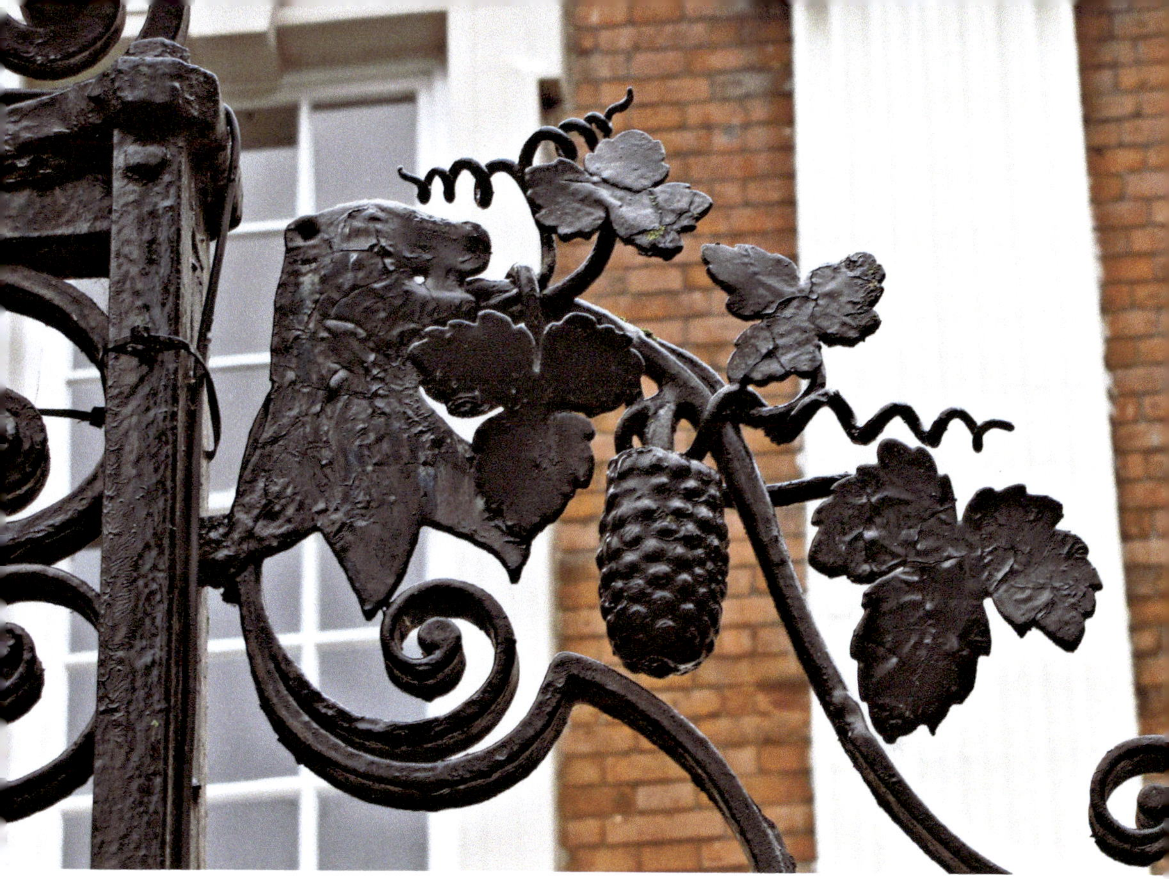

Detail of the wrought-iron decorative entrance and gate showing a leopard and grape vine symbols of Dionysus/Bacchus, god of wine, reflecting the owner's trade.

## 42. Spon Street

Spon Street has far too many interesting buildings so I have put them under one title. The Spon Street Townscape Scheme was launched in 1967 and proposed relocating buildings from Gosford Street, Far Gosford Street, Jordan Well, Much Park Street and parts of Spon Street and Spon End. Eventually only properties in Much Park Street and western/central Spon Street were relocated here. The first building restored in 1969 was No. 169, followed by the first relocated building, No. 9, previously No. 7 Much Park Street, which was re-erected in June 1972. The completed street finished in 1990 contained twelve buildings restored in situ and ten re-erected from other sites. Spon Street now has one of the most important groupings of medieval timber-framed buildings in the country.

Numbers 1 and 2, the last built, stand at the entrance to the street; both formerly stood beyond the ring road. Number 1 dates from the early to mid-fifteenth century and No. 2 from later that century. They were originally four hall houses (open hall to roof and upstairs bedroom), known as Wealden houses as they were common in East Anglia. These Wealden houses are normally bigger, but the Coventry version was adapted to fit into confined spaces. Number 9 was formerly No. 7 Much Park Street and dates from the late fifteenth to early sixteenth century. Number 10 is a two-bay hall house and is original to the site. It dates from the early fifteenth century with a seventeenth-century rear.

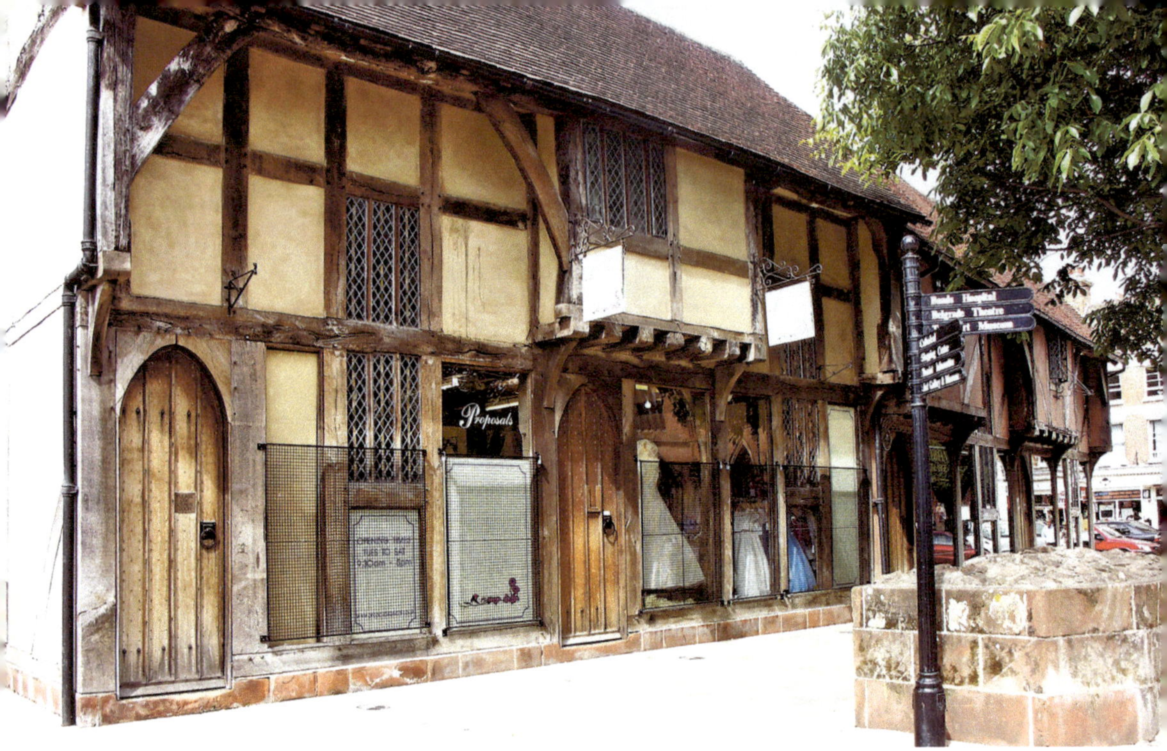


Nos 1 and 2 Spon Street, the last built facing a representation of the city wall, built on the excavated wall.

Number 11/12 was built in the mid-fourteenth century and is one of the oldest buildings standing on its original site in Spon Street. It's an incomplete Wealden house with a central hall and two-storey bays on either side. The left-hand bay was lost when No. 10 was built and the right bay is cut short. Number 14/15 is known as the Tudor House and dates to the mid- to late fifteenth century. It was formerly the Recruiting Sergeant Inn. One of the highest quality houses in the street it was originally a four-bayed hall house with oriel windows, a two-bay hall with fire in the centre.

Number 16 was formerly 142–43 Spon Street, which was dismantled in 1971 and moved here. It represents the last use of timber-framed building in Coventry with bricks. Numbers 20 and 21 were formerly 122–23 Much Park Street. The double-depth building has a mid-fifteenth-century front and mid-sixteenth-century rear. The front was jettied, and the rear an open hall. The building was originally the Green Dragon Inn, made famous by its many references in George Eliot's novel *Middlemarch*.

Numbers 22 and 23 are the Old Windmill, known as Ma Brown's from former publican Ann Brown. This plastered-over timbered building dates from around the sixteenth century and was originally two buildings. The present entrance originally led into a narrow courtyard that divided them. The left side was a shop into the late nineteenth century. The original inn was here in 1824, the other older Windmill inn was in Spon Causeway. Still a popular pub, it retains many original fittings. For the next building, see the Rotherham House.

Numbers 159–62 are a surviving section of a mid-fifteenth-century terrace. The original row was made up of six Coventry Wealden houses. Numbers 163 and 164 were formerly Nos 8, 9 and 10 Much Park Street. These are early fifteenth-century, three-storey, high-status buildings from the former merchant quarter, which originally formed the homes of two merchants. Number 167 dates from the fifteenth or sixteenth century and wasn't originally attached to No. 168, which dates from the fifteenth century. The curved-braced

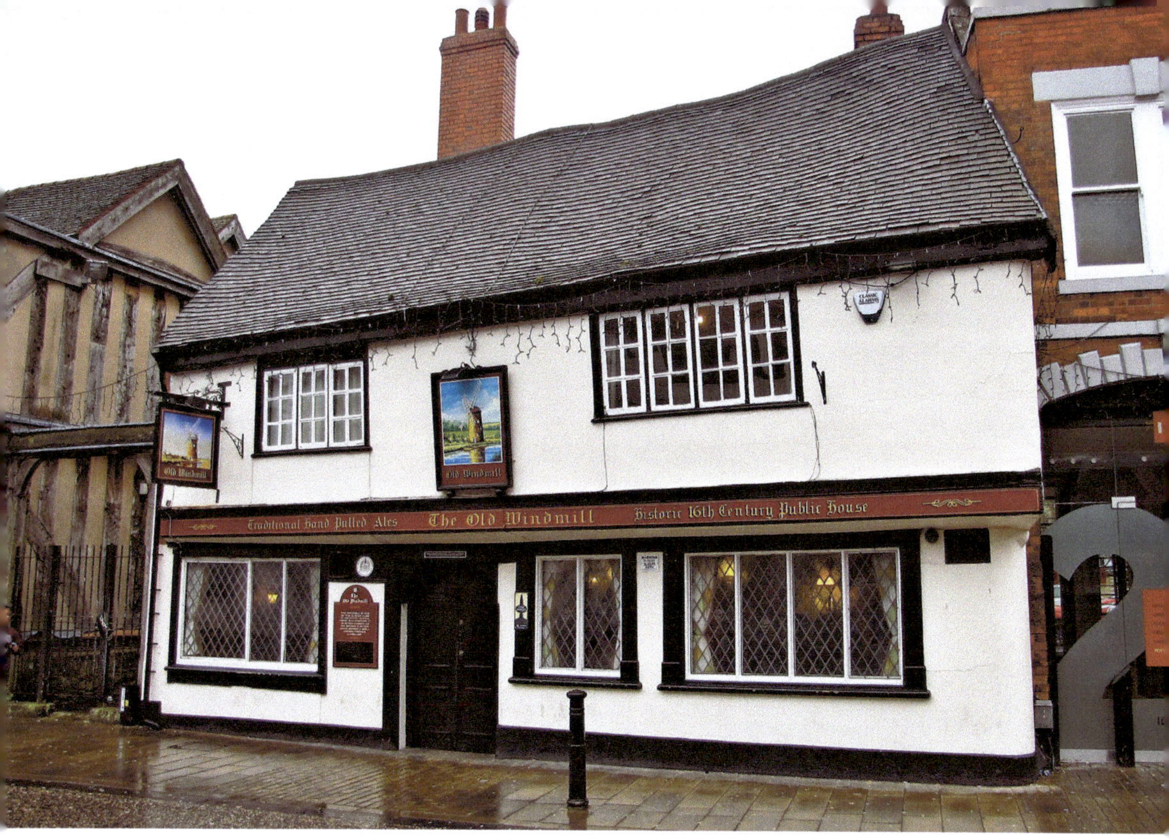


*Above*: The Windmill in Spon Street – one of the city's best-known pubs.

*Below*: Part of a late medieval terrace at the end of Spon Street.

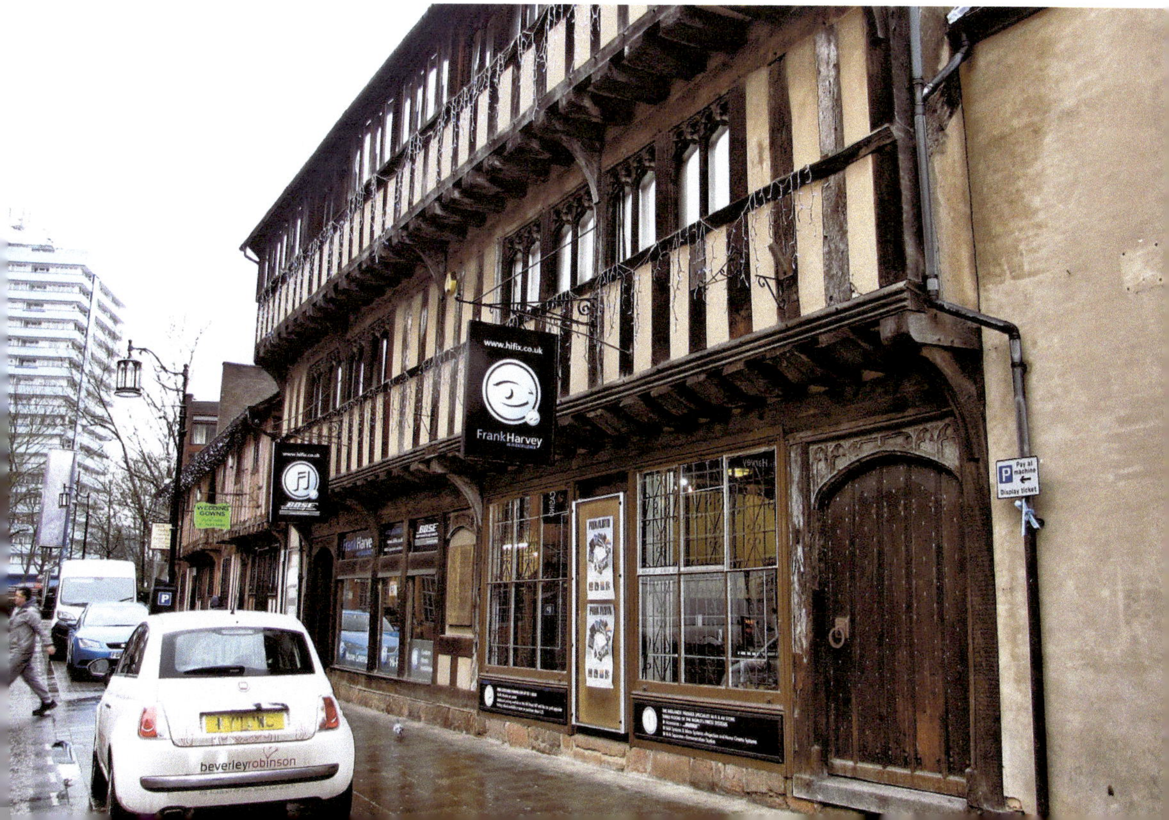

fourteenth-century building of No. 169 was the earliest and first building restored in the townscape scheme; it, and its neighbour, are believed to be the earliest surviving semis in the country. Numbers 171 and 172 are fifteenth to sixteenth century and original to the street.

## 43. Stivichall Church

Stivichall Church is dedicated to St James and originally seated 114 worshippers, but is now much larger. It was built at the cost of Francis Gregory of Stivichall Hall. The building took seven years to make and when completed replaced the Norman church that stood in the halls grounds. This was apparently dilapidated and pulled down in 1810. The new church was opened in 1815 and the twelfth-century font from the old church was placed in it. The nave measured 32 feet by 18 feet, the chancel was 14 feet by 13 feet, and western tower was 9 feet by 9 feet.

In 1851 the *Coventry Herald* reported,

> On Tuesday last, Bond's Hospital, in this City, of which he had been an inmate upwards of two years, Mr James Green, aged 73. Although of a reserved turn of mind, he was a man of amiable disposition and exemplary morals, he was by trade a stone-mason; and, as a very rare occurrence in the life of any single individual, it may be recorded of him that, with only the assistance of one labourer, he was the sole and entire builder of a Parish Church – that of Stivichall, near this City, which he completed about forty years ago.

Green's church, which he also designed, was extended in 1954. The 1815 building can still be clearly seen and now forms the chancel and nave of the present church.

Green's church on Leamington Road in Stivichall was extended in 1957 and now bears little resemblance to this image.

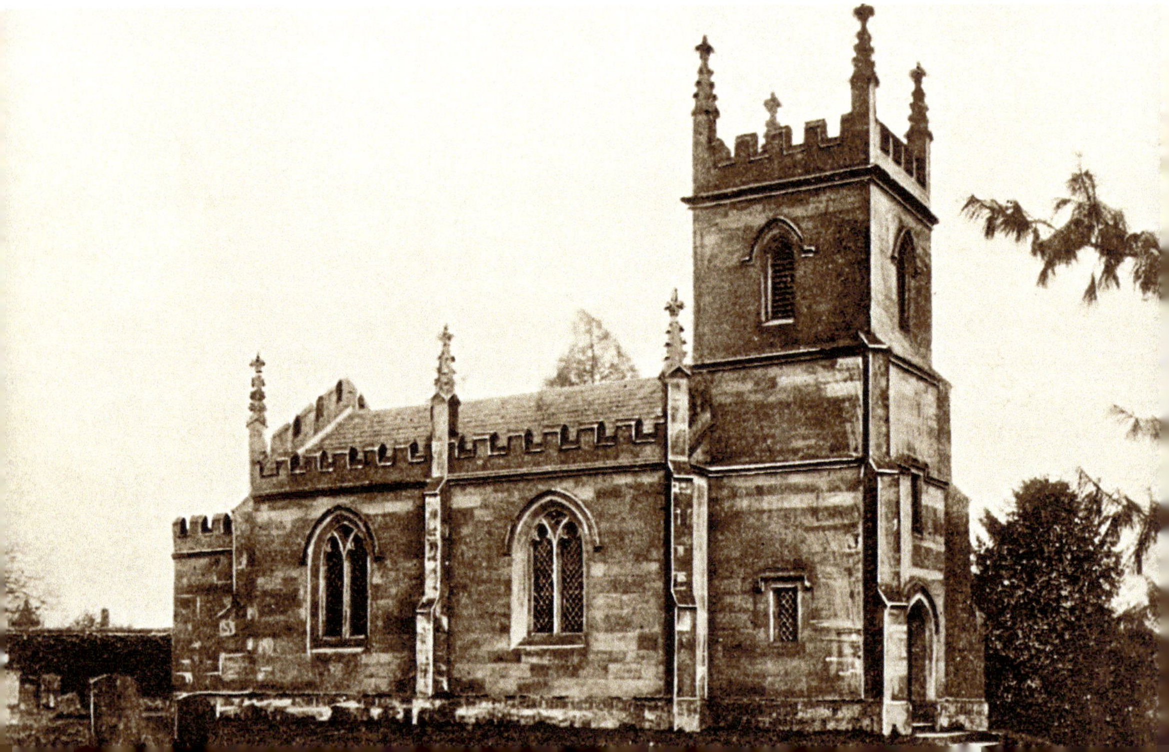

## 44. Stivichall Grange

A hidden gem, this beautiful fifteenth-century red sandstone and moated grange once belonged to Coventry Priory. After the Dissolution it was sold to the Gregory's of Stivichall Hall, and later became Stivichall Grange Farm. At the beginning of the nineteenth century James Weston farmed here and bred longhorns. Weston was still here in the 1850s and later the farm passed into the Swinnerton family through the marriage in 1832 of Joseph Swinnerton of Cryfield Grange to James' daughter.

In the later nineteenth century William Weston Swinnerton continued breeding longhorns here; he died in 1920 and the farm was taken over by Reginald Hollick who had married Catherine, William's daughter. He was the last to farm here and bred prize-winning Warwickshire longhorns and fine geldings for hunting. This was a picture book farm, mainly grazing land, with cowsheds, staddle stones and waggon sheds holding beautiful Warwickshire wagons. It had a near miss in 1940 when a landmine blew up the greenhouse. In 1961, aged eighty-seven, Mr Hollick was about to give the farm up as the land he had farmed was being overrun by housing. Ten years later Colonel Gregory-Hood applied to have the vandalised grange demolished, but the Coventry Civic Amenity Society fought against it. The demolition application was considered by the council who passed it on to the Department of the Environment, who blocked it. It was then passed by the Gregory-Hoods to the Coventry diocese at a peppercorn rent, they planned to put nuns in it. Later Stivichall Grange was extended and converted into flats.

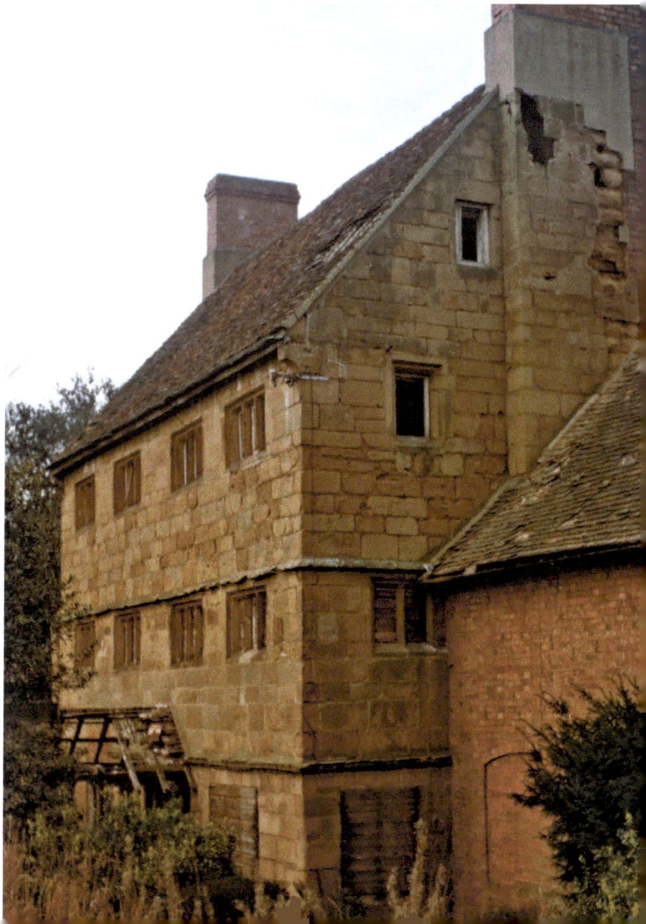

Stivichall Grange as it appeared in the late 1960s before restoration.

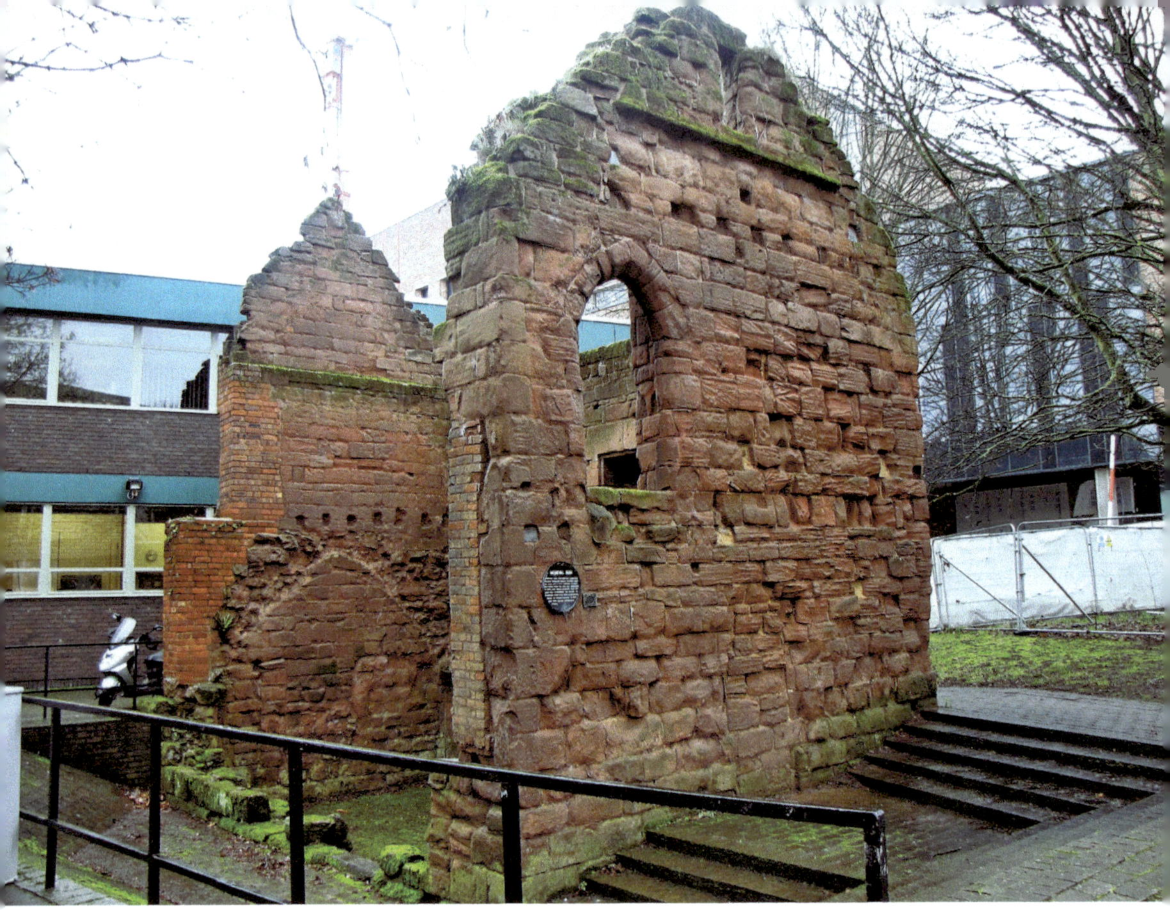

The Stone House, the oldest house in Coventry.

## 45. Stone House

During the Easter raids of 1941, Coventry was again hammered by the Luftwaffe; amid the ruins of Much Park Street an ancient building came to light. The bombs blasted away brick walls, exposing beneath a hidden sandstone gem dating back to 1350. Excavations in the 1970s proved it a rare thing, Coventry's only surviving fourteenth-century stone merchant's house. Archaeology shows that it was topped with red tiles and green glazed ridge tiles. Extending towards the street frontage was a timbered extension, probably the merchants shop or place of trade.

Despite its great rarity, in 1969 its demolition was planned for a university building. Thankfully this was blocked and one of Coventry's rarest buildings still stands, surrounded by university buildings, an important forgotten relic of the cities distant past.

## 46. Swanswell Gate, Hales Street

Also known as Priory Gate, this surviving minor gate probably dates from the second half of the fourteenth century. Some have suggested it dates from 1461 when Prior Shotteswell gained Corporation agreement to realign the city wall to take in the Priory

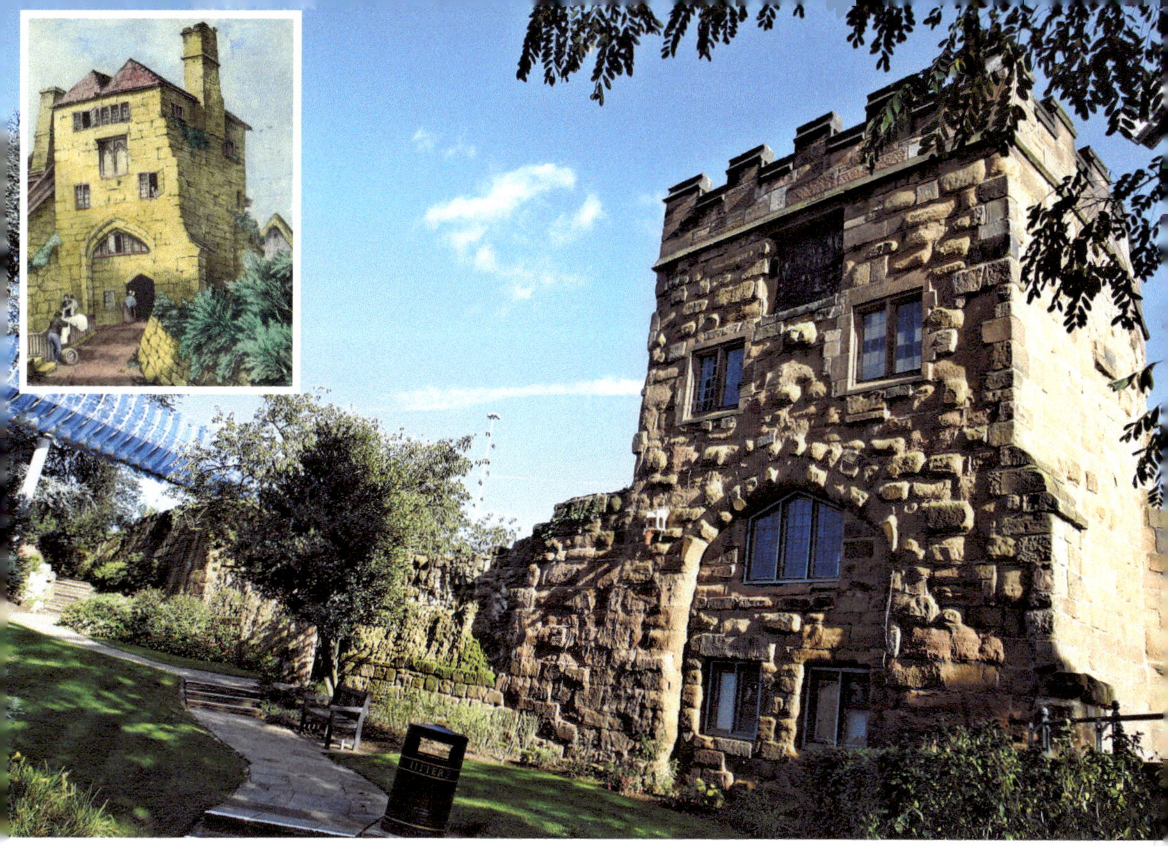

A more unusual view of Swanswell Gate from Lady Herbert's Garden.

*Inset*: An engraving of Swanswell Gate by Miss Eld, dating from 1840.

pools. There are, however, remains of a square tower buried nearby, which shows the original course. The wall itself was realigned from below the gate with no need to rebuild the actual gate. By 1820 the archway had been partially blocked and the upper section roofed and turned into a weavers shop. In 1851 it was in danger of collapse and the owner was told to make it good or demolish it. In 1852 Mr Dickinson had it re-roofed and the entrance blocked. It was converted into a shop in 1911, with the dwelling upstairs. This shop was still going in 1929.

The last owner of the gate, Sir Alfred Herbert, gave it to the city in 1931. It was restored in 1931–32: the double-pitched roof was removed and replaced, and battlements were added to the tower. In the late twentieth century it was occupied by an artist and was later used to store garden tools, before becoming a mini police station; it is now empty again.

## 47. University Engineering & Computing Block

This extraordinary building was completed in 2012 for Coventry University's Faculty of Engineering, Environment and Computing. The £55-million building uses a range of technologies, including integrated solar panels, rainwater harvesting, solar thermal energy and biomass boilers. It was designed by Arup Associates and its maze of multi-level floors cover 14,000 square metres, providing learning space for 4,000 students. It houses a

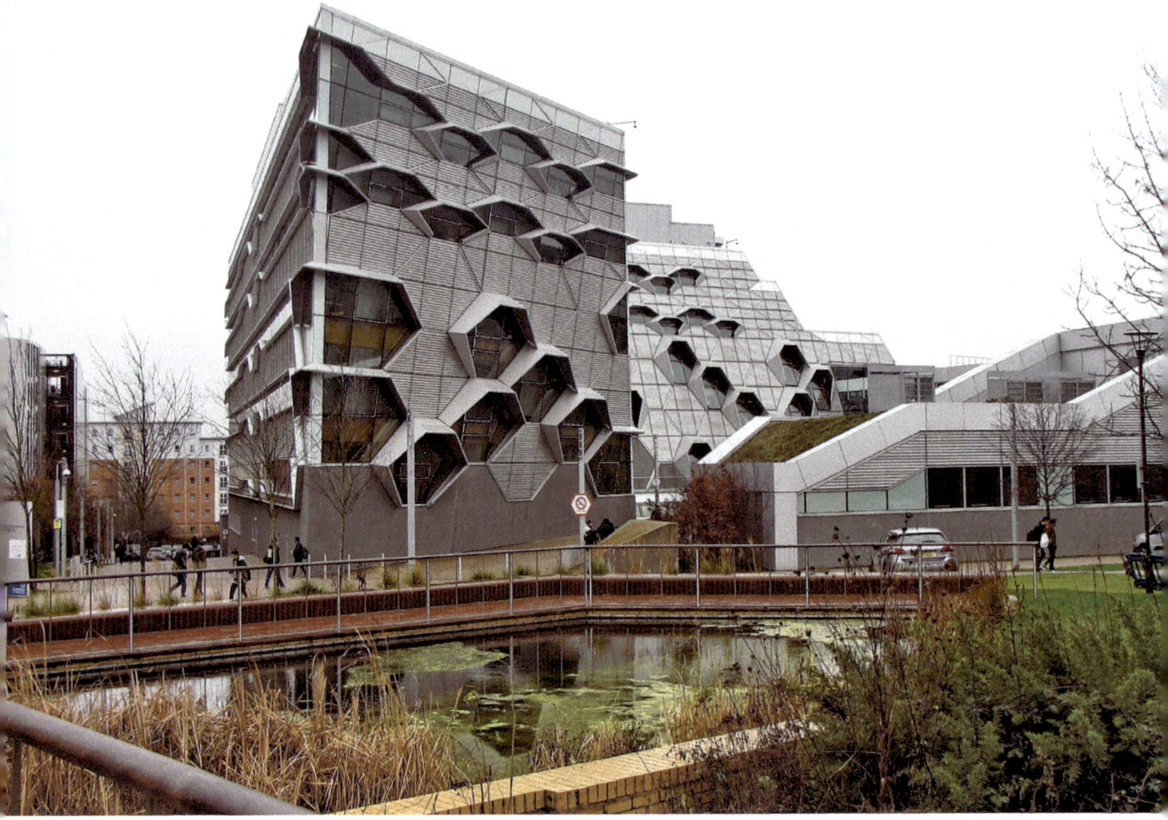

The Engineering, Environment and Computing block.

high-precision wind tunnel and a £3-million high-performance engineering centre. The basement houses a full size Harrier Jump Jet, three flight simulators, air traffic control suite and the largest cryogenic magnet in the UK. It also houses full-scale racing car prototypes, including one that can do 1,000 mpg.

The building was created to be a learning tool so students can see and understand the forces used within its engineering. Every steel beam is stamped with its structural loading capacity. In one zone, floating modular units known as 'the planets' are suspended from the structure to give students a feel for the forces at work. The building itself is clad in profiled aluminium panels, arranged into an interlocking hexagonal pattern with hexagonal openings shaded by aluminium hoods. The building consists of two interlocking L-shaped structures around a landscaped courtyard. The three-storey nature block to the south is a simple glass building with a planted green roof. The seven-storey science block to the north has a highly engineered canted façade comprising of a lightweight timber frame and aluminium composite cladding panels. The hexagonal windows with aluminium hoods reminds one of a beehive, and at certain angles it resembles an ocean liner.

## 48. Whitefriars, the Convent of Our Lady of Mount Carmel, London Road

The Carmelites, or Whitefriars, were set up in Coventry in 1342 by Sir John Poultney, merchant and mayor of London. They were a reaction to the wealthy worldliness of the Benedictines. Whitefriars' Friary stood in 10 acres and was intended to be an aid to the poor, along with a centre of theology and music. The white-robed friars lived an austere lifestyle and were well patronised. Their austerity wasn't carried into their 303-feet-long central towered church, which has been likened to a small cathedral and was one of the largest friary churches in England. Inside it was painted white, gold, red and blue and had much gilding. The windows were London glass and the floor was covered with an estimated 150,000 encaustic tiles. Some of its choir stalls survive in the grammar school.

The friars attended services every three hours – day and night. When not at services, they were either preaching, teaching or studying. One of note was William of Coventry, a fourteenth-century theologian and historical writer, who used the friary's extensive library and was buried in its chapter house. Edward III gave land to extend the church and in 1384 Lord Basset of Drayton gave £300; in 1506 Thomas Bond of Coventry gave 20 marks to rebuild the cloisters. The friary maintained the city wall around their house, which housed the Tower of Our Lady, a nationally known place of pilgrimage.

This huge complex holding fourteen friars was surrendered to the Crown on 1 October 1538 and was sold to a member of the royal household, George Pollard and local speculator Andrew Flamock. They sold some of it in 1543 to Coventry Corporation, who knocked most of it down, including the church in 1572. The rest of Whitefriars and its buildings were granted by Henry VIII to Sir Ralph Sadler. He sold it in 1544 to John Hales for £83 12*s* 6*d*.

Hales demolished some and turned the rest, mainly the cloistered section, into a private residence called Hales Place. He entertained Elizabeth I here over three nights. Mary Queen of Scots and James I both stayed here.

In his will Hales ordered the building to be sold but it remained in the family. Early in the eighteenth century when Christopher Hales died, his brother, Sir Edward, sold it to pay Christopher's debts. The Duke of Montague then became the owner and in 1722

Whitefriars from the ring road side.

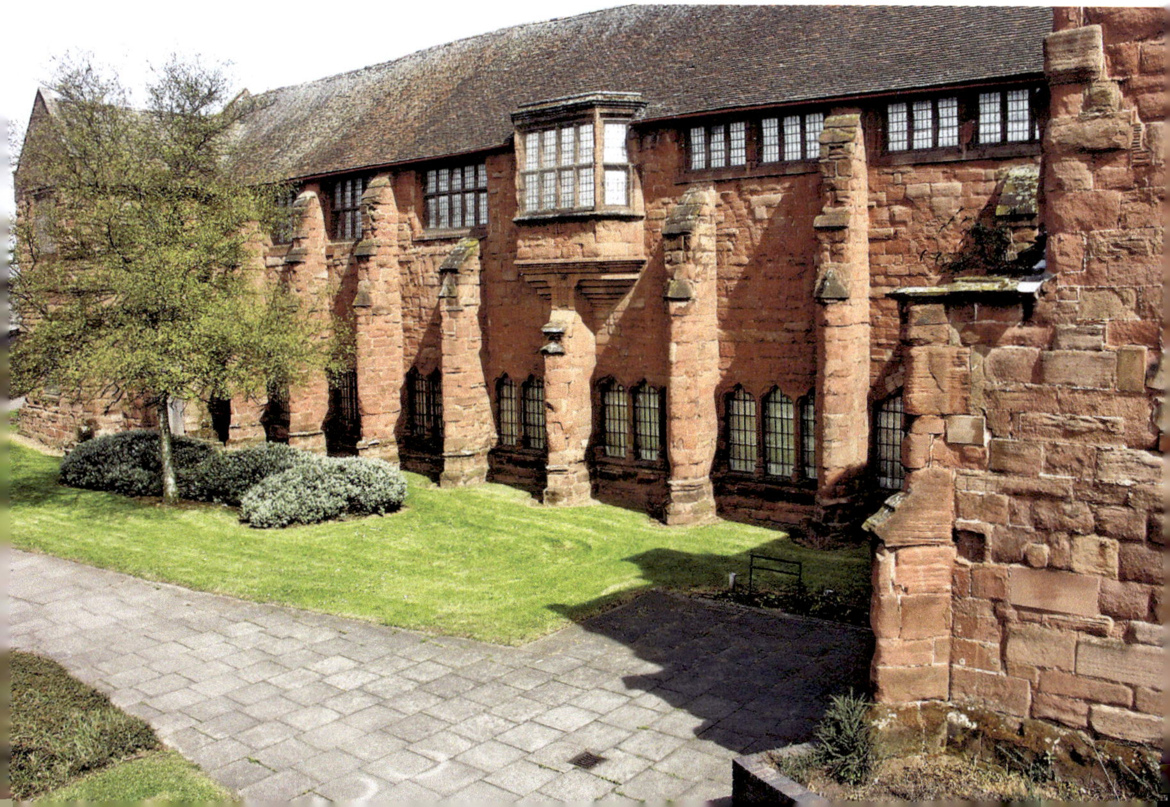

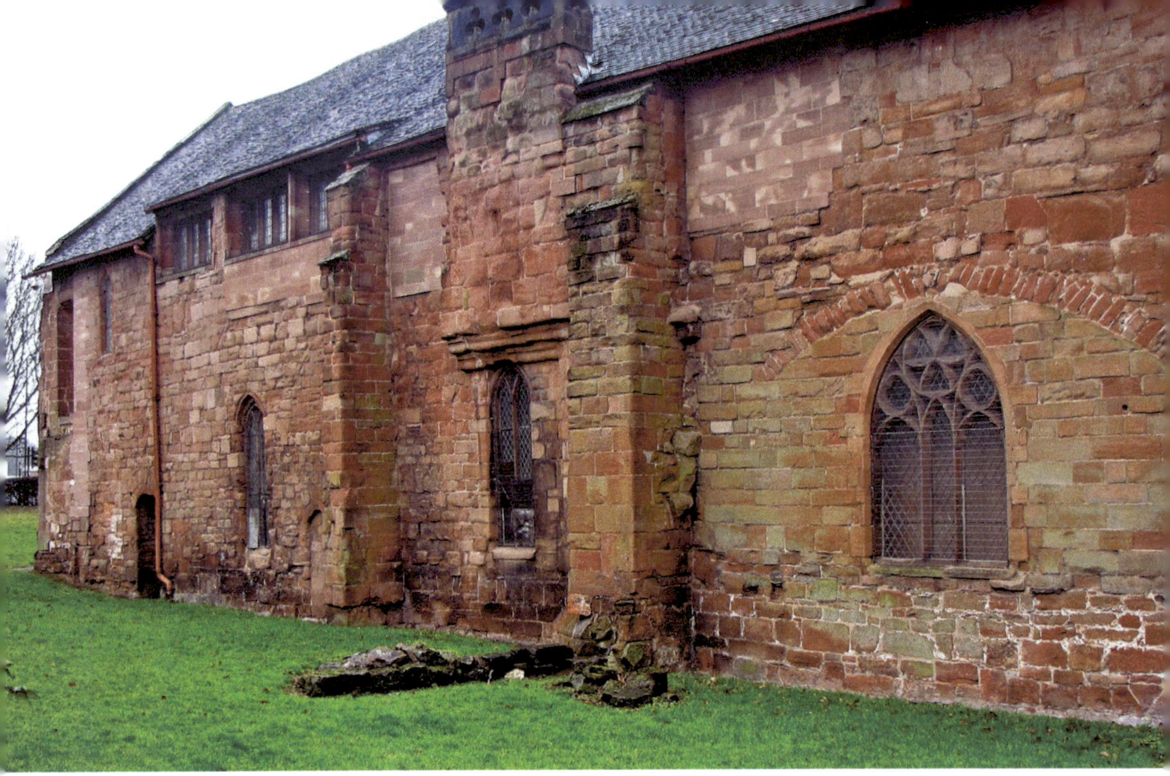

*Above*: Whitefriars from the university side.

*Below*: The beautiful cloisters of Whitefriars acted as a dining room for the inmates when it was a workhouse.

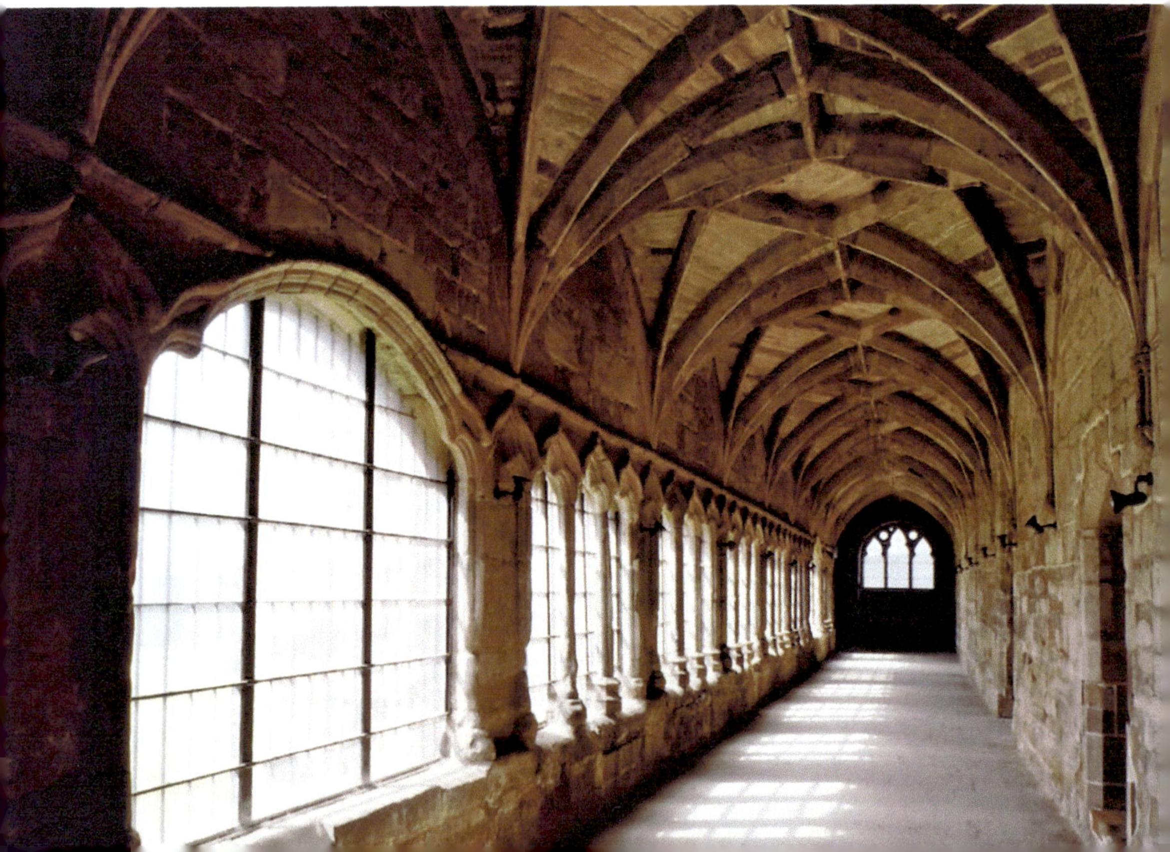

conveyed it to Mr Samuel Hill of Shenstone Park and it then passed to Mr Smith of Apsley, a clergyman. Smith sold it in 1801 to the Directors of Poor of the United Parishes of Coventry and the building was converted into a workhouse. The finely groined and arched cloisters became the dining hall of the inmates.

Whitefriars was restored in the 1960s and became a museum for a short period. Over recent years it's been a storeroom for the Herbert. Considering this is one of the most significant remains of a Carmelite building in Great Britain, one can only hope for a better future for this important historic building. It is now under negotiation to be taken over by the Historic Coventry Trust.

## 49. Whitefriars Gate, Much Park Street

Whitefriars Gate is the postern gatehouse of Coventry's Carmelite Friary. It now consists of one dwelling with a central pointed arch leading into Whitefriars Lane, the only kidney stone lane in the city. The building attached to it is timber framed. It was built in 1352 as the main entrance to the friary and through its arch have passed Elizabeth I, Mary Queen of Scots and James I. At the time of the Dissolution it became the property of John Hales. The narrow lane through the gate ran to the inner gate of the friary and was destroyed in 1940.

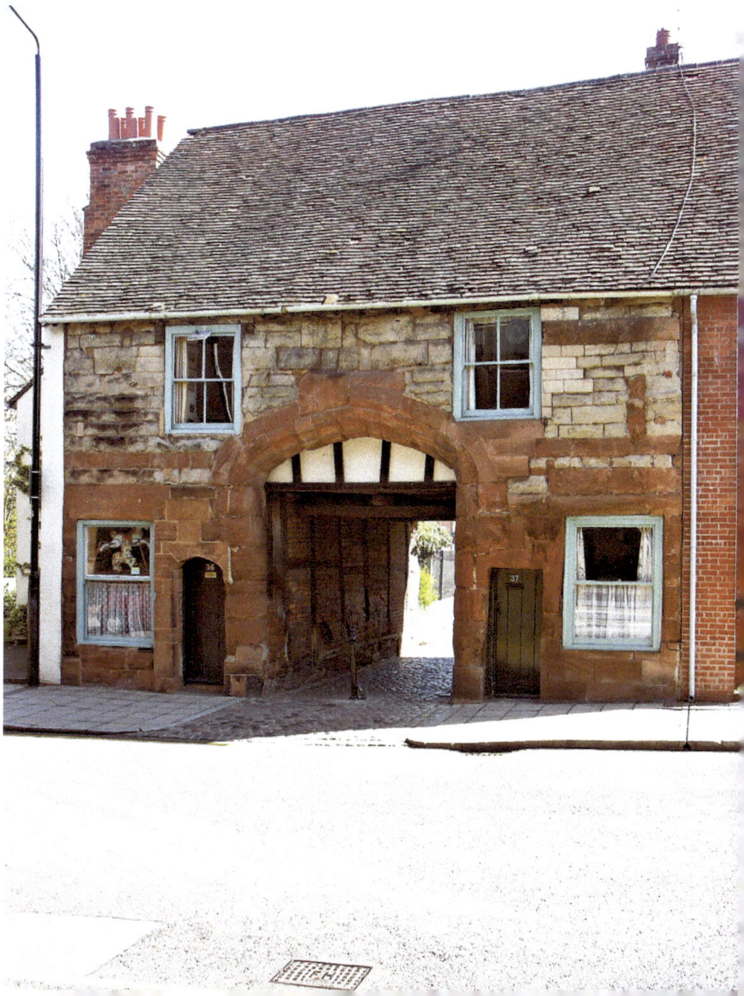

Front view of Whitefriars Gate when it was still in use.

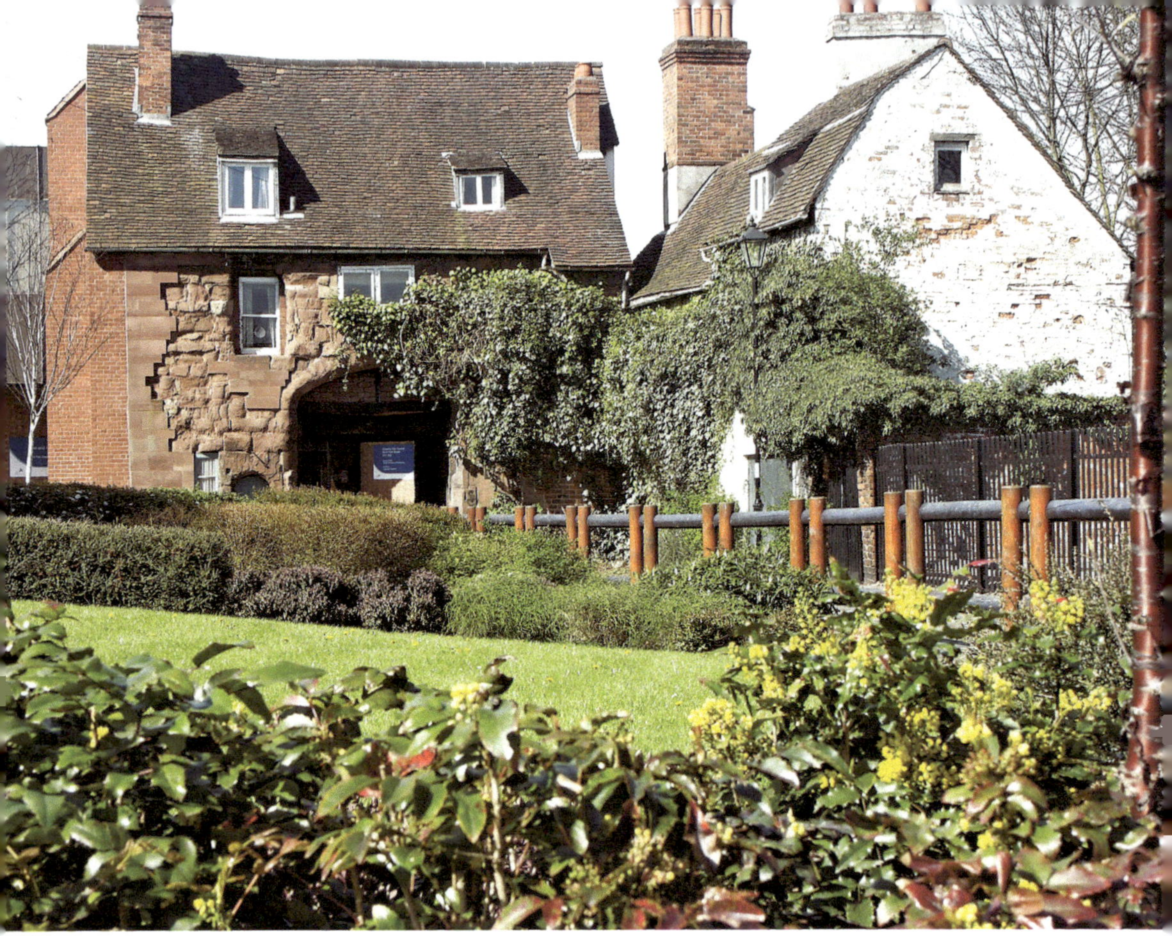

A rear view looking very pleasant. At the moment the building is impossible to photograph as it is encompassed by building materials for a university building.

After 1722 the building changed hands several times until, in 1801, the Directors of the Poor acquired it and converted it into two houses, which were used as a butchers, drapers and coal merchants. This gateway is traditionally associated with Charles Dickens. A scene in *The Old Curiosity Shop* claims to be based here. When Little Nell and her grandfather were travelling with Mrs Parley's exhibition, they came to a town late at night and their caravan turned on to a piece waste ground by a gate. The moon was shining down upon it, leaving the low archway very black and dark. There was an empty niche from which some old statue had fallen. Then Quilp appeared through the arch and asked at what hour the London coach passed the corner of the road. As Dickens knew, the London coach certainly passed this gate.

At the beginning of the twentieth century it was the residence of the Dickensian-sounding Zakeriah Peach. Half-owned by the council, it stood empty for many years and was in danger of collapse. In 1942 the council acquired all of the building including some attached houses, some of which they demolished; the gate continued its decline. In 1962 it was acquired by Ron Morgan, who carried out renovation work and set up his home here, incorporating a pottery, and in 1970 a popular toy museum. It closed ten years ago when Ron died.

After a number of years of deterioration and a fire the council restored it. A number of individuals with ideas for galleries and restaurants were turned down as tenants and the building began again to deteriorate. The university then took an interest, encompassed the gate with buildings then withdrew their interest. The gate is presently boarded up and surrounded by university building materials.

## 50. Wyken Church

Dedicated to St Mary Magdalene, it was built by Ranulf, Earl of Chester, in the early twelfth century. In 1260 priests were appointed to celebrate Divine Service three days a week and during church festivals. The chancel and nave are of Norman work; the tower is fifteenth century and was originally very low, its top section and spire were added in Victorian times. The billet-moulded doorway on the west of the tower is Norman and was moved from the south of the nave. There is one surviving Norman window in the chancel. The font is early Norman work, decorated with 'blind arches'.

The church, apart from being the oldest in the city, also has a fine medieval wall painting that shows St Christopher bearing Christ as a child on his shoulder. It was discovered in 1956 on the north wall during installation work. The painting faces the original blocked doorway (seen from the outside), a common trait relating to St Christopher, extending his protection to all who pass. The painting, although fragmented, dates from around 1480 and shows St Christopher wading through a river; behind him a medieval post mill can be seen. It was thought to have been plastered over in around 1547.

Wyken Church, Wyken Croft – Coventry's oldest church.

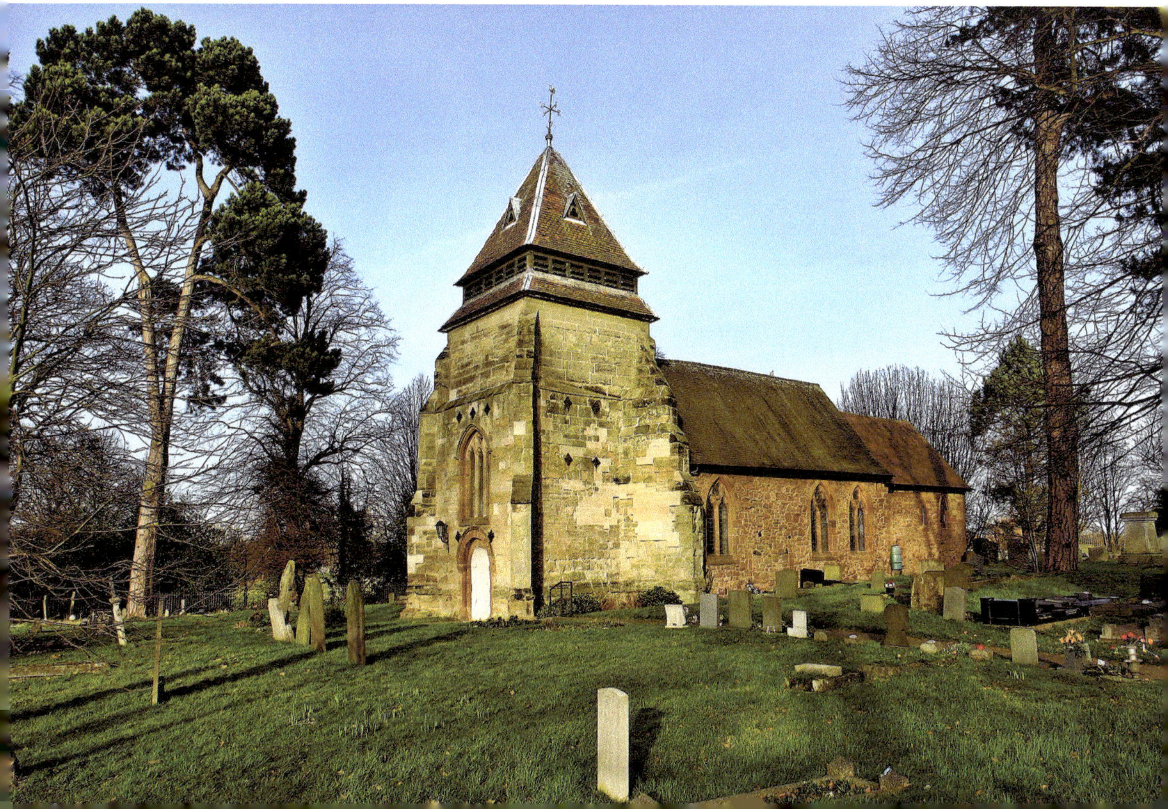

# Acknowledgements

Many thanks to Rob Orland, John Ashby, Paul Maddocks, Coventry City Council, British Library; photographs Rob Orland, Steve Orland and David McGrory.

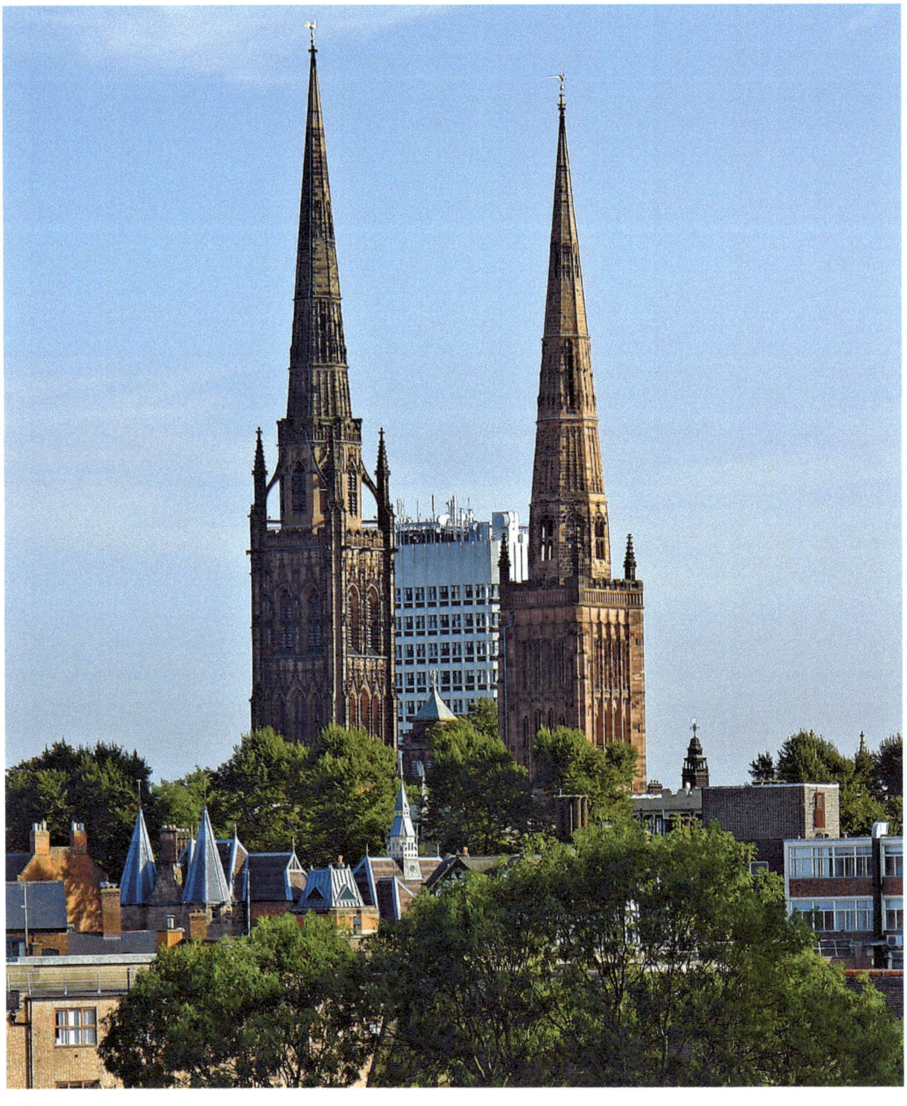

Beauty and brutalism, a classic example of how not to do it.